Mrs. T. J. V Owen

Mrs. Owen's Illinois Cook Book

Mrs. T. J. V Owen

Mrs. Owen's Illinois Cook Book

ISBN/EAN: 9783744764957

Printed in Europe, USA, Canada, Australia, Japan

Cover: Foto ©Andreas Hilbeck / pixelio.de

More available books at **www.hansebooks.com**

ADVERTISEMENT.

The undersigned having examined the manuscript copy of Mrs. T. J. V. Owen's "ILLINOIS COOK BOOK," heartily recommend it to the patronage of all housekeepers. The original and selected receipts are the choicest we have ever seen, and the materials called for are within the reach of all, and can be had, as a general thing, in any of our western towns. The greatest objection to the cook books now published is that the receipts call for material rarely to be obtained outside of the larger cities.

Mrs. B. S. EDWARDS, Springfield, Illinois.
" JACOB BUNN, " "
" CHARLES RYAN, " "
" J. C. ROBINSON, " "
" VIRGIL HICKOX, " "
" N. M. BROADWELL, " "
" JOHN S. BRADFORD, " "
" J. A. McCLERNAND, " "
" WM. A. TURNEY, " "
" W. F. KIMBER, " "
" J. A. CHESNUT, " "
" CHAS. D. HODGES, Carrollton, "
" Dr. WHITE, Bloomington, "
" ALEX. MOREAN, Brooklyn, New York.
Miss CARRIE HURST, Jacksonville, Illinois.
Mrs. P. B. PRICE, " "
" JACK WRIGHT, Petersburg, "

☞All orders addressed to Mrs. T. J. V. OWEN, Springfield, Illinois, will receive prompt attention. PRICE, $2.00 per copy.

MRS. OWEN'S

ILLINOIS COOK BOOK.

BY MRS. T. J. V. OWEN,

A PRACTICAL HOUSEWIFE.

"Whatever is worth doing is worth doing well."

SPRINGFIELD, ILL.:
JOHN H. JOHNSON, PRINTER.
1871

PREFACE.

In coming before the public with the "ILLINOIS COOK BOOK" I do so because years ago I felt the necessity of a book of this kind; one that would be a guide to young housekeepers, as well as a great convenience to older ones. There are a great many receipts published from time to time, that in all probability are very good; but we are often loth to try anything entirely new, through fear, not only of the disappointment, if it should not prove good, but the waste of material, which by a careful housekeeper should be a first consideration. Taking this into consideration, I have been careful of preserving all well-tried receipts, and in collecting such as, in my own judgment and the judgment and experience of my friends, would reach the necessities of all who may desire a good practical receipt book. In all general directions I have tried to be explicit, making them so plain that the most inexperienced can understand. Let all remember that care must be taken in order to produce nice dishes; so that with care and a liberal amount of good material we may all live well at least.

To the ladies of Springfield I owe much for their extreme kindness in supplying me with receipts from time to time, and for their voluntary recommendation of the book to the public. Allow me here to express my heartfelt thanks to all those who have shown me this kindness, and let me here say that I have KNOWN the truth of the adage that "a friend in NEED is a friend INDEED.

MRS. T. J. V. OWEN.

SPRINGFIELD, ILL., 1871.

ADVICE TO HOUSEKEEPERS.

To young beginners in housekeeping the following brief HINTS ON DOMESTIC ECONOMY in the management of a moderate income may perhaps prove acceptable.

Whenever anything is bought, a bill of the goods and a receipt should be required, even if the money be paid at the time of purchase; and to avoid mistakes the goods should be compared with these when brought home; if the money is to be paid at a future period, a bill should be sent with the articles and regularly filed.

An inventory of furniture, linen and china, should be kept, and the things examined frequently, especially if there be a change of servants often; the articles used by servants should be entrusted to their care with a list, as many persons do with silver.

In the purchase of glass and crockeryware, either the most customary patterns should be chosen, in order to secure their being easily matched, or, if a scarce design be adopted, an extra quantity should be bought to guard against the annoyance of the set being spoiled by breakage, which, in the course of time must be expected to happen. There should also be plenty of common dishes, that the table set may not be used for putting away cold meats, etc.

The cook should be instructed to be careful of coals and cinders. Small coal wetted makes the strongest fire for the back of the grate, but must remain untouched until it cakes. Cinders lightly wetted gives a great degree of heat, and are better for furnaces, ironing stoves and ovens.

The most durable linens for sheeting are the Russia, German or Irish fabrics; a good stock of which, as well as of table linen, should be laid in to avoid the necessity of frequent or irregular washing. When linen cannot be afforded, always buy the best muslin sheeting. Sheets that have a seam in the middle wear the best, as the seam strengthens that part; and as the sheets begin to wear, sew the two outside seams and open the middle seam, and they will wear twice as long.

A STORE ROOM is essential for the custody of articles in constant use, as well as for others which are only occasionally called for. These should be at hand when wanted, each in separate drawers, or on shelves and pegs, all under the lock and key of the mistress, and never given out to the servants but under her inspection. It is altogether a mistaken idea of letting servants have full sway over what is provided for the household; however honest they may be, their want of judgment often proves destructive; and every woman who considers her own and her husband's interest, will see that care is taken of what he works hard to provide. Pickles and preserves, prepared and purchased sauces, and all sorts of groceries, should be placed in the store room; spices pounded, bottled and corked tight; sugar in readiness for use; lemon and orange peel put in bags and stored away; thyme, parsley and all sorts of sweet herbs should be dried, rubbed through a sieve and bottled tight; the small bits of tongues saved and dried for grating into omelets; and care should be taken that nothing be wasted that can be turned to good account.

BREAD is so heavy an article of expense that all waste should be guarded against. Be careful to cut no more than will be wanted at a time; it is better to replenish the plate than to have a box full of dry bread going to waste; bread keeps better in earthen than in wooden ware. Make dry or dip toast of the dry bread, or use the receipt in this book for frying bread, which is delightful.

SUGAR being an article of considerable expense in all families, the purchase demands particular attention. The cheap sugar does not go so far as that more refined, and there is a difference even in the degree of sweetness. The close heavy, shining white sugar should be chosen. The best sort of brown has a bright crystalline appearance, as if mixed with salt; and, if feeling coarse when rubbed between the fingers, is better than when more powdery. Loaf should be cut in pieces when first purchased, and kept out of the air two or three weeks; for if it dries quickly it will crack, and when wet will break. Put it on a shelf with a space between each piece, and let it gradually dry, and it will save a full third in the consumption.

—2

Soda, by softening the water, saves a great deal of soap. It should be melted and put in a large jug and corked tight for use. If you soak your clothes over night use a little, and also in boiling.

The best starch will keep good in a dry place for years. Everything should be kept in the place best suited to it, as much waste may thereby be avoided.

Great care should be taken of jelly bags, which, if not properly washed and scalded, will give an unpleasant flavor when next used.

There are comparatively few among the middle classes of society who can afford to keep professional cooks, their wages being too high, and their methods too extravagant. In such cases a plain cook is alone attainable, who knows little beyond the commonest operations of the kitchen. The mistress, therefore, ought to make herself so far acquainted with cookery as to be competent to give proper directions for preparing a meal and having it properly served up.

Perhaps there are few points on which the responsibility of a man is more immediately felt than the style of dinner to which he may accidentally bring home a visitor. If the dishes are well served, with the proper accompaniments, the table linen clean, and all that is necessary be at hand, the comfort of both husband and friend will be greatly increased by the usual domestic arrangements not having been interfered with.

Hence, the DIRECTION OF A TABLE is no inconsiderable branch of a lady's duty, as it involves judgment in expenditure, respectability of appearance, and the comfort of her husband as well as of those who partake of their hospitality. Inattention to it is always inexcusable, and should be avoided for the lady's own sake, as it occasions a disagreeable degree of bustle, and evident annoyance to herself, which is never observable in a well regulated establishment.

The mode of setting out a table differs according to taste. It is not the multiplicity of dishes, but the choice, the dressing, and the neat looks of the whole, which gives an air of refinement to a table. There should always be more than the necessary quantity of plate or plated ware and glass, to afford a certain appearance of elegance; and these, with a clean cloth and neatly dressed attendants, will show that the habits of the family are those of gentility. Castors should be looked to and carefully wiped; cruets filled always before dinner time; and much trouble and irregularity are saved, when there is company, if servants are TRAINED to prepare the table and sideboard in a similar manner every day. Too many or too few dishes are extremes not uncommon: the former encumbering the dinner with a superfluity which partakes of vulgarity, whilst the latter has the appearance of poverty or penuriousness.

The mistress of a family should never forget that the welfare and good management of the house depends on the eye of the superior; and consequently that nothing is too trifling for her notice, whereby waste may be avoided, or order maintained. If she has never been accustomed, while single, to think of family management, let her not upon that account fear that she cannot attain it; she may consult others who are more experienced, and acquaint herself with the necessary quantities, qualities, and prices of the several articles of expenditure in a family in proportion to the number it consists of. The chief duties of life are within the reach of humble abilities, and she whose aim is to fulfil them will rarely ever fail to acquit herself well. United with, and perhaps crowning all the virtues of the female character is that well-directed ductility of mind which occasionally bends its attention to the smaller objects of life, knowing them to be often scarcely less essential than the greater.

TO YOUNG HOUSEKEEPERS.

Be satisfied to commence on a small scale. It is too common for young housekeepers to want to begin where their mothers ended. Buy all that is necessary to work skillfully with; adorn your home with all that will render it comfortable. Do not look at richer homes and covet their costly furniture. If secret dissatisfaction is ready to spring up, go a step farther and visit the homes of the suffering poor; behold dark cheerless apartments, insufficient clothing, and absence of all the comforts and refinements of social life, and then return to your own with a joyful spirit. You will then be prepared to meet your husband with a grateful heart, and be ready to appreciate the toil and self-denial which he has endured in the business world, to surround you with the delights of home, and you will co-operate cheerfully with him in so arranging your expenses that his mind will not be constantly harrassed lest his family expenditures may encroach upon public payment.

Be independent; a young housekeeper never needed greater moral courage than she does now, to resist the arrogance of fashion. Do not let the A's and B's decide what you shall have; neither let them hold the strings of your purse. You know best what you can and ought to afford. It matters but little what people think, provided you are true to yourself, to right and duty, and keep your expenses within your means.

HOUSE FURNISHING.

If you are about to furnish a house do not spend all your money, be it much or little. Do not let the beauty of this thing, and the cheapness of that, tempt you to buy unnecessary articles. Dr. Franklin's maxim was a wise one—"Nothing is cheap that we do not want." Buy what you can get along comfortably with at first. It is only by experience that you can tell what will be the wants of your family. If you spend all your money, you will find that you have purchased many things that you do not want, and have no means left to get the articles you really need. If you have enough, and more than enough, to get everything suitable to your situation, do not think you must spend it all, merely because you happen to have it. Begin plainly and humbly. As riches and prosperity increase it is easy and pleasant to increase in comforts; but it is always painful and inconvenient to decrease. After all, these things are viewed in their proper light by the truly judicious and respectable. Neatness, tastefulness and good sense may be shown in the management of a small household, and the arrangement of a little furniture, as well as upon a larger scale; and these qualities are always commendable. The consideration which many purchase, by living beyond their income, and of course, living upon others, is not worth the trouble it costs. The glare there is about this false parade is deceptive; it does not procure to any one valuable friends or extensive influence. The friends who flock around us in our prosperity, are generally the farthest from us when the clouds of adversity gather around us.

ADVICE TO MOTHERS.

I would here give a few words of advice to mothers, those who are training up families of daughters, and who wish not only to discharge well their own duties in the domestic circle, but to train up their daughters to make at a later day happy and comfortable firesides for their families; that they should watch well, and guard well, the notions which they imbibe and with which they grow up. There will be so many persons ready to fill their young heads with false notions and vain fancies; and there is so much afloat in society opposed to duty and common sense, that if mothers do not watch them well, they may contract ideas fatal to their future happiness and usefulness, and hold them till they grow into habits of thought or feeling. A wise mother will have her eyes open, and be ready for every case. A few words of common, downright, respectable, practicable sense, timely uttered by her, may be enough to counteract an erroneous idea, whilst if it be left unchecked, it may take such possession of the mind that it cannot later be corrected. One main falsity abroad in this age is the notion that women, unless compelled to it by absolute poverty, are out of place when engaged in domestic affairs. Now, mothers should have a care lest their daughters get hold of this conviction as regards themselves. There is danger of it; the fashion of the day endangers it, and the care that an affectionate family take to keep a girl, during the time of her education, free from other occupations than those of her tasks or her recreations, also endangers it. It is possible that affection may err in pushing this care too far; for as education means a fitting for life, and as a woman's life is much connected with domestic and family affairs, or ought to be so, if the indulgent consideration of parents abstains from all demands upon the young pupil of the school not connected with her books or her play, will she not naturally infer that the matters with which she is never asked to concern herself, are, in fact, no concern to her, and that any attention she may ever bestow on them is not a matter of simple duty, but of grace, or concession, on her part? Let mothers avoid such danger. If they would do so, they must bring up their daughters from the FIRST with the idea that in this world it is required to give as well as to receive, to minister as well as to enjoy; that every person is bound to be useful, practically, literally useful in their own sphere; and that a woman's first sphere is the house, and its concerns and demands. Once really imbued with this belief, and taught to see how much the happiness of woman herself, as well as her family, depends on this part of her discharge of duty, and a young girl will usually be anxious to learn all that her mother will teach her, and will be proud and happy to aid in any domestic occupations assigned to her, which need never be made so heavy as to interfere with the peculiar duties of her age, or its peculiar delights. If a mother wishes to see her daughter become a good, happy and rational woman, never let her admit of contempt for domestic occupations, or even suffer them to be deemed secondary. They may be raised in character by station, but they can never be secondary to a woman.

MODERN COOKERY AND HOUSEHOLD MANAGEMENT.

THE average of human felicity may not be much higher now than it has been; the world will most likely deserve its title of a "vale of tears" to the end of time; but one consolation, and that by no means a small one, has become stronger and of more general circulation in the present day—there is the possibility of getting good dinners OFTENER. Good dinners! excellent dinners! super-excellent dinners! have been cooked in all ages. Thanksgiving day, Christmas and New Years have secured good cheer for Christendom. Sunday dinners retain a comfortable superiority over the rest of their brethren; but their very association with plenty of good things suggests the "spare fast" of intermediate seasons, when a household was on salted meat for months; the frugal housewife being careful to use first the portions which were a "little touched" and going on with the remainder, as it stood in the most urgent need of being cooked. Certainly all that has been changed for the better. Set dinner parties are less thought of than the comfort of the family. The idea has been set forth and cherished that the HUSBAND and CHILDREN are entitled to as much consideration as occasional guests; and that the table ought to be set out as carefully and neatly every day as on special occasions. There is a self-respect in such a fact that goes deeper than the clean table-cloths and dinner napkins. One of the latest attainments of civilization is COMFORT. People are beginning to make themselves comfortable with such things as they have. The one point insisted upon in all works on household management ought not to be a love of show or extravagant expenditure; but the necessity of having everything that depends on personal thought or care done as well as possible.

—3

The table linen must not of necessity be fine, but to be clean and well spread is indispenssble. The dinner may be of scraps, but those scraps may be made savory; and certainly the receipts and directions for turning stale crusts into delicate puddings, morsels of cold, dry meat into delicious ENTREES, leave cooks and wives without excuse for "banyan days" or hungry dinners. Cookery is the art of turning every morsel to the best use; it is the exercise of skill, thought, ingenuity, to make every morsel of food yield the utmost nourishment and pleasure of which it is capable. A woman who is not essentially kind-hearted cannot be a comfortable housekeeper. A woman who has not judgment, firmness, forethought, and general good sense, cannot manage her house prudently or comfortably, no matter what amount of money she may have at her command. A woman who has not an eye for detecting and remedying disorder and carelessness, cannot keep her house fresh and pleasant, no matter how much money she may spend on furniture and upholstelry. It is not *money* but *management* that is the great requisite in procuring comfort in household arrangements. But the woman with limited means may make her things as perfect after their kind as the woman with ample means, only she will be obliged to put more of HERSELF into the management; and that element of personality has a charm which no appointments made through the best staff of servants can possess. The luxury of completeness must always depend on the individual care and skill of the mistress.

That a thing should be perfect after its kind is all that can be required. We are all so much creatures of imagination, that we think more of the signified than of the actual fact. When a man sees his table nicely set out, he believes in the goodness of his dinner in a way that it would be impossible with the self-same dinner on a soiled table cloth.

FOUR GOOD POINTS

Essentially necessary for the management of household concerns. These are—

    1st. Punctuality.
    2d. Accuracy.
    3d. Steadiness.
    4th. Dispatch.

Without the first, time is wasted. Without the second, mistakes, fatal to our own interest and that of others, may be committed. Without the third, nothing can be well done. Without the fourth, opportunities of good are lost which it is impossible to recall.

FOUR IMPORTANT RULES.

    1st. A suitable place for everything, and everything in its place.

    2d. A proper time for everything, and everything done in its time.

    3d. A distinct name for everything, and everything called by its name.

    4th. A certain use for everything, and everything put to its use.

REMARKS.

It may not be considered out of place to make a few remarks on the art of, as also on the principles of cookery. For nearly all will acknowledge cooking not only to be an art, but a science as well. To know how to cook economically is an art. Money making is an art. Now is there not more money made and lost in the kitchen than any where else? Does not many a hard-working man have his substance wasted in the kitchen? Does not many a shiftless man have his substance saved in the kitchen? A careless cook can waste as much as a man can earn, which might as well be saved. It is not what we earn, as much as what we save, that makes us well off. A long and happy life is the reward of obedience to natural laws; and to be independent of want, is not to want what we do not need. Prodigality and idleness constitute a crime against humanity. But frugality and industry combined with moral virtue and intelligence, will insure individual happiness and national prosperity. Economy is an instinct of nature, and enforced by Bible precept: "Gather up the fragments that nothing may be lost." Saving is a more difficult art than earning. Some put dimes into pies and puddings, where others only put in cents; the cent dishes are generally the most healthy. Almost any woman can cook well, if she have plenty with which to do it; but the real science of cooking is to be able to cook a good meal or dish with but little out of which to make it.

This is what the few receipts I have given will assist you in doing.

As to the principles of cooking, remember that water cannot be made more than boiling hot—no matter how much you hasten the fire, you cannot hasten the cooking of meat, potatoes, &c., one moment. When meat is to be boiled for eating, put it into boiling water at the beginning, by which its juices are preserved. But if you wish to extract these juices for soup or broth, put the meat into cold water, and let it simmer slowly. The same principle holds good in baking also. Make the oven the right heat and give it time to bake through, is the true plan; if you attempt to hurry it, you only burn instead of cooking it done.

There is one other process to which I must yet allude—the process of

SPOILING.

Many cooks know how to *produce* a good dish, but too many of them know how to *spoil*. They leave fifty things to be done just at the critical moment, when the chief dish should be watched with an eye of keenness, and attended by a hand thoroughly expert. Therefore too much care cannot be given to any dish we may prepare, remembering that it is but half done until it is taken from the stove or oven well cooked.

ILLINOIS COOK BOOK.

SOUPS.

Fresh meat of any kind is better for soups, for the reason that meats or fowls that have once been cooked have lost much of their sweetness.

Soups should never be allowed to boil too hard, as it has a great tendency to make the meat very tough. Many persons hold to the opinion that meat should always be boiled the day before it is wanted, so that the liquor may be set aside to cool, and let the grease rise to the top and be skimmed off. But very fine soup can be made the day it is to be used. A beef shank, or a knuckle of veal either, make splendid soup. Proper care should always be taken to have your soups well seasoned and flavored, as all depends upon this. One receipt for seasoning and flavoring soups will not suit for all, as there is such a diversity of tastes; but for those who like herbs, it is well to get such as they like; for instance, thyme, summer savory, sweet marjorem, sweet basil, sage, or such as suit their tastes; (they can be bought in ten cent packages at any drug store;) rub them well together, and then rub them through a sieve, and bottle them ready for use at any time. I have found this a very good plan. You can keep yourself supplied at a trifling cost, and always be ready to make a palatable soup.

Beef Soup.

Take the shin bone of the beef, wash it, and put it in a pot of cold water; put very little salt in, and let it boil; skim well. Have ready such vegetables as will suit the taste, such as carrots, onions, turnips, cabbage, potatoes, a little celery root; of course it takes but little of each. If the vegetables are not intended to be left in the soup, the meat should be taken out and the soup strained. If dumplings are liked, a little milk and flour, well beaten up, and a spoonful of butter, made stiffer than for batter-cakes. Drop these dumplings in the boiling soup, let them boil from five to ten minutes; flavor to suit the taste.

Mutton Soup.

A piece of forequarter of mutton is the best for a soup piece; throw a little salt into the water, just enough to raise the scum; let it simmer slowly; then prepare such vegetables as suit the taste; turnips, carrots, a little cabbage and onion, are very nice; a grated carrot or very little tomatoes give the soup a rich taste and color; this soup may be thickened with pearl barley or rice. Summer savory or thyme flavor any soup nicely.

Portable Soup.

Boil down any kind of meat to a jelly, season it

highly with salt, pepper and spices or herbs; let it set away till partly cold, then pour it into a clean, new tin or earthen vessel, and set it away to congeal; it can be used as you want to make soup by cutting a portion of the jelly and adding boiling water. Vegetables can be added and as much more seasoning as is required to make it palatable.

Mock Turtle Soup.

Take a nicely skinned and cleaned calf's head, soak it in a little salt and water over night, rinse it before putting it on the fire; have a large dinner pot of cold water with a little salt, put in the head and let it boil till tender; before putting the head in the pot remove the brain, which should be thrown into a little salt and water to whiten them; after the soup has been well boiled and skimmed, add pepper, salt, a little mace and cloves, and sweet herbs,. tied up in a thin piece of muslin. If you wish a dark soup brown the flour you use to thicken the soup with. Before taking it up for the table add the juice of two lemons, the yolks of eight eggs boiled hard and chopped. Take up the head, cut out the tongue, which must be skinned and dressed with egg and butter sauce, and served on a dish with a garnish of fresh parsley. Chop some of the meat from the head and season, mixing a little milk and flour and raw egg. Mix well, roll into balls and fry in hot lard, and drop with the brains into the soup.

Veal Soup.

Put a knuckle of veal into a pot of salted water with about a pound of ham. When the meat is cooked very tender take it out, and have a small head of chopped celery, one onion, one turnip, a carrot sliced very fine, four chopped tomatoes, a small piece of red pepper pod, black pepper and salt to suit your taste. Thicken with rice, vermicelli, or a thickening made of flour and butter. Noodles are very nice in this soup, if the vegetables are removed from the soup before the noodles are dropped in. Twenty minutes are sufficient to let them boil.

Giblet Soup.

A very nice soup is made from the neck, feet and giblets of fowls, with a little veal or nice beef bone added; put these all into a pot of cold water and boil gently. The giblets can be removed and chopped fine and put back into the soup; season like any other soup. Flavor to suit the taste.

Chicken Soup.

Have a fine large chicken, it can be put into the water whole, and then dressed for dinner, or it can be cut as for frying; in either case the chicken can be served on the table. Put in very little salt at first; remove all scum before putting in anything to flavor the soup; have a cup of rice well washed and soaked, and any sweet herbs, a small onion, and one or two potatoes cut fine. Chicken soup is much better if a little parsley is chopped and added; season with pepper and salt. Noodles may be substituted in place of the rice, or dumplings made of a little milk, flour and butter, and one egg; beat all well together, and make thicker than batter; drop in by the spoonful. Pearl barley is very nice in chicken soup, but should be well washed and put into the soup when it is first put on.

Gumbo Soup.

This is a Southern soup, and can be made in different ways. If made as it should be, it is one of the finest soups that can be made. If it is made of okra the chickens should be young and fried a delicate brown, with a few slices of nice bacon; when fried put them in a pot with boiling water. One must be governed by the quantity of soup that will be needed. Let the soup simmer slowly, skim well, and add pepper, salt, sweet herbs and rice a half teacupful; if the okra is green about half a teacupful of that. If this is made in the winter it will take a little more of the dried; it is nice with a few oysters added just before taking the soup from the fire. The best gumbo is made of young chickens, cut up as for frying, and put in a pot of cold water, and let them come to a boil; when boiled till very tender add salt and pepper to the taste. The gumbo is made of dried and powdered sassafras leaves, which should be gathered in the fall before the frost. One tablespoonful of the powder with the same quantity of flour, well rubbed together and dropped in the soup just before it is taken up. A nice pot of well cooked mush should be made to eat with this soup, serving a tablespoonful in each soup plate.

Noodles for Soup.

If you wish noodles for an ordinary pot of soup one egg is sufficient; have your flour sifted, make a hole in the centre, add one teaspoonful of salt, break in one egg, and with one hand stir them gently till the egg is well broken and mixed in a smooth dough; then work it quite stiff and roll out as thin as a wafer, keeping the board well floured; after it is rolled rub flour over the top and let it remain till it begins to dry, then roll it up tight and with a sharp knife cut (beginning at the end) into small shreds, and open them out as soon as you cut them, sprinkling flour over them.

Oyster Soup.

In making oyster soup great care should be taken not to have it made too long before it is used, as the oysters become hard and tough, and have an insipid taste. The water should be boiling; have a clean bright vessel; put in the water and a pint of new milk or good sweet milk; about one pint of milk to a gallon of boiling water; let it boil, then add the liquor from the oysters, butter, pepper and salt; have a dozen nice butter crackers rolled fine; if you can get it add one pint of good sweet cream, then the crackers, and last the oysters; as soon as they are heated through the soup is ready for use. In making oyster soup for company it should not be made in large quantities; if convenient it should not be made in larger quantities than one gallon, as it becomes tasteless and the oysters are hard and unfit to eat.

Veal Broth.

Stew a knuckle of veal of four or five pounds in three quarts of water, with two blades of mace, an onion, a head of celery, and a little parsley, pepper and salt; let the whole simmer very gently until the liquor is reduced to two quarts; then take out the meat when the mucilaginous parts are done, and serve it up with parsley and butter. Add to the broth either two ounces of rice separately boiled, or of vermicelli, put in only long enough to be stewed tender.

Winter Soup.

Take carrots, turnips, and the heart of a head of celery, cut into dice, with a dozen button onions; half boil them in salt and water, with a little sugar in it; then throw them into the broth; and, when tender serve up the soup; or use rice, dried peas, and lentils, and pulp them into the soup to thicken it.

With many of these soups, small suet dumplings, very lightly made, and not larger than an egg, are boiled either in broth or water and put into the tureen just before serving, and are by most persons thought an improvement, but are more usually put in plain gravy soup than any other, and should be made light enough to swim in it.

FISH.

Fish should be examined very carefully, as it is one of the most unhealthy things that can be eaten unless it is perfectly fresh. In selecting them examine the eyes; if they have a life-like appearance they are fresh; if the eyes are sunken and dark colored they are unfit to eat. A good way to test them is to examine the gills.

Crabs should be of a dark green color, and when fresh from the water are always lively; the same remark holds good with regard to lobsters.

Never buy a clam or oyster if the shells are parted. If the valves are tightly closed the oyster is fresh.

Boiled Fish.

Scale your fish first, take out the eyes and gills, draw and wash it well. Flour a cloth, wrap the fish in it, and boil in plenty of water strongly salted. A common sized fish of any kind requires about half a teacupful of salt. Put your fish kettle over a strong fire, and when the water boils put the fish in it. The fish can be stuffed with a stuffing made like turkey stuffing, and seasoned very much the same; it must be sewed up with a strong thread; let it boil 20 to 30 minutes. Take the fish out of the cloth carefully, place it on your dish and send it to the table. Have egg sauce served with it; garnish with parsley.

If any of the boiled fish is left from dinner it can be picked in small pieces, spiced and put into vinegar; it makes an excellent relish for breakfast or tea.

Boiled Cod Fish.

Soak a dried cod fish over night in cold water, scrape and wash it clean, then put in on to boil in as much cold water as will cover it.

Let it boil one hour. Drain it on your first dish and serve it with mashed potatoes, drawn butter, and hard boiled eggs.

Baked Fish.

Secure any nice fresh fish, such as fresh cod, trout, white fish, or any of the fresh or salt water fish; scale them and wash them clean, and let them remain in a little salt and water for a short time. Have a stuffing made of the crumbs of nice light bread—a baker's loaf is preferable for its lightness—put salt, pepper, butter, and sweet herbs in; with a spoon, as the hand makes it heavy, (as it does all stuffing,) fill your fish, sew it up, put bits of butter over the top, pepper, salt, flour; put in water enough to keep it from burning, and baste it often. For a fish of four pounds it will take about one hour to bake. If fish is left in any quantity from a meal it makes a splendid chowder. Make egg sauce.

Fish Sauce.

Take large tablespoonful of butter in as much flour, mix together and melt in a teacup of milk; beat the yolk of an egg, stir it in the butter and place it on the fire, stirring it all the time. Chopped parsley may be added.

Cod Fish Cakes.

Soak as much cod fish as will be required for a meal; after it is fresh enough pick it, removing all the bones; mash it with equal quantities of mashed potatoes, and season with salt and pepper to your taste, adding butter and two or three hard boiled eggs, chopped very fine, one raw egg helps to hold it together. Make it into cakes, flour and fry them in hot lard. Fry them a light brown.

Spiced Fish.

Fish of any kind, either boiled or baked, that has been left from a meal, is very nice spiced. Take salt, black pepper, a little cayenne pepper, two tablespoonfuls of whole allspice, mix through the fish and cover with good vinegar. This can be made by soaking a fresh shad, or other fish, and boiling it, and when cold, picking and spicing it; but it is a very nice way to use up cold fish.

Fried Fish.

Clean your fish well, wipe it with a dry cloth, split down the back, and fry it in halves, unless the fish is too large, then make four pieces of it; pepper, salt and flour, or rub on corn meal, and have your frying-pan with your lard in it very hot, and fry a nice light brown.

It is useless to enumerate the different kinds of fish, as this manner of frying holds good for all fish that is to be fried. It is fried as nicely by setting your skillet or frying-pan in the oven as it is on the top of the stove; many think it improves the taste.

Broiled Fish.

Cleanse them, of course, thoroughly, split them down the back, season with salt and pepper. Have your gridiron heated and well greased; put your fish on and let it broil slowly. It should be nice brown on both sides; have it well basted with butter, and lay the two sides together that it may assume its original shape.

Cat Fish.

This must be scalded with boiling (not hot) water, and the skin removed; cut down the back and cut in pieces as large as the hand; salt, pepper and flour each piece, and fry in hot lard to a nice brown. Some persons like it dressed with beaten egg and bread crumbs, or dipped in a batter and fried a nice brown.

Fried Oysters.

Select the largest for frying. Take them out of their liquor with a fork, being careful not to disfigure them, let them drain in a colander; when well drained put them in a dish, salt and pepper them well, have ready some nice butter crackers, rolled fine, and about one-third as much corn meal, mix them well together, and dip each oyster separately into the crackers; by putting two oysters together and frying them it will be found quite an improvement. Fry them in equal quantities of lard and butter. Have the lard hot and fry a nice light brown. Do not let them burn.

Stewed Oysters.

Put your oyster liquid in a stew-pan and add water according to the quantity to be stewed; put in salt, pepper, and a little butter; let this begin to boil, and then add a half-pint of good sweet cream, a little rolled cracker, if liked; then throw in your oysters, let it boil up once, and take it immediately to the table. This way is splendid if you have the cream.

Scalloped Oysters.

Take a nice tin or earthen baking dish and grease it well. Have ready good butter or pic-nic crackers well rolled, cover the bottom of the dish or pan first with the crackers, then the oysters, then lumps of butter over the top, then pepper and salt, next crackers and, so on, till all your oysters are in, putting butter, pepper and salt in each layer, put last a layer of crackers, with butter on top; put the oyster liquor in as you are putting it in the pan; put in water, not too hot, sufficient to cook them, set the pan in the oven and let it bake; for two cans of oysters it will take about one hour.

Fried Cod Fish.
(SENATOR SAMUEL CASEY'S RECEIPT.)

Take one pound of cod fish, four large potatoes, four eggs, one teaspoonful salt, and one of black pepper; cook fish and potatoes at the same time, (but in different vessels,) take the bones out of the fish, peel the potatoes, hot right out of the water, mash them and the fish well together, with a tablespoonful of flour; have the eggs well beaten, and add them to the mixture with a piece of butter as large as a walnut; mix all well together, and fry in cakes, in hot lard; send to the table hot. This mixture will be soft and must be dropped into the lard with a spoon, as it cannot be made out into balls. It is the nicest way I have ever prepared codfish for a breakfast dish. The water on the fish must be changed while it is boiling; once changing will perhaps be sufficient.

Boiled Fish.
(SENATOR SAMUEL CASEY'S WAY.)

Take cat fish, or any good kind of fish. After cleaning it well, rub it with salt, and wrap it in a cloth not too tight; have ready a kettle with boiling water well salted; drop your fish in and let it boil well, the length of time must be governed by the size of the fish, for a good-sized fish, (say three quarters of an hour,) pour melted butter over it.

To Make Stewed Oysters Tender.

Turn the oysters with the liquor into a convenient dish. With a fork remove each oyster into another dish, passing it as you do so through the oyster liquor, in order to wash off any bits of shell, etc. When all have been removed, strain the liquor through a fine sieve, which will retain the bits and yellow crabs. Some people eat these little crabs, but I reject them from the oyster stew, as they suggest carelessness. Put the strained liquor into the kettle with the quantity of water or milk you think proper, and set to boil. Add rolled cracker and salt. A little mace (only a little) is a great addition, as it brings out the oyster flavor; I do not put in pepper as some guests do not like it, and the color of the soup is not so good. Each person can suit his own taste by using either the black or cayenne. The clearer and whiter a soup appears, the better it will be relished. I omit cracker in a dinner soup; each guest must be supplied, however, at the table. Keep out the oysters until all the ingredients of the soup are added, and until it thoroughly boils. Now add the oysters. As soon as it comes to a good boil, the soup is ready to serve. If you have a very rich stew—a great many oysters and little soup—it may be well to put only part of the oysters in at a time, waiting until the first lot have had a good scald before adding the remainder. The idea is to give each oyster a good scald on the outside surface; it cooks them sufficiently and avoids the toughness that comes from overcooking. Treated according to these directions the oysters in a stew will be as tender as raw ones. It is very easy to spoil oysters by overdoing them.

French Stewed Oysters.

Wash fifty large oysters in their own liquor; strain the liquor into a stew pan, putting the oysters into a pan of cold water; season the liquor with a half pint of sherry or madeira, the juice of two lemons, and a little mace. Boil this liquor, and skim and stir it well; when it comes to a boil, put in the oysters well drained, let them get heated through, but do not boil them. Many people consider this the nicest way of stewing oysters.

Clam Fritters.

Put a sufficient quantity of clams into a pot of boiling water; when the shell opens wide take out the clams from the shells, and put them into a stew pan. Strain the liquor, and pour about half of it over the clams, adding a little black pepper; they will not need salt. Let them stew slowly for half an hour; then take them out. Drain off all the liquor, and mince the clams as fine as possible, leaving out the hardest parts. You should have as many clams as will make a pint when minced. Make a batter of seven eggs beaten till very light, mix with these gradually a quart of milk and a pint of sifted flour; make it perfectly smooth and free from lumps; mix gradually the minced clams with the batter, and stir the whole very hard. Have ready in a frying pan some boiling lard; put in the batter with a spoon, so as to form fritters, and fry them a light brown. Drain them well when done, and serve hot. Oyster fritters are made the same way, only they must be minced raw and mixed with the batter without having been stewed.

Potted Shad.

Take the backbone out of the shad, cut it in small

pieces, then put one layer of shad, one small piece of butter, some salt, pepper, and a very small piece of mace, clove, and allspice whole; cover with vinegar. Bake in an earthen pot, well sealed, eight hours. Six whole cloves and the same of allspice is enough for three shad; seal the cover with dough, so as to keep the air out.

Oyster Omelet.

Strain the liquor from twenty-five large oysters or forty small ones, chop them fine, leaving out the hard part. Break into a shallow pan, six, seven or eight eggs, according to the quantity of oysters, leaving out half the whites. Having beaten the eggs well, mix in the chopped oysters, adding a little cayenne pepper and nutmeg, if you like that spice. Put three ounces of the best butter into a frying pan, let it come to a boil, pour in the omelet mixture, stir it till it begins to harden; fry it a light brown, lifting from the edge several times by slipping a knife under it. Take care not to cook it too much, or it will be tough; serve immediately. This quantity will make one large, or two smaller omelets.

To Pot Trout.

Take from six to eight trout, from a quarter to half a pound in weight each. Gut, scale and wipe them dry in a clean cloth. Then dispose of them in a shallow dish, about two and a half inches in depth, containing a very small portion of water at the bottom, enough to supply a sufficiency of steam to pass through them. Add to them a supply of ground mace, ground black pepper, salt, and two or three bay-leaves, covering the dish over with a tin protection, and consign the same to a slow oven, to admit of the fish being steamed through. When the prongs of the fork will pass readily into them, they will be done and may be taken up. When cold, remove the bay-leaves, and let them be well covered with clarified butter.

Lobster Rissoles.

Extract the meat of a boiled lobster, mince it as fine as possible; mix it with the coral pounded smooth, and some yolks of hard-boiled eggs, pounded also. Season it with cayenne pepper, powdered mace, and a very little salt. Make a batter of beaten egg, milk and flour. To each egg allow two large tablespoonful of milk and a large teaspoonful of flour. Beat the batter well, and then mix the lobster with it gradually, till it is stiff enough to make into oval balls about the size of a large plum. Fry them in the best salad oil, and serve them up either warm or cold. Similar rissoles may be made of raw oysters minced fine, or of boiled clams. These should be fried in lard.

Champlain Chowder.

To four pounds fish, one pound fat pork to fry. Fry the pork gently in a bake kettle until the fat is out. Have ready the fish to put in when the scraps of pork are taken out, one quart boiling water to every four pounds of fish. Put in with the fish at the same time, pepper, salt, and a few sliced onions. Let it stew over a quick fire twenty minutes. Take off the cover then, and add one gill of milk. In five minutes take it up, and add crackers and oysters just before the chowder is done, if you wish.

Stewed Halibut.

Cut the fish into pieces about four inches square, leaving out the bone; season it slightly with salt, and let it stand half an hour. Take it out of the salt, put it in a deep dish, and scatter over it cayenne pepper, ground white ginger, and grated nutmeg; add a pint of vinegar, and a little butter rolled in grated bread. Put the dish in a slow oven, and let it cook till well done, basting it frequently with the liquid. When nearly done, add a tablespoon of capers.

Codfish Cakes---A Yankee Dish.

Take salt codfish that has been cooked slowly; *simmered*, not boiled, the day before. Remove the bones and mince it. Mix it with WARM mashed potatoes, mashed with butter and milk, in the proportion of one-third codfish, and two-thirds mashed potato; add sufficient beaten egg to make the whole into a smooth paste. If it seems dry, add a little butter. Make into cakes an inch thick, and as large round as a teacup. Fry in salt pork, and serve the slices with the fish cakes. These are very nice, if well made.

A Codfish Relish.

Sliver the codfish fine, pour on boiling water till it is freshened; then drain off water, add butter, pepper, and heat it a few minutes on the stove, but do not let it fry.

Fried Perch.

Egg and bread crumbs, hot lard. Scale and clean the fish, brush it over with egg, and cover with bread crumbs. Have ready some boiling lard; put the fish in, and fry a nice brown. Serve with melted butter or anchovy sauce.

Egg Sauce for Salt Fish.

Four eggs, half a pint of melted butter; when liked, a very little lemon juice. Boil the eggs until quite hard, which will be in about twenty minutes, and put them into cold water for half an hour. strip off the shells, chop the eggs into small pieces, not, however, too fine. Make the melted butter very smoothly, and when boiling, stir in the eggs, and serve very hot. Lemon juice may be added at pleasure.

Curry Fish.

Put into the pot four onions and two apples, in thin slices, some thyme, or savory, with a quarter of a pound of fat or dripping, three tablespoonfuls of salt, one tablespoonful of sugar, and fry for fifteen minutes; then pour in three quarts of water and one pound of rice; boil till tender; add one tablesoonful of curry-powder, mixed in a little water; cut up six pounds of cheap fish the size of an egg; add to the above, and boil for twenty or thirty minutes, according to the kind of fish. If salt fish is used, omit the salt. If no herbs, do without, but always use what you can.

Fish Sauce.

Take half a pint of milk and cream together, two eggs well beaten, salt, a little pepper, and the juice of half a lemon; put it over the fire, and stir it constantly until it begins to thicken.

MARKETING.

CARE AND USES OF MEATS. MANNER OF COOKING DIFFERENT PARTS OF MEATS AND FOWLS.

Beef Steaks.

The sirloin and porter-house steaks should always be *broiled* and broiled *quickly*. They should never be put on the gridiron till your meal is ready to serve up. Steaks should not be used the day they are cut; but if possible kept on ice a day or two, they then become tender; be governed of course by the weather in such matters. Always put your meat in a vessel of some kind, and set that on the ice. If the meat is put in contact with the ice it becomes white looking, and loses all its richness.

Roasting Pieces.

The sirloin roast is considered the best; the next piece forward of the sirloin is also a good roasting piece. The rib pieces of the forequarter are preferred by many; by removing the ribs and rolling the piece it makes a nice roast, and can be stuffed with bread crumbs and such seasoning as is used for any ordinary dressing for fowls.

Corned Beef Pieces.

The rump and round and etch bone are used expressly for corning. The flank and brisket are also good corning pieces; very many prefer the brisket, as it has a portion of the fat that is very sweet in boiled meat. It is well for persons who can do so, to select such pieces as they prefer, and have a large jar or keg, and make their own corned beef; they will find it much nicer. I have given a well tried receipt for corning beef, one that I have used for years, and one that cannot fail to please. Corned beef must be boiled tender; if used hot for dinner, take what is left and put it in some flat bottomed vessel and put a heavy weight over it; put a clean board or flat cover on, then the weight, and set it away till perfectly cold, and slice thin for supper; by pressing it it becomes firm and is more like tongue.

A Stuffed Flank.

Take a large, nice, well trimmed flank, put it in salt and let it remain over night. Then wash it in cold water, and wipe it dry. Have a stuffing made as for turkey or goose, and spread it well over the meat, putting on occasionally nicely cut strips of salt pork; season this dressing highly; roll your meat up and sew it very tight in a piece of strong muslin; put it in to boil as early as possible in the morning, and boil six hours. This is delightful. Put it in a vessel and press it, leaving the cloth on till cold; put a heavy weight on, let it remain till cold. Slice very thin. In winter when meat is firm and nice this makes a splendid supper dish.

Time for Boiling Meat.

The old rule of fifteen minutes to a pound of meat, is rather too little, I think; the slower it boils the tenderer, the plumper, and whiter it will be. For those who choose their food thoroughly cooked, (which all will who have any regard for their stomachs,) twenty minutes or more to a pound will not be found too much for gentle simmering over a good fire; allowing more or less time, according to the thickness of the joint; always remembering the slower it boils the better. Without some practice it is difficult to teach any art; and cooks seem to suppose they must be right if they put meat into a pot and set it over the fire for a certain time, making no allowance whether it simmers without a bubble, or boils at a gallop.

FRESH KILLED MEAT

Will take much longer time boiling than that which has been kept till it is what the butchers call ripe, and longer in cold than in warm weather. If it be frozen it must be thawed before boiling as before roasting; if it is too fresh killed it will be tough and hard. The size of the boiling pots should be adapted to what they are to contain; the larger the pot the more room it takes upon the fire; and a larger quantity of water requires a proportionate increase of fire to boil it. In small families I would recommend block tin sauce pans, &c., as the lightest and safest. If proper care is taken of them, and they are well dried after they are cleansed, they are far the cheapest. Take care that the covers of your boiling pots fit close, not only to prevent unnessary evaporation of the water, but that the smoke may not get under the edge of the lid, and give the meat a bad taste.

If you let meat or poultry remain in the water after it is done enough, it will become sodden and lose its flavor.

It is very important in boiling meats to keep the water constantly boiling, else it will cause the meat to soak the water up; if it is necessary to add more water, be sure to have it boiling, skim carefully; salt thrown in raises the scum; always put your meat into cold water, and let it gradually heat and boil at first; never let meat remain longer in the water than you can help, better to take it up and place it in a heater, if possible. The broth in which meat is boiled makes a most delicious soup by adding vegetables chopped fine, carrots, especially, give a fine flavor to soup. Bunches of mixed vegetables and parsly can be procured at the market, generally.

TAKE CARE OF THE LIQUOR

In which you have boiled meat or poultry; in a few minutes you may convert it into a most palatable soup.

IF THE LIQUOR IS TOO SALT,

Use only one half, saving the other half for the next day; people's tastes vary so much in regard to the flavor of soups. Add sufficient boiling water to the portion of broth you wish made into soup, then put in such vegetables and herbs as will suit the taste. Vermicelli, macaroni, or our home-made noodles may be added.

Boiled Ham.

If the ham is large, and to be boiled, it is much better to soak it in clear water over night, put it on to boil in cold water; when water is to be added to anything cooking, always add boiling water. Some persons think a boiled ham is much improved by setting it into the oven for a short time after you have removed the skin and before it has time to get cold. If you boil a whole ham, let it remain in the liquor in which it was boiled over night, it is a great improvement.

Tongues.

They are much better put in brine, and then smoked. Make an ordinary brine; use a little brown sugar and a small piece of saltpetre. Two weeks in the brine is sufficient; when taken out let them be washed off in clear, cold water, wiped dry, and hung up in a cool, dry place, for about two days; then they may be smoked.

Mutton Hams---To Pickle for Drying.

First take a weak brine and put the hams into it for two days, then pour off and apply the following, and let it remain on from two to three weeks, according to size: For each 100 pounds take six pounds salt; saltpetre, one ounce; saleratus, two ounces; molasses, one pint; water, six gallons; will cover these, if packed closely. The saleratus will keep the mutton from becoming hard. These, if properly selected and properly cured, are, according to my experience, equal to any dried venison I ever ate. I prefer the "corned beef brine" receipt, although there is but little difference between them.

For Corned Beef.

(MRS. WM. A. TURNEY.)

Take a large dinner pot of rain water and put in it—
    One pint salt,
    One pint molasses,
    One pint brown sugar,
    Five cents worth saltpetre.

Boil all together, skim till clear; let it cool. If it will bear an egg, it is all right. This will cover about 27 or 28 pounds of beef. Next, take—
    One tea cup brown sugar,
    One tea cup of salt,
    Five cents worth saltpetre.

Beat them and mix them well together, and rub each piece of the meat well with it; put the meat into your jar or keg, let it stand 24 hours; then pour over it the brine, which should be made the night before. In two weeks it is ready for use. This makes the finest corned beef I have tasted.

Sugar Cured Hams.

(MRS. S. FERGUSON.)

For eighteen or twenty hams—
    Fifteen ounces saltpetre,

Four ounces saleratus,
Four pounds brown sugar,
Eight quarts fine salt,
Two quarts molasses.

Mix well together in a tub, rub the mixture well on the face of the hams, putting it all on; put them in a tight barrel. Let them remain four days. Make a strong brine that will bear an egg, and pour over the hams. Let them remain in the brine from five to six weeks, or till well salted; changing them once in that time, putting those that are in the bottom of the barrel on the top, so that they will not have the juice pressed out of them. When they are sufficiently salted, take them out of the brine, wash them well in warm (not hot) water, wipe them quite dry and hang them up a day or two, before being smoked. When smoked, put black pepper on the joints, wrap them up in strong brown paper. You can wash them with common white-wash, colored with any of the common yellow colors, or pack them in a large dry box and cover each ham thoroughly with good dry ashes.

Beef and Mutton

A little under-done, (especially very large joints,) which will make the better hash or broil, is not a great fault, by some it is preferred; but lamb, pork and veal, are uneatable if not thoroughly boiled, but do not overdo them. A trivet, or fish drainer, put in the bottom of the boiling pot, raising the contents about an inch and a half from the bottom, will prevent that side of the meat which comes next the bottom from being done too much, and the lower part ot the meat will be as delicately done as the other part; and this will enable you to take out the contents without sticking a fork into your meat, which is no benefit to it.

Ribs of Beef

The three first ribs make an excellent roasting piece, many prefer it to the sirloin for roasting; if the ribs are taken out and it is rolled and skewered, it will be round, and can be filled with a stuffing of bread crumbs, seasoned and flavored to suit the different tastes. As the meat is more in a solid mass, it will require more time to roast it. A piece of ten or twelve pounds weight will not be well roasted in less than four or five hours. Salt, pepper and flour it well before putting in to roast.

Mutton Chops.

Mutton chops are better broiled than cooked in any other way, and should be broiled over a rather *slow* fire, as the fat that cooks from them usually increases the fire.

Leg of Mutton.

The leg of mutton is very nice boiled or roasted plainly, or can be stuffed and roasted. The loin is a roasting piece. The leg is often cured as you would cure beef to dry; it has a much finer grain than the beef, and is more like venison. I have cured mutton legs in the corned beef receipt, and found them so like venison that you could scarcely tell the difference; they chip nicely, the meat is close and firm, and looks beautiful on table.

Pork Steaks.

The best steaks are off the shoulder; the first ham steaks are considered too dry for steaks.

Spare Ribs.

Spare ribs are nice if broiled well, broiled without burning. They are also nice cut up and stewed, or roasted; a pan can be well filled with the spare ribs as they are cut from the hog—pepper and salt, and a very little well powdered sage, sprinkled over each layer, and then nicely roasted, occasionally changing the pieces so that each piece can be a little browned. Many persons like this dish cold.

Sausage Meat.

Take about two-thirds of nice lean pork, and one-third of fat, chop them nicely, and season with salt, black pepper, sage, and a little summer savory. The best way is to make out a little cake and fry it, adding such seasoning as is needed to give it the right taste. There are nice little sausage grinders now in use, which are a great convenience, and not costing over three or four dollars; with a little trouble and care every family can grind their own sausage and season it to the taste.

Tender-Loin.

During the slaughtering season families can live very much cheaper. The tender loin is a very nice breakfast dish, nicely fried, with a well made gravy. The backbone, or chine, salted down for a few days, and then washed and boiled till tender, makes a good dinner. Some persons boil cabbage, turnips and potatoes with it; it is very relishable, and makes a good *wash-day* dinner, giving you a sufficient variety, and very little labor in cleaning after it.

Pigs Feet.

They should be thoroughly cleaned, washed, and thrown into salt water over night, then boiled till they are almost to pieces; a little red pepper pod is nice thrown in, and a few whole cloves and allspice. When they are done, have a jar sufficiently large to hold them; put the feet one by one into the jar, (let them well drain first,) then have good, clear vinegar, and cover the feet with it; do not disturb them for a day or two, and then they are fit to eat. A nice dish for breakfast is made by cutting the feet into halves, dipping them into a nice batter, and frying till they are a nice brown; the grease for frying anything should always be *hot*.

Shoulder and Ham.

These are salted and smoked. Some rub them well with dry salt and let them remain till they are sufficently salted, and have them smoked; others prefer a brine to the dry salt. The weather has considerable to do with the length of time they remain in either salt or brine, if they freeze it takes longer for them to take the salt.

Curing, Smoking and Keeping Ham.

To a cask of hams, say from 25 to 30, after having packed them closely and sprinkled them slightly with salt, let them lie thus for three days; then make a brine sufficient to cover them, by putting salt into clear water, making it strong enough to bear up a sound egg or potato; then add one-half pound of saltpetre and a gallon of good molasses; let them lie in brine for six weeks—they are then exactly right. Take them out and let them drain; while damp, rub the flesh side and the end of the leg with finely pulverized black pepper, with a little cayenne pepper; let it be as fine as dust, and rub every part of the flesh side, then hang them up for a few days before smoking. They can then be kept well, after being well wrapped in strong brown paper and whitewashed, or they can be wrapped and packed in dry ashes; a little well pulverized charcoal mixed through the ashes is a great improvement. My own experience has taught me that it is very much cheaper, and certainly much safer, to have your hams and all meat to smoke marked so that you will always get your own meat, and then get your butcher to smoke them for you.

Packing Beef.

It is a very important thing to know how to keep a large quantity of beef. If you have a hind quarter of beef to put away, have it cut into steaks and roasts; take such pieces as you wish for dried beef and corned beef, put them into your brine. Have a nice, clean box, sufficient to hold your steaks and roasts, put this box into a larger box and pack that with ice or snow, first put a quantity in the bottom of the large box, pack the sides tight, cover it closely; let no ice or snow *touch* your meat, as it draws the blood out and renders the meat tasteless; it should be kept in some dry, cool place, smoke house, or any place where it is cold and dry, a cellar is too warm and would melt the ice.

To Try Out Lard.

It is much better in trying out lard, if you have a sufficient quantity to justify you doing so, to render out the leaf fat separately from the other fat; cut the fat into small pieces, put it into a clean pot over a slow fire, adding at first a little water to keep it from burning; let it cook till the cracklings are of a reddish brown; add a little salt, then strain into tin cans or stone jars; try out the other fat in the same way.

Mutton.

As beef requires a large, sound fire, mutton must have a brisk, sharp one; if you wish to have mutton tender, it should be hung as long as it will keep, and then good eight-tooth four years' old mutton is as good eating as venison. The leg, haunch and saddle will be the better for being hung up in a cool, airy place, for four or five days at least; in temperate weather a week, in cold weather, ten days. A leg of eight pounds will take about two hours, let it be well basted. A chine or saddle, the two loins, of ten or eleven pounds, two hours and a half. A shoulder of seven pounds, an hour and a half; they should be well watched and often basted. Potatoes, peeled, are very nice, roasted with any of the roasting pieces.

Shoulder of Mutton.

May be dressed in various ways, but the most usual is to roast it nicely, and send it up with onion sauce. It is an unsightly joint, but the appearance may be improved by cutting off the knuckle, when it may be called a shield; it has more different sorts of meat in the various cuts than the leg. The bone may also be taken out, and the mutton stuffed; it is very good baked, and is frequently served upon a pudding.

Leg of Mutton Boiled.

To prepare a leg of mutton for boiling, trim as for roasting; soak it for a couple of hours in cold water; then put only water enough to cover it, and let it boil gently for three hours, or according to its weight. Some cooks boil it in a cloth; but if the water be afterwards wanted for soup, that should not be done; some salt and an onion put in the water are far better. When nearly ready, take it from the fire, and, keeping the pot well covered, let it remain in the water for ten or fifteen minutes.

Cooking a Loin of Mutton.

From an hour and a half to an hour and three-quarters. The most elegant way of carving this is to cut it lengthwise, as you do a saddle. A neck about the same time as a loin. It must be carefully jointed, or it is very difficult to carve.

The Neck and Breast

Are, in small families, generally roasted together. The cook should crack the bones across the middle before they are put down to roast. If this is not done carefully, they are very troublesome to carve. A breast piece about an hour and a quarter to roast.

The Haunch.

The leg and part of the loin of mutton. Send to the table two sauce-boats of gravy; one of rich, drawn mutton gravy, seasoned high, and bruised mint to flavor; the other with plain gravy. Roast slowly and thoroughly.

Mutton, (Venison Fashion.)

Take a neck of good four or five year old wether

mutton, cut long in the bones; let it hang a few days, it will improve it. Two days before you dress it, take allspice and black pepper, ground and pounded fine, a quarter of an ounce each; rub them together, and then rub your mutton well with this mixture twice a day. When you dress your mutton to cook it, wash off the spice with warm water, rub salt and a little fresh black pepper over it, dredge on flour, and put it into the stove; put hot water in the roasting pan, baste frequently.

Beef a la Mode.

In making a la mode beef the round is generally preferred. I can only give directions for preparing it. The size of the meat must be selected according to the number to eat it. Every family knows about the number of pounds it will take. Select young and tender meat, cut holes entirely through the thick part, have long strips of salt fat pork, cut and rolled in a seasoning of thyme, sweet majorum, sweet basil, cloves, pepper, salt, half a teaspoonful of each; then open the holes already made in the beef, and draw the strips of fat through them. Some like onions; they can be used or not, as taste dictates. Put your meat in your pot, (or, if cooked in a stove, put it in a covered pan,) add sufficient water to cover it, and let it cook slowly three or four hours; make a rich gravy, and just before taking it out of the pan or pot, add a pint of either claret or port wine. If boiled it can be taken out and set in the oven a short time; sprinkle over the top powdered crackers.

Beef Patties.

This is a nice way to use cold roast beef. Chop fine the lean, and a little of the fat; season it with pepper, and mace, if you like, or sweet herbs. If you have any gravy left, moisten the meat with it. Make a nice plain paste, and cut it round about the size of a plate; do not roll it too thin; cover half of each sheet of paste with the mash, but do not get it too near the edge; fold the other half of the paste over, so as to form a half moon; wet your finger in cold water, and pinch together the two edges of the paste. Prick the patties with a fork, put them in a baking pan and bake a nice brown, or fry in hot fat, as you prefer. Serve hot. Cold veal or cold chicken make nice patties.

To Hash a Calf's Head.

Clean the head thoroughly, and boil it for a quarter of an hour. When cold, cut the meat into thin, broad slices, and put them into a pan with two quarts of gravy; and, after stewing three-quarters of an hour, add one anchovy, a little mace and cayenne, one spoonful of lemon pickle, and two of walnut catsup, some sweet herbs, lemon-peel, and a glass of sherry. Mix a quarter of a pound of fresh butter with flour, which add five minutes before the meat is sufficiently cooked. Take the brains and put them into hot water, skin them, and pound them well. Add to them two eggs, one spoonful of flour, a little grated lemon-peel, and finely chopped parsley, thyme and sage; mix well together with pepper and salt. Form this mixture into small cakes; boil some lard, and fry them in it until they are a light brown color, then lay them on a sieve to drain. Take the hash out of the pan, and lay it neatly on a hot dish, strain the gravy over it, and lay upon it a few mushrooms, forcemeat balls, the yolks of four hard-boiled eggs, and the brain-cakes. Garnish with slices of lemon and pickles.

Spoon Meats.

Calf's feet or mutton shanks make mild nourishing broth, but have but little richness or flavor of meat. To clean them, have a kettle of boiling water on the fire, and throw in the feet all at once, or in succession, as the size of the vessel allows. Let them boil about three minutes, then take one out, when the hoofs and hairs will easily come off; loosen the hoof at the root and turn it back, scrape the hairs, carrying the knife upwards. This must be done immediately on taking out of the boiling water, therefore only one at a time must be taken out. Feet, and all gristly parts, require long boiling, or baking, and consume a large quantity of water in the process.

Minced Beef.

Cut into small pieces the remains of cold meat; the gravy reserved from it, on the first day of its being served, should be put into the stew-pan, with the addition of warm water, pepper, salt, and a little butter. Let the whole simmer slowly for an hour. A few minutes before it is served, take out the meat; add to the gravy some walnut catsup, or a little lemon or walnut pickle. Boil up the gravy once more, and pour over the meat. This is a very nice way to use up any kind of cold meats or fowl. A little curry powder may be used by those who love high seasoning.

Beef and Mashed Potatoes.

Mash some well cooked potatoes, add a little cream or sweet milk, butter, salt and black pepper. Slice cold beef and lay it at the bottom of a deep pie dish, with salt, pepper, butter, and a little beef gravy, which should always be saved; cover the whole with a layer of the potatoes, then another quantity of the meat, and then potatoes, and seasoning, having potatoes reserved for the top; make it higher in the middle of the dish than at the edges; put butter on the top and bake a light brown.

Beef's Heart.

Get a heart of a nice young ox, wash it carefully, and with a sharp knife remove from the inside of it all sinews; lay it in salt and water, and let it remain over night; put it on very early in the morning, and boil till quite tender; then take out, put strips of ham fat, as in a la mode beef, cut the holes with a long, slim knife, or make them with a table steel; make a dressing with bread crumbs and a little onion, pepper, salt, and any herbs preferred; fill the heart, and roll it in a dough made as for soda biscuit; roll about an inch thick, and secure the edges with flour, that it will not come open; put in a pan, add water, and cover with butter, baste well while roasting. This way is very nice. It can be pinned in a cloth and boiled, if preferred. Make a nice gravy.

Beef Collops.

Cut the inside of a sirloin, or any other convenient piece, into small circular shapes, flour and fry them; sprinkle with pepper, salt, chopped parsley, and shalot; make a little gravy in the pan; send to table with gherkin or tomato sauce. Or: Cut thin slices of beef from the rump, or any other tender part, and divide them into pieces three inches long, beat them with the blade of a knife, and flour them. Fry the collops in butter two minutes; then lay them into a small stewpan, and cover them with a pint of gravy, add a bit of butter rubbed in flour.

Beef a la Mode.

Take a nice piece of round of beef, the size must be regulated to the size of the family, cut holes about an inch and a half apart, all through the meat; have nice long narrow strips of pork fat, and draw through the holes, (that from the fat of ham is nicest;) salt your meat and let it remain an hour or two; then put it into vinegar, (not too strong,) let it remain 24 hours; then have in a stove pot a nice large piece of butter, let it get hot; put in your meat and let it brown nicely in this butter, turning it often, and watching it carefully that the butter does not scorch, (*attention must be paid* to this to have it nice;) then set the pot on the back of the stove, and pour in the vinegar in which the meat had stood over night, and add pepper and spices, (whole) cloves and allspice; let this *simmer* slowly several hours till done tender; strain the liquor it has boiled in, and make gravy of it. In cutting slices of the meat, cut it so you will have the bits of pork all through the slice of meat. This is very nice for tea cold.

Beefsteak Pie.

Take rump steaks that have been well hung, cut in small scallops; beat them gently with a rolling pin; season with pepper, salt, and a little shalot, minced very fine; put in a layer of sliced potatoes, place the slices in layers with a good piece of fat and a sliced mutton kidney; fill the dish; put some crust on the edge, and about an inch below it, and a cup of water or broth in the dish. Cover with rather a thick crust, and set in a moderate oven.

Staffordshire Beefsteak.

Beat them a little with a rolling pin, flour and season, then fry with sliced onion of a fine light brown; lay the steaks into a stew pan, and pour as much boiling water over them as will serve for sauce; stew them very gently half an hour, and add a spoonful of catsup, before you serve.

To Mince Beef.

Shred the underdone part fine, with some of the fat; put it into a small stew pan, with some onion, (a very little will do,) a little water, pepper and salt; boil it till the onion is quite soft, then put some of the gravy of the meat to it, and the mince; don't let it boil. Have a small hot dish with bits of bread ready, and pour the mince into it, but first mix a large spoonful of vinegar with it.

Potted Beef.

Take three pounds of beef well salted, pick out any gristle or skin that may be in it; pound the meat carefully in a stone mortar, with a little butter, until it becomes a fine paste; season it by degress as you are beating it, with black pepper, allspice, or pounded cloves, mace, or grated untmeg. Put in pots, pressing it down as closely as possible, and covering it about a quarter of an inch thick with clarified butter.

To Stew a Brisket of Beef.

Put the part that has the hard fat into a stew pot, with a small quantity of water; let it boil up, and skim it thoroughly; then add carrots, turnips, onions, celery, and a few pepper corns. Stew till extremely tender; then take out all the flat bones, and remove all the fat from the soup. Either serve that and the meat in a tureen; or the soup alone, and the meat on a dish, garnished with some vegetables. The following sauce is much admired, served with the beef: Take half a pint of the soup, and mix it with a spoonful of ketchup, a teaspoonful of made mustard, a little flour, a bit of butter, and salt; boil all together a few minutes, then pour it round the meat.

Beef Balls.

Mince very fine a piece of tender beef, fat and lean; mince an onion, with some boiled parsley; add grated bread crumbs, and season with pepper, salt, grated nutmeg and lemon peel; mix all together and moisten it with an egg beaten; roll it into balls, flour and fry them in boiling fresh dripping. Serve them with fried bread crumbs.

Beef Steak Smothered with Onions.

Cut up six onions very fine; put them in a saucepan with two cupsful of hot water, about two ounces of good butter, some pepper and salt; dredge in flour. Let it stew until the onions are quite soft, then have the steak broiled, put into the saucepan with the onions; then simmer about ten minutes, and send to the table very hot.

Head Cheese.

Take a nice hog's head; have it nicely quartered and washed well; let it remain in salt water a few hours; then put on to boil, throw in a little salt at first, it will bring up the scum which must be removed; boil till the meat will drop from the bones; throw in, while boiling, cloves, allspice, and some red pepper pod. When done, remove from the fire, take out the meat with a ladle, carefully remove all bones; then with a spoon or stick mash up all the meat, and mix well; put in a bag, and tie, then put a weight on it, and press it; when cold remove a portion of the bag and cut into thin slices, and serve with vinegar. The ears should be cut off closely, and very carefully washed before it is put on to cook.

Roast Pig.

Take a pig that the weight is from seven to twelve pounds, let it be about five weeks old. Have your butcher kill and clean it; a great deal depends on the way it is dressed. Wash it thoroughly inside and outside. Take some nice salt pork and chop it fine; take bakers loaf bread, pour cold water on it; have some potatoes boiled and mashed fine, one large chopped onion, plenty of pepper, salt and butter, one raw egg, and thyme, sweet basil, summer savory and sweet marjorum; mix all well together; salt and pepper your pig; fill it with the stuffing, and sew it up; bend the knee joints up to the body, and tie the feet close, so they will appear well when it comes to the table. Put it in your dripping pan, salt and pepper and flour; cut nice large pieces of the fat of a raw ham and cover over the top, it prevents its browning too fast. It should be well basted, and often. It will take about from three to four hours to roast it well. Have the liver, lights, and heart boiled tender and chopped for the gravy. Put a lemon in its mouth before putting it on the table.

Tripe Stewed.

Cut tripe into strips, put them in rich gravy, with a lump of butter size of a hen's egg, rolled in flour; shake until the butter is melted. Add a tablespoonful of white wine, some chopped parsley, pepper, salt, pickled mushrooms, and a squeeze of a lemon. Shake well together, and stir until tender.

Lamb to Fry.

Fry slices of lamb in lard till they are a nice brown. They are nice served on a dish of spinach, or on slices of nicely toasted bread.

Calf's Head Pie.

Boil the head an hour and a half, or even longer; put it into cold water, pepper, salt, and add a part of a red pepper pod while boiling, remove the meat from the bones. Boil the bones again in the same liquor for an hour longer; then strain it off, and set it away till the next day. To make the pie, boil two eggs for five minutes; let them get cold, then lay them in slices at the bottom of a pie dish, and put alternate layers of meat and currant jelly, with pepper and chopped lemon alternate, till the dish is full, sprinkling each layer with pepper, salt and butter. Cover with a crust, and bake, adding the liquor that was strained the day before. This makes a delicious pot pie.

Mock Venison.

(MRS. DR. PRICE, KY.)

Boil a quarter of mutton until tender. (For evening companies.) Take a quarter of a pound of butter, a pint of tomato cutsup, two tumblers of blackberry or plum jelly, half tea cup of mixed mustard, (more if it is not very strong,) one bunch of celery chopped fine, (if you cannot get the celery, use the seed,) one teaspoonful of black pepper, a fourth of a teaspoonful of cayenne pepper, half pint Madeira wine or any good cooking wine, a tablespoonful of sugar, more if the jelly is acid; stew the whole well together; slice the mutton in thin slices in a chafing dish, pour the sauce over it, and serve hot. This will be sufficient for a dinner or an ordinary evening party.

Mutton Hash.

Cut cold mutton into small pieces, fat and lean together; make a gravy with the bones that you have taken the meat from; put on a little water, add pepper, salt, an onion, butter, and a few potatoes cut up raw; let it boil till these are cooked; take out the bones; take a little of the gravy up and thicken it with flour; put in your meat and let it boil up once, stirring it well, and it is ready to be served up.

Veal

Requires particular care to roast it brown and nice. Let the fire be the same as for beef; it should cook slowly at first, and requires to be well cooked. When first put in the oven it should be well basted. It should be salted and peppered, a little flour and pieces of butter put over the top; as veal is seldom fat, it requires either butter or any nice fryings.

A FILLET OF VEAL,

Of from ten to twelve pounds, will require from four to five hours at a good fire; some make a stuffing, or forcemeat, and put it under the flap; it is nice left to eat cold or to make into a hash; in cooking it, let it brown nicely.

A LOIN

Is the best part of the calf, and will take about three hours roasting; cover the kidney fat with heavy, brown paper; some cooks send kidneys to the table on buttered toast, which is eaten with the kidney and the fat, which is much more delicate than any marrow. Take care to keep up a good fire, so that your meat may brown well.

A SHOULDER OF VEAL

Will take from three to three and a half hours to roast; stuff it with the forcemeat, as you would a fillet of veal.

NECK,

Best end, will take two hours. The scrag part is best made into a pot pie or into broth; season same as any of the other pieces. If cut up nicely, it makes a nice dish of curry; put in potatoes, salt and pepper; let it boil till quite tender, and just before taking up, rub together a little butter and flour to make a nice gravy; a teaspoonful of curry powder is a great improvement.

The hock and shin are used for soups. The legs, too, are good soup pieces.

The chump end of the loin and the loin are roasting pieces. The hind leg and flank are used for cutlets, or can be used to stuff and roast. Neck pieces are generally used for stews, pot pies and curries. There are few dishes nicer than a nice dish of curried veal.

Curried Veal.

Cut your veal into small pieces, say three or four inches long, just as you would for any other stew; wash nicely, put into a clean iron pot or saucepan, with water enough to cover it; add pepper, salt, a few pieces of nice salt pork, half a teacup of well washed rice, butter the size of a hen's egg, and any kind of herbs, if you like their flavor; let it cook slowly—you can put in a few potatoes, they help to thicken the gravy; if it should not be thick enough, wet up a little flour, (be sure there are no lumps in it,) and turn in; then add a little curry powder, and you have a most palatable dish. You can make nice curries frequently of cold meats, such as are too often thrown into the swill bucket.

Veal Patties.

(MRS. N. W. BROADWELL.)

Three pounds veal, chopped very fine; one slice of salt pork; one onion, all chopped very fine; six crackers, rolled fine; a piece of butter the size of an egg; two eggs; one teaspoonful salt, and one of pepper; half a nutmeg; mix well together, form into a round loaf; sprinkle bread crumbs, or rolled cracker, over the top, with butter; bake three hours, baste while baking. It is very nice cold, sliced for supper; the pork can be left out, and more butter added, if you like.

A Plain Veal Pie.

Cut the meat from an uncooked breast of veal, and stew it in a little water. Have ready a pie dish lined with paste. Put in a layer of stewed veal with its gravy, and a layer of sausage meat; then veal again, and then sausage meat. Repeat till the dish is full. Cover with paste, and bake it brown. A cheap and good family pie.

Southern Stewed Veal.

Peel and boil a half dozen fresh spring onions, drain them and slice thin and comely. Put the veal in a stew pan, season with salt and a little cayenne; cover the veal with the onions, and lay on them some bits of fresh butter rolled in flour. Flavor with nutmeg and lemon, if you like. This stew is very nice, and lamb or chicken will make an equally nice one.

Veal Cutlets---To Stew.

Cut them about half an inch thick, flatten them with a chopper, and fry them in fresh butter or dripping. When brown on one side turn and do them on the other, continuing to do so till they are thoroughly done, which will be in about a quarter of an hour. Make a gravy of some trimmings, which put into a stewpan with a bit of soft butter, an onion, a roll of lemon peel, a blade of mace, some thyme, parsley, and stew the whole over a slow fire for an hour, and then strain it; put one ounce of butter into another pan, and when melted mix with as much flour as will dry it up; stir this for a few minutes, then add the gravy by degrees till the whole is mixed; boil it five minutes, then strain it through a sieve and put it to the cutlets. Some browning may be added, together with mushroom or walnut cutsup, or lemon pickle.

Fricandeau of Veal.
(MRS. R. E. GOODELL.)

Three pounds and a quarter of raw veal; three-fourths of a pound of salt pork, chopped very fine; one teaspoonful salt; one teaspoon black pepper; a little sweet marjoram, rubbed fine; four soda crackers, powdered very fine; three eggs, (raw,) mix well together with the hands, to make adhere; form into a large ball or roll, rub with butter, strew pounded cracker over it, place it in a pan and bake slowly two and a half hours. Slice, when cold, for tea. This is used for evening parties.

Veal Sweatbread.

Trim a fine sweetbread (it cannot be too fresh); parboil it for five minutes, and throw it into a basin of cold water. Roast it plain, or beat up the yolk of an egg, and prepare some fine bread crumbs. When the sweetbread is cold, dry it thoroughly in a cloth; run a lark-spit or a skewer through it, and tie it on the ordinary spit; egg it with a paste brush, powder it well with bread crumbs, and roast it. For sauce, fried bread crumbs round it, and melted butter, with a little mushroom catsup and lemon juice, or serve them on buttered toast, garnished with egg sauce or with gravy.

Veal and Oyster Pie.

Make a seasoning of pepper, salt, and a small quantity of grated lemon peel. Cut some veal cutlets, and beat them until they are tender; spread over them a layer of pounded ham, and roll them round; then cover them with oysters, and put another layer of the veal fillets, and oysters on the top. Make a gravy of the bones and trimmings, or with a lump of butter, onion, a little flour, and water; stew the osyter liquor, and put to it, and fill up the dish, reserving a portion to put into the pie when it comes from the oven.

Veal Loaf.

Take a cold fillet of veal, omit the fat and mince as fine as possible, mix with one-fourth pound of fat ham, chopped fine; a teacup grated bread crumbs, a grated nutmeg, two beaten eggs, a saltspoon of salt, and a half saltspoon cayenne; mix well together in the form of a loaf. Glaze over with the yelk of egg, and strew over pounded cracker. Set the dish in an oven, and bake half an hour. Make a gravy of the trimmings of veal, or some of the gravy left when the meat was served the first day. Heat up the gravy, thickened with the yelk of an egg dropped in just before taken up, and serve the loaf with the gravy poured round it.

Veal Pie.

Take a shoulder of veal, cut it up and boil one hour, then add a quarter pound of butter, pepper and salt, cover the meat with biscuit dough, cover close and stew half an hour, and it will be ready.

Veal Stuffing.

Chop half a pound of suet, put it in a basin with three-quarters of a pound of bread crumbs, a teaspoonful of salt, a quarter of pepper, a little thyme, three whole eggs, mix well. A pound of bread crumbs and one more egg may be used, it will make it cut firmer.

Minced Veal.

Chop fine the pieces of cold roast veal; heat over the gravy, or if none is left, melt a piece of butter the size of an egg in a gill of hot water, stir till it is melted, lest it become oily; when it boils, put in the veal and cover it, stir it several times while cooking; season with pepper and salt. Toast a few slices of bread and lay on the dish, put the veal on the toast.

Veal Patty.
(MRS. HERVEY ELLIOTT.)

Four pounds of veal,
One pound and a half of pickled pork,
Three eggs,
Six crackers.

Chop the pork and veal about as fine as mincemeat; then add the eggs, well beaten, and the crackers finely rolled; season with salt and pepper to suit the taste. Bake about two hours, occasionally basting it.

Breast of Veal.

Cover it with the caul, and, if you retain the sweetbread, skewer it to the back, but take off the caul when the meat is nearly done; it will take two and a half to three hours' roasting; serve with melted butter and gravy.

Veal Dressed with White Sauce.

Boil milk, or cream, with a thickening of flour and butter; put into it thin slices of cold veal, and simmer it in the gravy till it is made hot without boiling. When nearly done, beat up the yolk of an egg with any nice table sauce that suits the taste; pour it gently to the rest, stirring all the time; let it just come to a boil, and it is done.

Sandwiches, (Very Fine.)

Chop the ham or tongue very fine; add mustard, pepper, extract of celery, and melted butter to taste, and hot water enough to make it spread. Have fresh, light bread, (or beaten biscuits,) cut thin, butter, and then spread on the prepared meat.

Veal Minced.

Cut veal from the bone into small pieces; put in veal or mutton gravy, pepper, salt, a little butter, catsup, if it is liked. Put it into a saucepan, and simmer it slowly; when nearly done thicken with a little flour rubbed up with butter, stir in, giving it time to thicken well.

Fricasseed Chicken.

Cut up chicken, and boil with a slice or two of pork in sufficient water to cover, till quite tender. Fry some pork, and when cooked a little, drain the chicken and fry with the pork till quite brown. Then take out, and pour the broth into the frying pan, with the pork fat, and make a gravy thickened with browned flour; season well with butter, and put the chicken into the gravy. Be sure and have the fat quite hot when the chicken is put in, so it will brown readily.

Roast Turkey.

See that your turkey is washed and free from all small feathers; examine the inside well that nothing is left there that ought to be removed; remove the craw and wind pipe, that is often carelessly left in. Make a stuffing as for "roast pig," if it is liked, if not, any plainer dressing will do; fill your turkey, and sew it up. Salt and pepper to your taste, dredge on flour; put bits of butter on the top. A turkey of ten pounds will take about three hours to cook. It should be well basted and kept from blistering, if it blisters it is cooking too fast. Turkey should be cooked very thoroughly, if it browns to rapidly, put a paper of three or four thicknesses over it. The giblets should be put on early and boiled very tenderly, and then chopped as fine as it can be chopped and the gravy made of it. To make the gravy, take the giblets after they have been chopped, put pepper, salt and butter, and dredge in sufficient flour to make it thick enough. When your turkey is removed from the pan, pour in sufficient gravy from the pan on the giblets, and boil it.

Roast Goose.

A goose should be roasted in the same manner as a turkey. It is better to make the stuffing with some mashed potatoes; always an onion, as a goose is not good without it, (the onion can be omitted in a turkey.) Put salt, pepper, butter, and a little sage; stuff and roast well. Some like goose a little rare, that is a matter of taste. Apple sauce is good to eat with goose.

Roast Ducks.

Ducks should be, as well as all other fowls, washed with great care; they should be wiped dry and singed well, then wiped again. They should be stuffed with a stuffing as for goose. A pair of ducks will cook in about an hour. Baste them well, and dredge them well with flour to make them brown. Canvass back ducks are generally cooked without stuffing.

Egg Frizzle.

Pour boiling water on to dried beef, that has been slivered very fine; change the water a time or two, if the beef is too salt, then pour off the water, and frizzle the beef in butter. When done, break in two or three eggs, and stir till the egg is hardened. This may be done without the egg, if preferred.

Sauce for Roast Beef or Mutton.

Grate horseradish on a bread grater into a basin; then add two tablespoonsful of cream, with a little mustard and salt; mix them well together; then add four tablespoonsful of the best vinegar, and mix the whole thoroughly. The vinegar and cream are both to be cold; add a little powdered white sugar. This is a very fine sauce, it may be served in a small tureen.

Croquettes.

These are a sort of mince meat dumpling. Take some cold veal, chicken, lobster, or tender cold beef, chopped fine. Put a half tablespoon butter in a saucepan on the fire. When melted, put in a piece of onion chopped fine; fry a little; add half a tablespoon of flour. When it browns put in the minced meat; stir it steadily, and add salt and pepper. Then add a gill and a half of broth, and set the pan a little off the fire to simmer. Chop three stalks of parsley fine, and mix it on the fire, stirring all the time. Then break in two eggs, stirring faster; in two or three minutes take it from the fire and set it to cool. Thus far has occupied about ten minutes. When the meat is cold, sift some flour on the board; take a lump of the mince the size of an egg, or larger, roll it in the fine flour, dip it in a cup of beaten egg, drain and roll it in bread crumbs; have a quantity of boiling suet, or drippings in a frying pan, and fry the croquettes in them for a couple of minutes, till brown. Put in a colander, and let the fat drain off.

An Economical Dish.

Steam or boil some mealy potatoes; mash them together with some butter or cream, season them, and place a layer at the bottom of the pie dish; upon this place a layer of finely chopped cold meat, or fish of any kind, well seasoned; then add another layer of potatoes, and continue alternating these with more chopped meat until the dish is filled. Smooth down the top, strew bread crumbs upon it, and bake until it is brown. A very small quantity of meat serves in this manner to make a nice, presentable little dish. A sprinkling of chopped pickles may be added, if convenient, and when fish is employed, it eats better if first beaten up with raw eggs.

French Stew.

Cut into pieces two or three pounds of the lean of fresh, tender beef, veal or pork, and peel and slice a quarter of a peck of ripe tomatoes; season the whole with a little pepper and salt. Put the whole into a stew pot, and cover it close, opening it only occasionally to see how it is cooking. Put no water to stew, the juice of the tomatoes is enough liquid. When the tomatoes are dissolved, stir in a piece of fresh butter dredged with flour. Let it stew about a quarter of an hour longer. When the meat is done through, have ready some bits of very dry toast cut in a three-cornered shape, leaving the crust off. Dip the toast for a moment in some hot water, butter it, and stand it up around the inside of a deep dish. Fill in the stew and serve hot.

Potatoes Roasted under Meat.

Half boil large potatoes, drain the water from them, and put them into an earthen dish or small tin pan, under meat that is roasting, and baste them with some of the dripping. When they are browned on one side, turn them and brown the other, send them up round the meat, or in a small dish.

For a French Pot au Feu.

Put into a large earthen pot or pipkin six pounds of good fresh beef, and four quarts of water. Set it on a slow fire, skim it when it simmers, and when nearly boiling add one teaspoonful salt, half a pound of liver cut in pieces, and some black pepper; add two or three large carrots sliced, four turnips pared and quartered, eight young onions peeled and sliced thick, two onions roasted whole, a head of celery cut up, a parsnip sliced, and six potatoes pared and quartered; also a bunch of sweet herbs. Let all boil slowly and steadily, skimming well; let it simmer five or six hours. Lay some large slices of bread in the bottom of a tureen, pour the soup upon it. This is a very good, plain dish.

Good, Plain Family Irish Stew.

Take about two pounds of scrag or neck of mutton; divide it into ten pieces, lay them in the pan; cut eight large potatoes and four onions in slices, season with one teaspoonful and a half of pepper, and three of salt; cover all with water; put it into a slow oven for two hours, then stir it all up well, and dish up in deep dishes. If you add a little more water at the commencement, you can take out when half done a nice cup of broth.

How to Cut a Chicken to Fry.

Have a sharp knife to begin with; then cut the wings off first; then the legs, cutting them carefully and neatly; throw each leg toward the back of the chicken and sever it from the body through the hip joint; next cut the chicken through the back; remove the lower portion of the back, then the neck piece, cutting it off through the rib joints; this leaves the breast piece, which should be cut in two lengthwise. A chicken cut up in this way looks much neater than to cut it in any other way. The leg can be cut in two pieces, making it more handy to serve at the table. With care, and a little practice, this art may be easily learned.

Stewed Rabbits.

Cut the shoulders of the rabbits, and throw them into a little salt and water to draw out the blood; when ready, cut them in pieces and put them in a pot with water enough to cook them; wash and peel some nice potatoes and cut them in pieces, and put in with the rabbit; let it stew till the rabbit is cooked very tender; then take flour and butter and rub them well together, and stir in; let it boil up till it makes a nice gravy; pepper and salt to suit the taste.

Rabbit Pot Pie.

Prepare the rabbits by cutting them up and putting them into a little salt and water; let them remain till cleansed from all blood spots. Make a dough, not too short, and if you wish a boiled pot pie, put in your rabbits and potatoes intermixed with pieces of the dough, that should be rolled out about half an inch and cut in oblong pieces; put in the dough alternately with the potatoes and rabbits; put salt, pepper and butter, and water enough to cook it and make the gravy;

put a crust on the top of the pot; let it boil slowly, and if you wish the top crust browned, heat a griddle or cover and put on till it is brown. When your dinner is ready to serve, have your dish or platter ready, take off the top crust, and with a ladle dip up the rabbits; the gravy will be thick enough, unless there was too much water put in. When all is out, pour in your gravy and put on the top crust. Pot pies are made the same way to be baked.

Chicken, veal, pigeons, squirrels and quails are made into pot pies, the same directions answering for all. Care should be taken not to put to put too much water, and there should be quite enough to cook the pie, leaving enough to make enough gravy or the pie will be very dry. All such pies or stews should be well seasoned.

Broiled Rabbits.

Take the hind quarters of the rabbit and pound them well; salt and pepper, and have your gridiron well greased and heated; put them on and let them broil slowly. When done, butter and send to the table hot. The butter should be melted in a pan, with a little sprinkle of flour and a good deal of pepper. Put the rabbits in a piece at a time, and with the pounder mash them into the butter.

Broiled Quails.

These are the nicest of birds, and require great care to have them nicely cooked. They are considered best when nicely broiled. Each quail should be picked over carefully, then they should be pounded slightly with the steak pounder, to break the bones and give them an opportunity to broil. A very nice way to serve them is to toast bread a light brown, and butter each piece well; lay a bird on each piece of the toast, and pour the butter in which they were dipped over the whole. If the toast is not liked, serve without.

Potted Rabbit.

Take very young fat hares or rabbits; wash and soak them in salt and water; then take them out of the water and wipe each piece quite dry; pepper, salt, and flour them well, and fry them nicely in hot lard; then take them from the stove and put them in a stone jar; pour the gravy, which should be made like chicken gravy, over them, adding one pint of boiling water; set this jar, which must be covered tight, in the oven, and let it remain about an hour and a half. The English think this a choice dish, and add one tumbler of good port wine.

Stewed Prairie Chicken.

Cut the chickens in pieces, wash and pick off all small feathers; put them in a pot, with just enough water to cook them, with salt, pepper and butter. Make a nice gravy of flour and butter, and stir in just before taking them up. Prairie chickens, if young, are splendid broiled.

Fried Chickens.

This is one of nicest ways that chickens can be cooked, and there is no way that requires more attention. If chickens are killed and picked at home, they should not be allowed to remain in the boiling water in which they are scalded; they should be picked as quick as possible, and then as soon as they are thoroughly cleaned, throw them into cold water till you are ready to cut them up ready for frying. Each piece should be salted and peppered, and dredged with flour; have the lard hot, and after all the pieces are in, cover with a tight fitting cover, let it fry slowly. Make a gravy by putting a little flour in the skillet, (after you have taken up the chickens.) Pour in boiling water and then a little milk or cream; pour gravy over the chickens, or serve in a gravy boat.

Chicken Salad.

For two chickens, take—
    The yolks of eight hard boiled eggs,
    One small teaspoonful of salt,
    One-half of a teaspoonful of cayenne pepper.
    One-half a wine glass made mustard,
    One wine glass and a half of vinegar,
    Two wine glasses of sweet olive oil.
As much celery as there is chopped chicken.
The chicken can be chopped very fine, or in larger pieces, as taste may dictate; chop celery fine; chop eggs very fine, mix with the chicken; then add the

celery and other ingredients; add more vinegar, if too dry, and black pepper. To this quantity about eight good sized pickles may be chopped fine and added, many think them an improvement.

Mayonaise.

A SUPPER DISH.

Six hard boiled eggs, (yolks only,)
Four tablespoonsful mixed mustard,
One teaspoonful salt,
One teaspoonful sugar,
Ten tablespoonsful of vinegar,
Ten tablespoonsful of rich cream,
One teaspoonful celery seed.

Slice cold fowl, or other delicate meat, and lay in the above mixture two or three hours before tea; wash lettuce and put on ice; just before tea is ready lay alternate layers of meat and lettuce, leaving lettuce for the top. Pour dressing over the whole.

Smothered or Baked Chickens.

Your chickens should be large and fat; split them down the back and put them in your dripping pan; salt and pepper, with plenty of butter put over the top; set them in the stove, with water sufficient to cook them. This is baked chicken. If you wish them smothered, cover a closely fitting pan over them, and let them cook slowly; put flour over the top before you put them in the stove. Make gravy with flour in the dripping pan in which they are cooked.

To Cook Calf's or Beef's Liver.

Cut the slices half an inch thick; put in a pan and pour over them some boiling water till it becomes white; pour off the water; salt, pepper, and flour each slice, and fry in hot lard; turn often, that it may not become hard when done; take up on your dish; shake flour into skillet; add a little salt and pepper, and sweet milk enough to make a nice, thick gravy; let it boil up once and pour over your liver. Always remove the skin from the liver before frying it.

VEGETABLES.

There is nothing in which the difference between an elegant and an ordinary table is more seen than in the dressing of vegetables, more especially of greens. They may be equally as fine at first, at one place as at another, but their look and taste are afterward very different, entirely from the careless way in which they have been cooked. They are in greatest perfection when in greatest plenty—when in full season. By season, we do not mean those early days, that luxury in the buyers and avarice in the sellers, force the various vegetables; but the time of year in which, by nature and common culture, and the mere operation of the sun and climate, they are in most plenty and perfection.

Potatoes and peas are scarcely worth eating before mid-summer.

Unripe vegetables are as insipid and unwholesome as unripe fruits. As to the quality of vegetables, the middle size are preferred to the largest or the smallest; they are more tender, juicy, and full of flavor just before they are quite full grown; freshness is their chief value and excellence, and I should as soon think of roasting an animal alive as of boiling a vegetable after it is dead. The eye easily discovers if they have been kept too long. They soon lose their beauty in all respects.

Roots, greens, salads, etc., and the various productions of the garden, when first gathered, are plump and firm, and have a fragrant freshness no art can give them again; though it will refresh them a little to put them into cold spring water for some time before they are dressed.

TO BOIL THEM

In soft water will preserve the color best of such as are green. If you only have hard water put to it a teaspoonful of soda.

TAKE CARE TO WASH

And cleanse them thoroughly from dust, dirt and insects. This requires great attention. Pick off all the outside leaves; trim them nicely; lay them in a pan of clear, cold water, with a little salt in it, and let them remain an hour at least before cooking.

TO HAVE VEGETABLES DELICATELY CLEAN,

Put on your pot with sufficient water and a little salt; make it boil and skim it perfectly clean before you put on greens of any kind to cook. They should not be put in till the water boils briskly. The quicker greens boil the greener they will be.

WHEN VEGETABLES SINK

to the bottom of the pot they are generally done enough, if the water has been kept boiling Take them up immediately or they will lose their color and goodness; drain off all the water before sending to the table. This branch of cooking requires the most vigilant attention. If vegetables are a minute or two too long over the fire, they lose all their beauty and flavor. If they are not thoroughly boiled tender, they are very indigestible.

TO PRESERVE OR GIVE COLOR

in cookery, many good dishes are spoiled; but the rational epicure who makes *nourishment* the main end of eating, will be content to sacrifice the shadow to enjoy the substance. Once for all, take care that your vegetables are *fresh;* for the fishmonger often suffers for the sins of the cook, so the cook often gets undeservedly blamed instead of the green grocer.

Potato Cakes.

Peel enough good sized potatoes for a meal for the family; grate on a coarse grater, and stir in from three to five eggs; then add a little flour—more eggs will not hurt them; stir well, and fry in hot lard, and, if tried once, my word for it, they will be tried again and often.

Potatoes.

There are few articles in families more subject to waste, both in paring, boiling, and being actually thrown away, than potatoes; and there are few cooks but what boil twice as many potatoes every day as are wanted, and fewer still that do not throw the residue away as totally unfit, in any shape, for the next day's

—10

meal; and yet, if they would take the trouble to heat up the despised cold potatoes in many or any of the various dishes recommended, they would find a cheap and very agreeable appendage to either the breakfast or dinner table. We are all potato eaters, (and esteem them beyond any other vegetable,) yet few know how to cook them well.

Plain Boiled Potatoes.

Put them into a saucepan with scarcely sufficient water to cover them. Directly the skin begins to break, lift them from the fire, and as quick as possible pour off *every drop* of the water. Then place a coarse (we need not say clean) towel over them, and return them to the fire again until they are thoroughly done and quite dry. A little salt should have been added to the water before boiling. Care should, of course, be used that they do not scorch or burn.

Potatoes to Mash.

These should be boiled in the same manner as the above directions; peeled, and mashed till there are no lumps of the potato left; salt to the taste; butter the size of an egg for about a dozen potatoes; a little good sweet cream or new milk; mash well together and serve while hot.

Mashed Potatoes

May be put into a pie plate of tin or earthenware,

smoothed over the top till quite round; make a hole in the centre, put in a lump of butter, and set it in the stove and let it brown nicely. Some persons beat up the yolk of an egg and put over it, this is a matter of fancy altogether.

Baked Potatoes.

Wash very clean your potatoes, cutting a small piece from each end, by so doing the steam or heat escapes, and the potatoes are more dry and mealy. Do not let let them remain in the oven to get too hard and dry; judgment should be used to have them just done in time to serve, as they will be spoiled if they remain long in the oven.

Potatoes Fried Whole.

When nearly boiled enough, put them into a stew pan with a bit of butter or some clean beef drippings; shake them about often to prevent burning, till they are brown and crisp; clear them from the fat. It will be an improvement if they are floured and dipped into the yolk of an egg, and then rolled in finely sifted crumbs.

Tomato Omelet.

Select your tomatoes; pour over them boiling water to remove the skins; then chop them, and put them in a saucepan without any water; put one or two onions chopped fine, a lump of butter the size of an egg, pepper and salt to the taste; cook slowly, and till they are pretty well cooked; then have ready the yelks of two eggs, well beaten, with half a teacup of sweet cream, and pour this into the cooked tomatoes, just before you take them from the stove, stir well; do not leave this on the stove after the eggs are stirred in, else the eggs and cream will curdle.

Potatoes Escolloped.

Mash potatoes in the usual way; then butter some nice, clean scollop shells, patty pans or saucers; put in your potatoes; make them smooth at the top, strew some bread crumbs over them; rub, or pour, over each a little melted butter; set them in the oven to brown; when done, take them out and turn them over, and if the under side is not browned, set them again into the oven a few minutes.

Saratoga Fried Potatoes.

Peel and slice large, nice potatoes, slice them very thin; have a kettle with lard, and when it boils, put in a portion of the potatoes, and fry them a light brown; keep moving them about till they are crisp; take them from the lard with a skimmer, let them drip free of the lard; send them to the table hot; salt may be added after they are taken up, or they can be salted before frying. When they are used in winter for breakfast, they should be prepared over night and thrown into salt water; in the morning, dip them from the water; lay them in a clean, dry cloth, and wipe off all the water, then fry them as above. This way of preparing them over night in winter is better, as the mornings are so very short, and it takes considerable time to prepare them. This way is preferred to almost any other way of frying potatoes. It would not do for an every day dish, as it takes considerable lard, and would be rather expensive at the end of a year.

Potato Fritters.

(MRS. RYAN.)

Three eggs, one quart sweet milk, and a little flour; rub in the flour with the eggs, salt to the taste. The batter must not be too thin. Then add well mashed potatoes; have a little lard in a skillet, it must be hot, and drop the mixture in by spoonful in small cakes; fry a light brown. They must be eaten hot.

Plain Fried Potatoes.

Potatoes can be par-boiled, and the skins removed; then sliced and fried, for either breakfast or dinner; and the potatoes left from dinner, put away carefully, are nice sliced and fried.

French Batter for Frying Vegetables.

Moisten a little flour with water, and add to it a small quantity of salt, a tablespoonful of olive oil, and a spoonful and a half of French brandy; beat up the mixture thoroughly, and when you are ready to use it, beat into it the white of an egg previously beaten to a strong froth. This batter may be used for frying sweet *entremets*, in which case sugar must be put instead of salt.

Potato Snow.

Pick out the whitest potatoes, put them on in cold water; when they begin to crack open, pour off the water and put them in a clean saucepan before the fire till they are quite dry, and fall to pieces; rub them through a wire sieve on the dish they are to be sent to the table in, and do not mash them, but let them remain as they fall from the sieve. They should be salted, of course, while they are boiling.

Squash.

Gather the summer squashes when young and tender. If the scallop, the seeds will do no harm; cut it in quarters, and boil in a bag until tender; squeeze out all the water, and season with salt and butter; pepper can be added at the table.

Turnips

Should always be boiled whole, and put in much after either carrots or parsnips, as they require less boiling. When used in stews, they are cut into small pieces the size of dice, or made into shapes with a little instrument to be found at all cutlery shops. They may be mashed in the same manner as parsnips, but some persons add the yelk of a raw egg or two. They are also frequently made into a *puree* to thicken mutton broth.

String Beans.

Gather them while young enough to break crispy; break off both ends, and string them; break in halves, and boil in water with a little salt, until tender; drain free from water, and season with butter.

Succotash, or Corn and Beans.

If old beans are used, they must be soaked over night, and parboiled in two waters before putting in the pork. The corn should be added to the beans and pork about fifteen minutes before the hour for serving the dinner. It is well to boil the cobs with the beans and pork in the last water. Remove them before adding the corn. For using beans not fully ripe, one change of water is sufficient; the pork can be parboiled at the same time. Beans for succotash should remain whole; care must be taken that they boil gently, so as not to break them. Considerable water is generally used in boiling the beans, that no more need be added when the corn is put in; most persons like considerable soup in this dish. Families can be governed by taste in this. Dish the corn and beans in a deep dish with the broth, and season with butter and a very little salt; use no pepper, if any person desire it, it is easily added. Serve the pork on a platter, after taking off the skin and dotting it with pepper, by dipping the little finger in ground pepper and pressing it on the pork.

Tomato Stew.

Take large, ripe tomatoes, scald, peel and quarter them, and sprinkle them with a little salt and pepper. Put in a stewpan some thin, tender beef steaks, lamb or mutton chops. Bury the meat in the tomato, and add bits of fresh butter rolled in flour and sugar, if you do not like the acid of the tomatoes; add a chopped onion or two, if you like it. Cook slowly till the meat is done and tomatoes all dissolved to a pulp. Add *no water* to this stew. A very wholesome dish.

Sweetbreads and Cauliflowers.

Take four large sweetbreads and two cauliflowers. Split open the sweetbreads and remove the gristle. Soak them awhile in lukewarm water; put them into a saucepan of boiling water, and set them to boil ten minutes. Afterward lay them in a pan of cold water to make them firm. The parboiling is to whiten them. Wash, drain and quarter the cauliflowers. Put them in a broad stewpan with the sweetbreads on them; season with a little cayenne and a little nutmeg —add water to cover them. Put on the lid of the pan and stew one hour. Take a quarter of a pound of fresh butter and roll in two tablespoons of flour; add this with a teacup of milk to the stew, and give it one boil up, and no more. Serve hot, in a deep dish. This stew will be found delicious.

To Stew Red Cabbage.

Slice a small, or half a large red cabbage, wash and put it into a saucepan with pepper, salt, no water but what hangs about it, and a piece of butter; stew till quite tender, and when going to serve, add two or three spoonsful of vinegar, and give one boil over the fire. Serve it for cold meat, or with sausages on it.

Fried Egg Plant.

Peel the egg plants, slice them thin, sprinkle a little salt over them, and let them remain half an hour; wipe the slices dry, dip them into beaten yelk of egg, then into grated cracker, and fry them a light brown in boiling lard, seasoning them slightly with pepper while they are cooking. Another way is to parboil the egg plants, after they are peeled, in water with a little salt, then slice thin, dust them with corn meal, flour, or corn starch, and fry them brown.

Green Corn Dumplings.

A quart of young corn grated from the cob,
Half a pint of wheat flour sifted,
Half a pint of milk,
Six tablespoonsful of butter,
Two eggs,
A saltspoonful of salt,
A saltspoonful of pepper,
Butter for frying.

Having grated as fine as possible sufficient young fresh

corn to make a quart, mix with it the wheat flour, and add the salt and pepper. Warm the milk in a small saucepan, and soften the butter in it. Then add them gradually to the pan of corn, stirring very hard, and set it away to cool. Beat the eggs light, and stir them into the mixture when it has cooled. Flour your hands and make it into little dumplings. Put into a fryingpan a sufficiency of fresh butter, (or lard and butter in equal proportions,) and when it is boiling hot, and has been skimmed, put in the dumplings, and fry them ten minutes or more, in proportion to their thickness. Then drain them, and send them hot to the dinner table.

Green Corn in Winter.

Take tender green corn, (sweet corn is best,) boil it ten minutes. Then cut it from the cob and dry it in the sun. Corn preserved in this way will keep for years, and will be perfectly fresh when brought on the table. To prepare for use, cook it until tender in as little water as possible. When nearly done, add milk, butter and salt to taste.

Tomato Pudding.

Pour boiling water on tomatoes, remove the skins; put in the bottom of the pudding dish some bread crumbs, them slice the tomatoes on them, season with sugar, butter, pepper and salt; add some more bread crumbs, then the sliced tomatoes and seasoning; and if the tomato does not wet the bread crumbs, add a little water. Then, for a small pudding, beat up two eggs, and pour over the top. Bake about twenty minutes.

To Broil Tomatoes.

Wash and wipe the tomatoes, and put them on the gridiron over live coals, with the stem down. When that side is brown turn them and let them cook through. Put them on a hot dish and send quickly to table, to be there seasoned to taste.

To Bake Tomatoes.

Season them with salt and pepper; flour them over, put them in a deep plate with a little butter, and bake in a stove.

Fricasseed Egg Plant.

Having peeled and sliced the egg plants, boil them in water with a saltspoonful of salt, until they are thoroughly cooked. Drain off the water, pour in sufficient milk to cover the slices, and add a few bits of butter rolled in flour; let it simmer gently, shaking the pan over the fire till the sauce is thick, and stir in the beaten yolks of two or three eggs just before it is served.

Beets.

These should be, as all other vegetables should be, fresh gathered, carefully selected, well washed, and they should be put into cold water. In cutting off the tops, do not cut too closely, or you will lose the rich, red color. They should be salted while boiling, and when done, taken up and thrown a few moments into clear, cold water, the skin will then slip off easily; slice them thin, and dress with butter and pepper; vinegar, if it is preferred.

Parsnips.

These are a nice winter vegetable, and are very nice boiled and dressed with butter, pepper and salt. They should be sliced lengthwise. A very nice way is to have butter hot in a skillet, and lay each piece nicely in the butter, and fry, turning over, that both sides may be browned.

Cabbage.

The Early York is a nice summer cabbage, and should be boiled with nice salt pork or corned beef, or a piece of brisket, either is nice, and makes a good family dinner.

Asparagus

Should be young, and freshly cut; boil in a little salted water; they should be tied carefully before putting in the water; (have nice bread toasted, if it is liked that way;) when done, take up, cut off the string, pour over the toast, if used, and if not, dress it with melted butter.

Peas.

Boil peas in salted water, and dress with butter. Some make a drawn butter, and some put cream and butter; all tastes are not alike. In the manner of cooking, that must be left to the tastes of those who are to eat them; but one thing should always be looked carefully to, that is to be sure they have not lain in the market for a week or more; they are not only unfit to eat, but are very unhealthy.

String Beans.

These should always be gathered fresh; string them, by breaking off both ends and pulling off the string that is on either side; they should then be broken. Always boil bacon with these.

To Preserve Mushrooms.

To each quart of mushrooms allow three ounces of butter, pepper and salt to taste, the juice of one lemon, clarified butter. Peel the mushrooms, put them into cold water, with a little lemon juice; take them out and dry them very carefully in a cloth. Put the butter into a stewpan capable of holding the mushrooms; when it is melted, add the mushrooms, lemon juice, and a seasoning of pepper and salt; draw them down over a slow fire, and let them remain until their liquor is boiled away, and they have become quite dry, but be careful in not allowing them to the stick to the bottom of the stewpan. When done, put them into pots, and pour over the top clarified butter. If wanted for immediate use, they will keep good a few days without being covered over. To re-warm them, put the mushrooms into a stewpan, strain the butter from them, and they will be ready for use.

Mushrooms Stewed in Gravy.

One pint of mushroom buttons, one pint of brown gravy, quarter of a teaspoonful of grated nutmeg, cayenne and salt to taste. Make a pint of brown gravy, cut nearly all the stalks away from the mushrooms and peel the tops; put them into a stewpan, with the gravy, and simmer them gently from twenty minutes to half an hour. Add the nutmeg and a seasoning of cayenne and salt, and serve very hot.

Baked Sweet Potatoes.

Wash them perfectly clean, wipe dry, and bake in a quick oven, according to their size—half an hour for small ones, and from three-quarters to an hour for larger ones. Let the oven have a good heat, and do not open any more than necessary to turn them, until they are done.

Roasted Sweet Potatoes.

Having washed them clean and wiped them dry; cover them with ashes, and then with hot coals; watch them closely that they do not burn. (This can only be done when you burn wood, and can be done in the hearth of the stove.)

Boiled Sweet Potatoes.

Wash them clean, put them in a pot or stewpan and pour boiling water over to cover them; cover the pot close, and boil fast for half an hour or more, according the size; try them with a fork; when done, drain off the water, take off the skin and serve.

Fried Sweet Potatoes.

Cold sweet potatoes may be cut in slices, across or lengthwise, and fried in hot lard or butter.

Summer Squash.

Squashes to be fit to eat, must be fresh, if they are not, the outside will be crisp when cut with the nail. Cut them in small pieces, and if not very tender, pare off the outside skin, scrape the seed from the inside; wash them and put them in a saucepan and cook till tender; add salt to make them palatable. After they are cooked well, let them cook down slowly till all the water is all cooked out and they are thick; then dress them with butter and pepper; put them in a dish; smooth them over the top, and they are ready for the table.

Young Beets.

Wash fresh pulled young beets; break the tops

from them, pick from them all the withered leaves, and put them with the beets into a pot of hot water; cover it, and let them boil fast for half an hour, or longer, if the beets are large; then take the tops into a colander, and press all the water from them; take the beets into a pan of cold water and rub off the skin with the hand; put the pressed tops into a dish, slice the beets over them; make a small cup of vinegar hot, with a bit of butter the size of an egg; add salt and pepper to the taste; add a teaspoonful of made mustard, if liked. If the stalks of beet tops are long, cut them from the beets and the leaves, tie them in bunches and boil, and serve like asparagus.

Greens and Sprouts.

Cabbage sprouts, young beet tops and the green, young turnips, are boiled with salt meats or in clear, salt water.

Spinage.

Spinage should be carefully picked over and well washed, and let remain in cold water till ready to cook; have your water *boiling* and salted; put in your spinage, and do not let it boil more than twenty minutes. When time to serve, drain in a colander till all the water has drained off; then dress with butter and pepper. Another way to dress it, is to drain it as dry as you can, and put it in a chopping bowl, chop it very fine indeed; have ready eight or ten hard boiled eggs, chopped as fine as you can chop them; mix the the eggs well through the spinage; put butter and pepper. It will have to be returned to the stove and warmed again before putting it on the table.

Slaw.

Two eggs, well beaten,
One teaspoonful dry mustard,
One teaspoonful salt,
One teaspoonful sugar,
One-half teaspoonful flour,
One-half teaspoonful black pepper,
A little cayenne,
Three-fourths of a teacupful vinegar,
Three-fourths of a teacupful cream or new milk,
One tablespoonful butter,
One-half teaspoonful celery seed.

Mix and beat all well together, and place the mixture in a another vessel containing boiling water till it is the consistency of thick cream; stir well; pour hot over cabbage.

Hot Slaw.

Cut the cabbage with a slaw cutter, or very fine with a knife; put a little vinegar, butter, pepper and salt, into a skillet, let them get hot; put in your cabbage, and when heated thoroughly, add a little cream, if you have it, and dish up. It is nice without cream.

To Bake Beans.

Boil the beans, (of course the quantity must be regulated by the size of the family,) say one quart in two or three quarts of water, till they begin to crack open; put in a teaspoonful of soda while they are boiling; when ready to bake, drain off all the water in which they were cooked; then put them in a pan large enough to hold them, and a piece of nice, fat salted pork which will weigh one or two pounds; score the pork across the top and settle it in the middle of the beans; cover all with water, and two tablespoonsful of molasses or sugar, and bake in a moderate oven two hours. Do not forget the sweetening, or you will not have Yankee baked beans.

Corn.

Corn, for boiling, should be full grown, but young and tender. When the grains become yellow, it is too old. Strip off the leaves and all the silk; some leave the inner leaves and pull them up over the corn before putting it in the water; have plenty of water; add salt, and let the pot boil briskly for half an hour.

Hominy.

Wash the hominy clean, through two or three waters; then put it into a pot, allowing two quarts of water to one quart of hominy; let it boil slowly three or four hours. When done, take a portion up in a dish, dress with butter, and serve hot. The rest can be put away, to keep cool, and be used the next day; add salt while it is boiling. Hominy is very nice fried as a breakfast dish.

Cucumbers.

Have them fresh gathered; pare them and lay them in cold water till near dinner; slice them very thin; pepper, salt, and vinegar to the taste.

Salsify.

Scrape the salsify roots, and wash them in cold water; parboil them, and if preferred, cut in small slices and fry. The nicest way is to boil tender, and add salt, pepper, butter and cream. If exposed to to the air it will turn blackish.

Corn on the Cob.

Corn to boil should be young and tender; remove the husks, and carefully take off all the silk; have a pot of boiling water salted sufficient for the corn, and boil from twenty minutes to three-quarters of an hour, according to the age of the corn.

ANOTHER WAY TO COOK CORN.

After removing silk and husks, cut the corn from the cob, but do not cut too closely into the cob, but take a knife and scrape it down; cook it well till all the water is cooked out, then dress it with pepper, salt and butter. It is also good to cook in this way, adding tomatoes, and is a very nice dish baked in the stove, adding butter and bread crumbs as you put it in the pan.

Celery.

Pick over and wash celery well, and let it lie in cold water till time to put it on the table, then wipe each piece dry. Send it to the table in a celery glass, and eat with salt only; or, as many prefer, chop fine, and use a salad dressing.

To Boil Onions.

Take off the tops and tails and peel them; put on water sufficient to cover them; throw in a little salt; boil till perfectly done; then pour off the water and throw in a little sweet milk to whiten them; take up and dress with butter and pepper.

Onions Fried.

Peel and slice your onions, and put them into a skillet with very hot lard in it, cover tight; or, throw them in with a beef steak as you are frying it. They are very fine in this way.

Potato Cakes.

Take two pounds of very mealy boiled potatoes, mash them very fine with a little salt, mix them with two pounds of flour, add milk enough to make this into dough, beating it with a spoon, and put a little yeast. Set it before the fire to rise, and when it has risen divide it into cakes the size of a muffin, and bake them. These cakes may be cut open and buttered hot. They are particularly nice.

Cold Peas.

Mash them; boil cream, and thicken it with the peas; add a little butter, pepper and salt to the taste. Beans can be used in the same manner.

Cold Corn.

Grate it, and make it into cakes, with egg and a little flour; fry in hot lard a light brown.

Green Corn Pudding for Meat.

Grate about twelve large, full ears of sweet corn, to this add one quart of sweet milk, one quarter of a pound of fresh butter, four well beaten eggs, as much pepper and salt as is necessary to season it well; stir well together and bake in a well greased pudding dish. This is an excellent dish to eat with meat.

Egg Plant.

The best directions are as follows: Cut the plant across into thin slices, lay them in salt over night; in the morning take them from the brine, wash them and wipe each piece dry, and sprinkle finely powdered crackers over both sides of the slices; then fry brown (not black) in just enough grease to keep them from sticking to the griddle. Some use corn meal instead of crackers. A friend says: Cut them in slices nearly an inch thick; sprinkle on salt, and let them lay one on the other all night, with a light weight on the top. In the morning drain off the brine, roll in flour and fry in hot butter, and they can't be beat.

COOKING EGGS.

Omelet with Cheese.

Beat six eggs very light; add two tablespoonsful of cream, butter the size of a walnut, a little chopped parsley, pepper, salt, and two ounces of grated cheese. Beat all well together, and pour into a pan in which a small piece of butter is melting; let it cook until of a light brown, then fold it over and dish for the table. Shake the pan while the omelet is cooking.

Omelet.

Three teaspoonsful milk to one egg, beat the eggs

light, then pour into a pan in which a little butter is melted hot, lifting the bottom with a knife so the softer parts can run in; cook three or four minutes. Salt to taste.

Hard Boiled Eggs.

Those who like hard boiled eggs, and want them to digest well, should boil them hard for *thirty minutes*, and they are then fit to eat. I thought this out of reason till I tried it myself; the eggs thus cooked are mealy and delightful.

Egg Omelet, (Very Fine.)

Take six eggs for each omelet, beat the yelks and whites separately; salt and pepper the yelks, and beat till they are very light; have the whites beaten stiff; have a long handled frying pan, or one that flares out at the edge; put in about a tablespoonful of butter, have it hot; put in the yelks, and quickly put in the whites; stir together till it is well mixed, and in a few moments turn one half up over the other and put into an oblong dish, and serve as hot as possible. This is a most excellent omelet, and is very nice with a little onion chopped very fine fried in the butter quickly before putting in the egg. This omelet must be made very quickly.

Poached Eggs.

Have a skillet with water boiling, a little vinegar

added; break in the eggs carefully; dress with butter, pepper and salt.

Pickled Eggs.

The eggs should be boiled hard, and then divested of their shells; when cold, put them in a jar, and pour over them (sufficient to cover them) vinegar in which has been boiled the usual spices for pickling. Tie the jar down tight; do not make many at a time, especially in warm weather; in winter, first pour the vinegar over red cabbage, and when it is a bright color pour it off and strain it over the eggs. It is nice to have a jar of white and a jar of the red eggs, they look handsome mixed on the table.

To Keep Eggs.

To four quarts air-slacked lime, put two tablespoonsful cream tartar, two of salt, and four quarts cold water. Put fresh eggs into a stone jar, and pour this mixture over them. This will keep nine dozen, and if fresh when laid down, they will keep many months. If the water settles away so as to leave the upper layer uncovered, add more water. Cover close, and keep in a cool place.

Eggs Plain Boiled.

This being beyond question the most popular way of serving eggs, we must commence by giving it in the approved French method. Get ready a saucepan of boiling water, place in it some fresh eggs, immediately remove the saucepan from the fire, put on the lid, and let the eggs remain exactly four minutes. Take them up, and serve them, while warm, in a dish. The eggs, if so preferred, may be put into cold water over a quick fire, and when the water comes to a boil, they are done.

Eggs a l'Ardennaise.

Break the shells of a dozen eggs. Separate the yelks from the whites, and keep each yelk by itself. Beat the whites to a froth; add to them a little salt, pepper, and thick cream. Pour this into a well buttered, deep dish, and arrange the yelks upon the top. Put the dish into a gentle oven, and, when set, serve them hot.

Eggs sur le Plat.

Heat some butter upon a tin or pewter dish; carefully break into it as many eggs as you think sufficient, arranging them neatly; season with salt and pepper; add a few teaspoonsful of good thick cream, and place the dish for six minutes over a clear fire, and serve directly.

Buttered Eggs.

Take three eggs, beat them up well, then add to them a gill of sweet milk. Place some butter (about the size of a large walnut) at the bottom of pan, pour the mixture into it, and boil until quite thick. Pour it upon buttered toast, and grate some ham or beef over it.

Egg Balls.

Take the yelks of six hard boiled eggs; pound them in a mortar, together with a little salt, one dessert-spoonful of flour, and a small quantity of pepper. When a smooth, but stiff paste is formed, add as much raw yelk of egg as will serve to mix it of the consistency required. Make it into balls, poach them, and serve them upon buttered toast, or any sauce approved of.

BREAD MAKING AND YEAST.

Good bread depends as much on having good yeast, as on having good flour. The cheapest flour in the *end* is always the *best* There is no one thing on which the health of a family so much depends as on good, well-baked bread. Biscuits made of baking powder, or soda and cream tartar, are, when made right, very nice, and often it is very convenient to make them, but they are not so healthy as biscuit made of good yeast. In order to secure good bread, great care should be taken to make the yeast a *special* object. There are a great variety of ways of making good yeast. I will give a number of receipts, all having been tried and found good

Hop Yeast.

Take a good handful of fresh hops, pour boiling water, let it boil till the water is sufficiently strong of the hops; have sifted flour enough to make a batter, not too thin, by straining the boiling hop water over it; let it cool; if you have a quart, put half teacupful of white sugar, a spoonful of salt and a teacupful of good, fresh yeast. Set it away to rise. When you wish to make your bread, take flour enough to make a sponge sufficient to make the amount of dough you wish, wet it to a batter with warm (not hot) water; have three or four well mashed potatoes and a teacupful of the hop yeast; let this rise well, and then make up your bread; add salt; work your bread well, but not too stiff. When you make out your rolls, give them ample time to rise well.

Grated Potato Yeast.

Take two or three potatoes, if not large, two if good size; grate them and pour boiling water on them, and set it in a vessel on the stove, and stir like starch till it is well cooked and clear; while it is hot stir in flour sufficient to make a strong batter; when cool, if too thick, thin it with the water in which your potatoes have been boiled, (if they have been peeled;) add a teacupful of good yeast; let it rise well, and it is fit for use. It is well to make your yeast, or sponge, for bread, near dinner time, in order to have the potato water to put into it.

Bottled or Jug Yeast.

(MRS. ZIMMERMAN.)

Yeast that will Keep Six Months.—Take ten or twelve good sized ripe potatoes, wash them well and put them to boil with the skins on in a gallon of water, boil till done; take them out of the water, and wash them while hot, (peeling them;) then take two good handsful of hops and boil well in the potato water, then strain the water over the mashed potatoes; add one cupful of brown sugar and one of salt, and a half cupful of ginger; boil the hops through one or two waters, to get all the strength out of them; let it cool; add a half pint of the same kind of yeast or of baker's yeast; after standing in a jar 24 hours, put in bottles or in a jug, and cork tight; set in the cellar for use. One large spoonful is enough for one loaf of bread. Make sufficient sponge to make the bread; add your yeast, and let it lighten; it will be salt enough.

Bottled Yeast.

Thicken two quarts of water with fine flour, four or five spoonsful; wet the flour with a little water till it is smooth and free from lumps, boil near half an hour, sweeten with half a pound brown sugar; when near cold, put into it four spoonsful of fresh yeast; put it into a jug, shake well together; let it stand one day to ferment near the fire, without being corked. There will be a thin liquor on the top, which must be poured off; shake the remainder, and cork it up for use. Take, always, four spoonsful of the old to ferment the next quantity, keeping it always on hand.

Potato Yeast, with Mashed Potatoes.

Boil well, and mash six or seven good sized potatoes; stir in flour while they are hot, and save the water in which they were boiled to thin it with; add a little salt, a half cupful white sugar, and a teacupful of good, fresh yeast. I have learned from experience that it is a piece of economy to make yeast near dinner time, or make it so you can use the water in which your potatoes have been boiled for dinner. You can boil enough for dinner and your yeast, thus saving the water, which is the life of good bread. For buns, English tea cakes and Spanish buns, I always use the yeast made of the grated potatoes. It must be made and used fresh. Bread and rolls of all kinds *must* be *watched carefully*, kept warm but not *hot;* bread should never be allowed to be heated while it is rising. It is the *care* given to bread from the making of the yeast, till it is taken out of the oven, that gives *success* in bread making.

Sally Lunn.

One quart flour,
Piece of butter size of an egg,
Three tablespoonsful sugar, (white, if preferred,)
Two eggs,
Two teacupsful milk,
Two teaspoonsful cream tartar,
One teaspoonful soda,
A little salt.

Stir the cream tartar, salt, and sugar into the flour; add the eggs without beating, the butter melted, and one cup of the milk. Dissolve the soda in the other cup of milk, and stir all together. Bake in three pans, the size of a breakfast plate, fifteen or twenty minutes.

Soda Biscuit.

Into one quart of flour, stir two teaspoonsful cream tartar and a little salt, add two tablespoonful rich cream or one of butter, dissolve one teaspoonful soda in a little hot water; mix with milk soft.

Bread Cake.

(MRS. N. W. BROADWELL.)

One pint of bread sponge,
One pint of brown sugar,
Half a pint of butter,
Two eggs,
Spices to suit the taste.

Raisins, currents and citron, one pound of each, (or more or less to suit the convenience,) the more fruit, of course, the richer; stir in flour enough to make it stiff enough to drop clear from the spoon; one teaspoonful of soda; put it in pans, and let it rise as you would bead; bake slowly. This is nice without fruit.

Snails.

Make a sponge as for bread; add to one quart of the sponge—

Two eggs,
One teacupful of sugar,
Two-thirds of a cupful of butter,

Cinnamon and nutmeg, (if it suits the taste.)

Beat all well together; let this lighten well; then work in flour enough to make, as for any other rusk, (not too stiff;) set it where it will be warm enough to rise quickly; when thoroughly light take a piece of the dough, dredge flour on your breadboard and roll the dough out as for biscuits; then cut it into strips about an inch and a half wide; butter the top of each strip, sprinkle a little cinnamon and sugar on the butter, and then with the hands roll each strip till it is as large as an ordinary biscuit; grease a pan; set these endwise in the pan and set to lighten; then bake slowly, they resemble snails. The remainder of the dough can be made out in the same way. Some make a portion of the dough in this way, and roll the rest and cut out or make out with the hand. Rolling these snail fashion makes them very nice; the butter makes them flakey and easy to break open.

Soufle Biscuit.

Cut up four ounces of butter in a quart of flour; make it into a smooth paste with new milk; knead it well, add a little salt, and roll out as thin as paper; cut out the cakes with a tumbler, and bake quickly. Serve hot.

Cream Cakes.

Beat three eggs very light, stir them into a quart of cream, alternately with a quart of flour, and add one wine glass of strong yeast, (good potato yeast is best,) and a little salt. Cover the batter and set it near the fire to rise. When quite light, stir into it a large tablespoonful of butter that has been warmed (not melted) by the fire. Bake the cakes in muffin rings, and send to table hot. Split with your fingers and butter. A knife put into them makes them sodden.

To Make Yeast.

Five large potatoes, one quart of boiling water, one cup of brown sugar, one cup of yeast. Boil your potatoes, and sift them; add your sugar, when milk-warm, your yeast; half a cup is sufficient for two loaves.

Common Bread Cake.

Take the quantity of a loaf from the dough, when making white bread, and knead well into it two ounces of butter, two of sugar, and eight of currants. Warm the butter in a teacupful of good milk. By the addition of an ounce of butter or sugar, or an egg or two, you may make the cake better. A teacupful of raw cream improves it much. It is best to bake it in a pan, rather than as a loaf, the outside being less hard.

Milk Yeast.

In case you should get out of yeast, and are in a hurry, make milk yeast. Take one pint of new milk, one teaspoonful of salt, a tablespoonful of flour stirred in, stand it in a kettle of water by the stove, and keep it lukewarm all the time. When very light, add lukewarm water, make into loaves or biscuit, and let them rise by the fire before cooking.

Buns.

One cupful butter,
One cupful sugar,
Half cup of yeast,
Half pint milk.
Make it stiff with flour; add, if you like, nutmeg.

"Peculiars," or Graham Puffs.

To one pint of Graham flour, add one pint of milk and one egg. Stir in the flour slowly, till it becomes a smooth (not thick) batter. Use no soda, nor yeast. Bake immediately. The best bakepans are of cast iron, with twelve sockets which must first be heated, then greased, filled and instantly returned to the oven. If new, the pans should be first scoured with soap and sand, then greased, heated and rewashed. Puffs may also be made without the egg, with milk and water, or all water. They may also be made of rye flour or corn meal. The corn meal requires an egg. This receipt is sufficient for twenty-four puffs.

Butter Biscuit.

Sift one quart of flour in a pan, and make a hollow in the centre large enough to admit a pint of milk and one pint of yeast; mix into a sponge, set it to raise; in the morning add one pound of melted butter, and knead in as much flour as will, with another pint of warm milk make soft dough; make out the biscuit in pans to rise; when sufficiently light, bake in a well heated oven.

Rusk.

One quart flour,
One pint milk,
One-quarter pound of butter warmed in the milk,
Two well-beaten eggs,
One teaspoonful mace or cinammon,
One wine glass and a half of fresh yeast.

Mix well and set away to rise; divide into pieces of equal size; knead each piece separately, and put them into a pan to rise again. When quite light, bake in a moderate oven.

Dutch Rolls.

One quart flour,
Two eggs,
Half pint of milk,
One tablespoonful butter,
One gill yeast.

Beat the eggs, add the milk to them with the melted butter; pour this into the flour, having first put in the yeast. It must be mixed softer than bread, and if not moist enough, add more milk. Let it rise before baking.

Raised Muffins.

Melt a tablespoonful of butter in one pint of milk,
A little salt,
Two eggs,
Half gill yeast.
Flour, to make a thick batter.

Rye Drop Cakes.

One egg,
Two cupsful rye,
Two cupsful flour,
Half a cupful sugar,
A teaspoonful salt,
A teaspoonful cream tartar,
Half a teaspoonful soda,
A teaspoonful melted butter,
A cupful and a half of milk.

Drop from a spoon on a flat pan, and bake half an hour.

German Waffles.

Warm a quart of milk, cut up and soften in it one-quarter pound of butter. Beat eight eggs, and stir in with one-half pound of sifted flour, two tablespoonsful of good, strong yeast; set it in a warm place to rise. When well risen it is time to bake in greased waffle irons.

Pop Overs.

(ELLA MOREAN, ST. LOUIS.)

One teacupful sweet milk,
One teacupful flour,
One egg.

Beat till very light, and have well greased your muffin pans and drop them in; set them in the oven. It takes but a few minutes, they will puff up, and are done.

Sour Milk Griddle Cakes.

To one quart thick, sour milk, stir in wheat flour until it is quite a batter, add a little salt. When the griddle is hot enough, dissolve one teaspoonful of soda in a little hot water; stir it into the batter quickly and bake the cakes. Soda should never be put into any kind of cakes or corn bread until it is just ready to go into the oven, as the effervescence takes place, and if it is put in before, its effect is in a great measure lost.

Muffins.

One teacupful yeast,
Three eggs,
One teacupful flour,
One pint sweet milk,
A little salt.

Let it rise until it is quite light, and bake in well greased muffin rings.

Buckwheat Cakes.

To a quart of buckwheat flour an even teaspoonful of salt; stir in warm water till it is the consistency of thin batter; beat it thoroughly, add half a cupful of good yeast; set the batter where it will be a little warm, if made over night. A spoonful of soda dissolved in hot water and stirred in in the morning, improves them very much.

Buckwheat Cakes with Sour Milk.

This can be made at any time, and at a moment's notice. Take your buckwheat and mix it with good, sour milk, a little salt, a teacupful of indian meal; mix it just stiff enough for cakes; add a teaspoonful of soda dissolved in warm water, stir in and bake.

Corn Meal Cakes.

Take one or two eggs, according to the quantity you wish to make; beat well; add salt, then sour milk, and next your corn meal; beat all together. Dissolve a spoonful soda in hot water, and stir in well. Have your griddle hot and well-greased with a piece of salt pork, if you have it.

Waffles.

Have three eggs, well beaten, sour milk and a little salt; stir in flour till it is sufficiently thick, a very little thicker than for griddle cakes. Dissolve soda in hot water, stir it in the batter, and beat all well together. Have your waffle irons well heated on both sides before putting the batter in; bake them a nice, light brown.

Brown Bread.

(MRS. ELIZA M'DONALD.)

Make a sponge at night as for any other bread; in the morning sift enough flour to make two small loaves; add half a cupful of molasses and the same of brown sugar, and a little lard; work well; put into pans to lighten.

French Brown Bread.

Half a teacupful molasses,
One pint Graham flour,
One pint corn meal,
One pint hop yeast sponge.

Add sweet milk to make a stiff batter, like mush. Let it stand till light. Bake slowly.

Steamed Brown Bread.

(MRS. MACKENZIE.)

Two teacupsful and a half sweet milk,
One teacupful sour milk.
Three teacupsful corn meal,
Two-thirds of teacupful molasses,
One teaspoonful soda,
One teacupful flour,
A little salt.

Steam three hours; then put into the oven ten minutes to form a crust. Eat it fresh and cut it in the pan, it is apt to crumble. Grease the pan well before putting it in to steam.

Boston Brown Bread.

One quart Graham flour,
One tablespoonful molasses,
One tablespoonful lard,
Two teaspoonsful cream tartar,
One teaspoonful soda,
Milk to make a tolerable stiff batter,
A little salt.

English Tea Cakes.

(MISS SNAPE.)

Half pint sweet milk,
Half pound butter, (melted in the milk,)
Two tablespoonsful of sugar,
One pint of sponge of potato yeast,
Four eggs,
Flour sufficient to make it into soft dough.

Boiled Brown Bread.

(MRS. DR. RYAN.)

Four teacupsful corn meal,
Two teacupsful flour,
One teacupful molasses,
Four teacupsful sour milk,

One teaspoonful soda,
A little salt.

Boil four hours in a tight covered tin bucket in water kept at a boiling rate. When done, the bucket can be set in a hot oven for ten minutes. Grease the bucket well.

French Rolls.

One pint flour, and make of it a thick batter with warm water; to this add:

One well beaten egg,
One tablespoonful lard, (or butter,)
A little salt,
One teaspoonful white sugar, dissolved in a teacupful potato yeast.

Make this when risen into a dough by adding more flour; let this rise again and make into rolls; let it rise in the pans, and then bake.

English Buns.

(MISS SNAPE.)

One quart potato sponge,
One pint new milk,
Half cup white sugar,
Half pound butter,
A little salt.

Flour enough to make a dough, (not so stiff as common dough;) cut out large, after they are light; let them rise in the pan; wet with sugar and milk before taking out of oven.

Breakfast Biscuit.

Sift one quart flour into a pan, and make a hole in the middle; pour in not quite a pint of hot milk into which a tablespoonful of butter has been dissolved; stir this into the flour gradually, and when lukewarm add one well beaten egg, two-thirds of a cupful of good potato yeast, into which a teaspoonful of sugar and a little salt has been dissolved.

Sally Lunn without Yeast.

One pint of flour,
One egg,
One tablespoonful melted butter,
One teacupful of sugar,
One teacupful of sweet milk,
One teaspoonful of soda,
Two teaspoonsful of cream tartar.

Beat the butter, egg, and sugar, well together; add a little salt; then put in flour and milk till all is in; bake in tins in a quick oven; split open and butter each side, and lay one piece on the other.

French Tea Biscuit.

(MRS. M. SIMPSON.)

Take bread dough, about as much as would make a moderate sized loaf; a lump of butter, or lard, as large as an egg, two eggs, and a tablespoonful of sugar; mix well, and let rise. About an hour before tea, roll and cut an inch thick with a biscuit cutter; then spread the top with butter and fold double; let them rise the hour, and when light, bake twenty minutes.

Rusk.

(MRS. EVA CRAVEN.)

Melt half a pound of butter and mix it well with two-thirds of a pint of milk, flour enough to make a stiff batter; add three or four tablespoonsful of good yeast, and set in a warm place to rise; when light, beat two eggs with half a pound of powdered white sugar; work into the batter with the hand; add a little salt, (unless the butter is very salty,) and a teaspoonful of ground cinnamon, and flour enough to make a stiff dough. Let it lighten thoroughly, make out with the hand, and when light, have ready one yelk of an egg, a little sugar and milk, well beaten; as you take them out of the oven wet the top with it.

Rice Corn Bread.

One pint well cooked rice,
One pint corn meal,
One ounce butter,
One pint milk,
Two eggs, beaten light.

Then add the milk and melted butter; beat the rice till smooth; add the egg and milk, and lastly add the corn meal; beat all well together until light, and bake in shallow pans.

Raised Muffins.

Melt a tablespoonful of butter in one pint of milk, two eggs, half a gill of yeast; flour to make a thick batter.

Johnny Cake.

Two teacupsful Indian meal,
Half a teacupful flour,
Two teacupsful sweet milk,
One tablespoonful molasses,
One teaspoonful of soda.
Bake in a hot oven. Will be light.

Spanish Buns.

Half a pint of rich milk and half a pound of butter; let the butter warm in the milk, but not melt to oil; stir it through the milk, and set it away to cool. Beat four eggs well, and add to this milk, with half a pound of flour; stir in half a nutmeg, and two wine-glassesful of good, fresh yeast; stir all well, and add very gradually half a pound of white sugar. If this is not put in by degrees, the buns will be heavy; add, also, by degrees, another quarter of a pound of flour, making three-fourths of a pound in all. Butter a pan, put in the buns, and set them in a warm place to rise. The time required for rising will depend a good deal on the quality of the yeast. They can be made out with the hand, or cut with a rather large cutter. When they are light and covered with bubbles, put in a moderate oven and bake. Just before taking out of the oven, take a small, soft brush, or piece of muslin, and rub them over with a little egg and milk, with a little sugar, which will give them a nice gloss. If made according to directions, they are very nice.

Light Cakes.

To three-quarters of a pound of fine flour, add one-half pint of lukewarm milk, mix in three spoonsful of light yeast, cover it over, and set it by the fire for half an hour to rise Work in the paste four ounces of sugar, and the same quantity of butter; make into tea cakes with as little flour as possible, and bake them in a quick oven.

Hominy Muffins.

Having washed a pint of small hominy through two or three waters, pour boiling water on it, cover and let it soak for several hours. Then put it into a thick saucepan with half a pint of boiling water, and let it boil until soft enough to mash; drain it, and mix it well with a pint of white corn meal or wheat flour, a little salt, and a pint and one-half of milk in which two tablespoonsful of butter have been melted. When the butter is nearly cold add four tablespoonsful of yeast, cover it, and set it in a warm place, until very light, with the surface covered with bubbles. Butter some muffin rings, set them on a hot griddle, pour into each a portion of the mixture and bake them brown on both sides. Send them to table accordingly as they are done, pull them open with your fingers and butter them quickly.

Tomato Toast.

This is a nice breakfast dish; prepare the tomatoes, and stew them as directed. Toast a slice of light bread for each member of the family, and spread the stewed tomatoes evenly on each slice. If any is left, pour it over the whole; serve immediately.

Little Milk Cake for Breakfast.

Place on a table or slab—
    One pound of flour,
    Half a teaspoonful of salt,
    Two teaspoonsful of sugar,
    Three teaspoonsful of fresh yeast,
    Two ounces of butter,
    One egg.

Have some new milk, pour in a gill, mix all together, adding more milk to form a nice dough; then put some flour in a cloth, put the dough in, and lay it in a warm place; let it rise for about two hours, cut it in pieces the size of eggs, roll them even, and mark the top with a sharp knife; egg over and bake quick; serve hot or cold.

New England Pancakes.

Mix a pint of milk, five spoonsful of fine flour,

seven yelks and four whites of eggs, and a very little salt; fry them very thin in fresh butter, and between each strew sugar and cinnamon. Send up six or eight at once.

Fritters.

Make any plain batter as for pancakes; put pared apples, sliced and cored, into the batter, and fry some of it with each slice. Currants, or sliced lemon as thin as paper, make an agreeable change, Any sort of sweetmeat, or ripe fruit, may be made into fritters.

Spanish Fritters.

Cut the crumb of a French roll into lengths as thick as your finger, in what shape you will. Soak in some cream or milk, nutmeg, sugar, pounded cinnamon, and an egg. When well soaked, fry of a nice brown, and serve with butter, wine, and sugar sauce.

Corn Oysters.

 One pint grated sweet corn,
 Half a cupful sweet milk,
 One teaspoonful salt,
 Half a teaspoonful black pepper,
 Two-thirds of a cupful of flour,
 One egg.
Beat up and fry like griddle cakes.

Potato Fritters.

Boil two large potatoes, scrape them fine; beat four yelks and three whites of eggs, and add to the above one large spoonful of cream, another of sweet wine, a squeeze of lemon, and a little nutmeg. Beat this batter half an hour at least; will be extremely light.

French Toast.

One loaf of stale bakers' break; take off the crust; cut in slices; one pint of milk, two eggs, a little salt. Have ready a hot griddle, well buttered; then dip the bread in the custard and fry immediately on the griddle. To be eaten with a rich sauce.

German Waffles.

Warm a quart of milk, cut up and soften in it one-quarter pound of butter. Beat eight eggs, and stir in with one-half pound of sifted flour, two tablespoonsful of good, strong yeast; set it in a warm place to rise. When well risen, it is time to bake in greased waffle irons.

Yankee Waffles.

One quart milk,
Six eggs,
One-quarter pound butter,
A large gill of yeast,
Salt.

Flour, to make a batter as thick as for griddle cakes. Bake in waffle irons, as long again as you would need to bake them on a griddle.

Rye Drop Cakes.

One pint sour milk or buttermilk,
Three eggs,
One scant teaspoonful soda,
A little salt.

Meal to make a batter that will spread a little, but not run. Drop with a spoon into round tins, and bake fifteen minutes.

Flour Griddle Cakes.

Four eggs,
One quart milk,
A little salt,
One tablespoonful of butter,
One gill yeast.

Flour to make a batter as thick as for buckwheat cakes. Raise over night, and if sour, add a little soda in the morning.

Graham Gems.

These must be baked in iron pans, each little pan partitioned by itself, as they will not rise if baked in a mass. Remove the cream from sweet milk, and for a sufficient quantity for two pans, add one egg and salt; stir in the flour slowly until somewhat thicker than pancake batter; beat thoroughly, as it will add to their lightness; have the oven very hot, as they must bake in fifteen or twenty minutes, or they will not be light; place the pans on the stove, and when hot, butter, and with the spoon, drop each little pan full; place immediately in the oven. Carry to table hot. Cold gems steamed or warmed are nearly as good as when fresh. They should be on every table, for even dyspeptics can eat them with impunity.

Potato Fritters.

Three eggs,
One quart of milk,
A little flour and salt.

Thicken with mashed potatoes. Drop in tablespoonsful into boiling hot lard, and fry a light brown.

Fried Bread.

Take cold light bread, (baker's bread is best,) cut it in slices about an inch thick, pour a little sweet milk over each piece, to soften it; do this just as you are ready to fry the bread, or it will be too soft if it soaks in the milk; have a batter made of one egg, a little milk and flour, salt, and a small quantity of baking powder; beat this till light; it should be about the consistency of thick cream. Have a frying pan with hot lard in it, and dip each piece of the bread into the batter, and cover both sides with it, and then fry it quickly; be careful not to have the bread too wet with the milk or it will break. Each piece should go the table whole. It is a splendid breakfast dish.

Beat Biscuit.

Two quarts of flour,
Half pint lard, (well rubbed together,)
One pint of cold water,
One tablespoonful of salt.

Mix well, knead, and beat with a rolling pin till smooth and light.

Kentucky Yeast for French Rolls.

Boil six large potatoes; mash them fine in the water in which they were boiled; add a small teacupful of sugar, a teacupful of yeast, let it rise in a moderately warm place. Take a quart of flour, a lump of lard the size of a hen's egg, one teacupful of the above yeast; mix with water; make into rolls; let them rise and bake in a quick oven.

Kentucky Buttermilk Yeast.

Boil a quart of buttermilk, throw in a teaspoonful salt; take from the fire and let it cool; stir in a sufficient quantity of flour to make the consistency of common yeast, put in a half teacupful of yeast; let it rise in a moderately warm place. Take a quart of flour, a piece of butter or lard the size of a hen's egg; mix it entirely with the yeast, work well; set it to rise, work over; make into rolls; rise and bake.

Boiled Bread.

Four cupsful of sour milk or cold water,
One cupful molasses,
One teaspoonful soda,
Four cupsful of indian meal,
Two cupsful of flour,
One teaspoonful salt.

Steam four hours.

Graham Flour Cakes.

One cupful sweet milk,
Two eggs, beaten light,
A small lump of butter,
One teaspoonful soda,
Two tablespoonsful molasses,
A little salt,
Graham flour.

Mix well and soft enough to drop into greased muffin pans.

Mush Muffins.

(MRS. ABLE.)

Four tablespoonsful mush,
One tablespoonful lard or butter,
A little salt,
One quart milk,
Six eggs, beaten seperately, the whites very light, and added last.

Flour to make the consistency of pound cake. Bake in muffin pans quickly.

Brown Bread.

(MRS. ABLE.)

Scald one teacupful corn meal; when cold, stir in one cupful molasses, one pint yeast; stiffen with unbolted flour; mix it soft, it will look rough; it should not be kneaded, but mixed as soft as possible, and when put in the pan to rise, smooth it over with the hand. Let it rise, and bake slowly.

Milk Biscuit.

(MRS. ABLE.)

Two pounds flour,
A quarter of a pound lard,
One teaspoonful salt,
One pint milk,
One teacupful yeast.

Put salt into the flour, then rub in the lard; add the milk and yeast, mixing well with a spoon as the dough is soft. Set it to rise at 10 o'clock in the morning; at 3 p. m. stir well with a spoon; at 5 p. m. roll them out with just sufficient flour to prevent sticking to the board; cut, put them in pans to rise. Bake twenty minutes.

Sally Lunn.

Seven cupsful flour,
Three eggs,
One pint milk,

Half cupful butter,
One cupful yeast.

Mix well, and set to rise for supper; roll thin, put in pie pans; when done split them open and butter each half, laying one upon the other.

Cheap Waffles.

Two pints flour,
Two pints sweet milk,
One teaspoonful lard,
One teaspoonful soda,
One teacupful butter milk,
One teacupful mush.

Salt to the taste; have irons hot, and bake quickly.

Corn Bread.

One quart of corn meal; pour boiling water over it, just enough to wet it through, beat it well; then beat three eggs separately, and add to the meal, when cool, a little salt, and a tablespoonful of lard; grease a pan well, and put the dough in large spoonsful an inch apart.

Good Corn Bread.

One quart corn meal,
One pint sour milk,
Three eggs,
One small teaspoonful of soda.

Take a part of the meal, and enough milk to wet

the meal; then put in the yelks of the eggs and beat till light; add the rest of the milk and meal alternately; dissolve the soda in a tablespoonful of boiling water, and stir in; add salt, and a tablespoonful of melted lard, have it hot, and stir in briskly; grease your pan, and have it hot before pouring in the meal.

Cream Pancakes.

Mix the yelks of two eggs with half a pint of good cream and a very little sugar, flour enough to make a thin batter; beat the eggs till very light; add a little cream; then flour till free from lumps, and beat to a smooth paste; add sugar, and the rest of the cream; have your griddles well-greased and *hot;* fry the cakes as thin as possible. Send to the table hot.

Quire of Paper Pancakes.

Beat sixteen eggs till very light; one quart sweet milk; take a half pound sifted flour, a little sugar, and half a pound melted butter, half a grated nutmeg, and two gills of wine; add a little of the milk to the eggs; then the flour, till all is in; beat till free from lumps, and perfectly smooth and very light; then add nutmeg, wine, butter, and the rest of the milk, a teaspoonful of salt. Have a long-handled frying pan; grease well, have it hot; put in but little batter, let it run all over the pan and very thin; they must be cooked very lightly. Some do not turn them; if turned, shake the pan three or four times and tip it upward, and if expert, the cake will turn over. Lay one on the other as they are cooked. Eat hot.

Crackers.

 One cupful and a half of butter,
 Two cupsful and a half of sugar,
 Four eggs,
 Three tablespoonsful rose water,
 One tablespoonful cinnamon.

Roll thin, and bake.

Corn Cake.

 Three cupsful of meal,
 Half cupful of flour.

Mix with sweet milk and water; let it stand all night, in the morning add—

 One teaspoonful of soda,
 One tablespoonful of sugar,
 One tablespoonful melted butter,
 A little salt.

Beaten Biscuit.

To make good beaten biscuits, the proportions are—

 Two quarts of flour,
 One tablespoon oval-full of lard,
 A good spoonful of salt.

Mix them as dry as possible, just using water enough to make a hard dough; then work them well, and beat them with a rolling pin; work them well, beat again, make in biscuits, and bake slowly.

French Rolls.

Warm a pint of new milk with two tablespoonsful butter, a little salt; when cool, add one pound of flour, one egg, well-beaten, one tablespoonful yeast; beat all well together; let it rise; when very light, make in rolls and bake.

Brown Bread.

Three cupsful corn meal,
Three cupsful rye flour,
One cupful wheat flour,
Two cupsful molasses,
Three cupsful sour milk,
One teaspoonful soda,
A little salt. Bake.

Muffins.

One quart of flour,
Half teacupful of potato yeast,
Two eggs,
One teaspoonful of salt,
One pint and a half of lukewarm milk,
Two tablespoonsful melted butter.
Let it rise, and when very light, bake.

Corn Bread.

One pint sour milk,
One pint corn meal,
One pint white flour,

Two teaspoonsful of soda,
One teacupful of sugar, (brown,)
One teaspoonful salt.
Bake one hour.

Sally Lunn.

One quart of milk,
Half teaspoonful of soda,
Three eggs,
One teacupful sugar,
One tablespoonful butter,
Half cupful of yeast.
Make into a stiff batter, and bake in pie pans.

Cracked Wheat for Breakfast.

Get your wheat at the mill, that which is cleaned for grinding; unscrew your coffee mill, so that it will grind coarse, and grind a little of the wheat first to clear out the mill; then grind one or two mills full, as may be needed; put it in a saucepan, and set that in another containing boiling water; sweeten it and grate in nutmeg; let it cook as long as it would take rice to cook. When done, dish it up and eat with cream. Do not have it too stiff, but stiff enough to dish up well. This is an elegant breakfast dish, and very nourishing.

Mush.

Sift your meal, and wet up as much as you wish to

make into mush with cold water, and beat it well to break the lumps; make it the consistency of a thick batter; grease a tin bucket well, put this in it, and set it in a pot of boiling water, and let it cook three or four hours. This is the finest way to make mush, all the raw meal taste is entirely destroyed, and will pour out smooth and not adhere io the bucket. When the mush is to be used for breakfast, cut it in thin slices and fry in hot lard; never put it in till the lard is smoking hot, or it will absorb the grease and be unfit to use.

Rice.

Wash your rice well in two or three waters, put it into a pan and add a little water to it; set it in a steamer over a pot of boiling water, and let it cook till done; as the water cooks out of the rice, add a little at a time of boiling water. There is no way so nice to cook rice.

PASTRY.

Very Rich Crust for Tarts.

Eight ounces flour,
Six ounces butter,
One dessertspoonful pounded sugar,
One to two spoonsful water.

Break lightly, with the least possible handling, six ounces of butter into eight ounces of flour; add a dessertspoonful of pounded sugar, and two or three of water; roll the paste for several minutes, to blend the ingredients well, folding it together like puff crust, and touch it as little as possible:

Pie Crust.

In making pie crust or paste, care should be taken not to work or knead the crust at all; it should be mixed quickly, and with as little handling as possible.

FAMILY PIE CRUST.

Such as most persons like for common use, a good proportion is—

Half a pound of lard,
One pound of flour,
A spoonful of salt.

Mix with cold water. This makes a very nice crust. If it is needed to be any richer, roll it out quite thin, or as thin as you would to put in a pie plate, and rub the crust all over with butter, and then dredge on a little flour and roll it all up; take a knife and cut it into pieces, and roll out for pies.

Puff Paste

Is made in the same manner, only using butter instead of lard, and rolling out and spreading with butter in the same manner as the above. This makes it leafy and more light than common crust.

Apple Pies.

It takes the best cooking apples to make good pies: these that are tart and will cook well. Stew or steam them till done, adding sugar and flour, with nutmeg or lemon. Make the pastry to suit the taste, either rich or plain; roll thin, put in your apples; put on another crust, and bake in a rather quick oven.

French Pastry.

(MRS. DR. JOEL PRICE, KY.)

One teacupful of butter,
Two teacupsful of white sugar,
Three teacupsful of flour,
Four eggs beaten separately,
Half teaspoonful of soda dissolved in half a teacupful of sour cream or buttermilk.

Bake in jelly cake pans. Put one cake on a pie plate and spread raspberry or strawberry preserves upon it, then a layer of meringue on the top; set it in the stove to lightly brown; continue in the same way till you have it is large as you wish, finishing the top with the preserves and meringue.

Belleflower Apple Pie.

Make a nice crust; put it in your pie plate; peel nice belleflower apples, slice them the round way of the apple, take out the core, take the slices and lay them in your crust; put sugar, nutmeg, and bits of butter; put two or three layers of apples, with sugar and butter over each; one crust. Bake slowly.

French Apple Pies.

Roll a crust as for other pies; put your apples on one half of the crust, and turn the other half over, pressing the edges together so that the fruit will not escape; take a knife or fork and make a few holes in the top; fry in hot lard. Do not make them too large.

Pumpkin Pies.

The pumpkin should be cooked slowly, (of course the rind should be cut off and the seeds scraped out,) then put in a kettle over a gentle fire until the pumpkin is thoroughly cooked; it should be taken from the fire and cooled, then run through a wire sieve; when it is all rubbed through, add milk till it is a little thicker than batter; to every quart add four or six eggs, if eggs are plenty, six; beat the eggs well with the sugar before it is stirred in the pumpkin and milk; grate in nutmeg, put allspice and ground ginger; line your pie plates, and fill them with the pumpkin mixture. One crust.

Mince Meat.

(MRS. DR. PRICE, KY.)

Six pounds meat, well boiled and beaten in a mortar,
Six pounds beef suet, chopped fine,
Two pounds raisins,
Two pounds currants,
One pound of citron,
Half dozen oranges,
Half dozen lemons, (grate the peel of each, or chop it, use pulp and juice, sweeten to the taste,)
One peck of apples, chopped fine, (can use preserved fruits if it suits the taste,)
Three quarts of whisky.

Mix all well together. Put into stone jars, tie or cork tight, and use as you desire for pies, adding a little water when you go to make the pies. Make a rich pastry and roll thin; spread your mince meat nicely in the crust before putting on the top crust. If necessary, when you take out of the jar for pies, before pouring into the crusts, add a little whisky, and sweeten the water. Add sugar to the taste, two grated nutmegs, powdered allspice, a good deal of cinnamon and ground cloves. These must be used according to taste and judgment.

Dried Peach Pies.

These can be made as either the baked or fried apple pies. The peaches should be well cooked, sweetened while cooking, and flavored to suit the taste, and should be worked well with the hand. These are delicious fried.

Pie Crust.

In making pies, frequently there is a portion of the crust left over, in such cases work in all the flour possible, beat them well, roll and make into crackers.

Cranberry Pie.

Take the choicest cultivated cranberries, wash them clean, remove all imperfect ones, select the largest. Line your pie plate with a rich puff paste, take the cranberries, and with a sharp knife split each one, and lay them carefully in your crust, sprinkle plenty of white sugar over them, put on another crust, and bake slowly. This makes the nicest cranberry pie I have ever eaten.

Pie Plant Pie, or Short Cake.

Wash your pie plant, remove the skin, and cut them up in small pieces; put them in a pan, and set the pan in a steamer over a pot of boiling water; cover, and in a short time it will be well cooked; let it get nearly done before you add the sugar. The nicest way I have ever made the pie plant, is to make a rich puff paste, roll it out as thick as for a pie; put it into a long tin baking pan; then with the hand rub butter all over the crust, then a very little flour on that; roll out another piece just the same size, and put it on top of the crust in the pan. Bake this in time to have it hot for dinner. Have your pie plant ready steamed and sweetened, with a nice lump of butter stirred into it; when the crust is baked, take a knife and lift off the upper crust, and spread on your pie plant, then put on your upper crust. By buttering the first crust you put in the pan, the top comes off without cutting or splitting it with a knife, as a knife put into hot crust or bread of any kind always makes it clammy. Try this way, and I venture you will never make pie plant pie any other way. In this way the fruit is not in the crust long enough to moisten or make it soggy.

Strawberry Short Cake

Is made in the same manner, with the exception that the strawberries are not cooked.

Cocoanut Pie.

Take a large, nice cocoanut, break off the outer shell, peel off the brown skin, wash it, dry it, and grate. Take—

—14

Six eggs,
One quart sweet milk,
One-quarter of a pound melted butter,
Sugar to the taste.

Beat eggs and sugar well together, then add melted butter, then cocoanut and milk; stir well, bake in pie plates with one crust.

Soda Cracker Pie.

Take four soda crackers, put them side by side in a plate and pour boiling water over them, and let them remain till they are quite soft. Make a nice crust, line pie pan, and then pour off the water from the crackers and slip them gently into the crust; trim off the corners after they are in the crust, to make them round; then have a bowl and pour a half cupful of water and a large cupful of white or brown sugar, and one teaspoonful of tartaric acid; stir all together, and pour over the crackers; put on an upper crust. Bake slowly. In the spring, when apples are scarce, this comes very near an apple pie.

Cream Pies.

Scald a quart of sweet cream; beat four or five eggs light, then stir them into the scalding cream; add a saltspoonful of salt, a teaspoonful of the extract of lemon or peach water, and half a nutmeg grated, if liked; sweeten to the taste, (about two tablespoonful of sugar is enough;) have flat pie dishes with nearly perpendicular sides; grease them well; line with pie paste rolled thin; set them in quick oven for ten mintes, then put in the cream nearly to fill them, and bake.

Cream Pies.

(MRS. DAVIS, CARROLLTON.)

One cupful of butter,
Two cupsful of white sugar,
Two cupsful of corn starch,
Two cupsful of flour,
Eight whites of eggs,
Two teaspoonsful soda, in
One cupful sour milk, or soda and cream tartar with sweet milk.

Bake in cakes an inch in thickness, allowing two cakes for each pie, with custard between them, made as follows:

Yelks of eight eggs,
Twelve tablespoonsful of white sugar,
Six tablespoonsful of flour,
One quart of sweet milk,
Flavor with lemon.

Golden Pie, (A Splendid Pie.)

(MRS. BROADWELL)

Take one lemon, grate the rind and squeeze the juice in a bowl, to which add

One teacupful of sugar,
One teacupful new milk,

One tablespoonful corn starch,
The yelks of three eggs, well beaten.

Pour into a nice paste, and bake slowly. When done, beat the whites of the eggs with a little sugar, and spread over the top, and return to the oven to slightly brown.

Cream Pie.

Half pound butter,
Four eggs,
Sugar, salt, and nutmeg to the taste,
Two tablespoonsful arrowroot.

Then pour on it a quart of boiling milk; stir all together; put in one crust.

Transparent Pie.

The yelks of three eggs, (this makes one pie,)
Three tablespoonsful white sugar,
One tablespoonful butter.

Beat till very light. Only one crust.

Delicate Pie.

(MRS. N. W. BROADWELL.)

The grated rind of a lemon and the juice,
One cupful of powdered sugar,
The yelks of three eggs,
Two tablespoonsful of flour,
Two-thirds of a cupful of water.

Take the whites of the eggs and three tablespoonsful of sugar, beat well together. When the pie is done, spread on the whites, and return to the oven to brown.

Cracker Pie.

(MRS. ABLE.)

One cupful sugar,
One cupful molasses,
Twelve small crackers, well rolled,
Half cupful hot water,
Two cupsful *hard cider*,
Half pound **raisins**,
One teaspoonful cloves,
Two dessertspoonsful allspice,
Two dessertspoonsful cinnamon,
One large tablespoonful of butter,
A little salt and pepper.
Bake in two crusts.

Lemon Pie.

(MRS. ABLE.)

One pint white sugar,
One cupful butter,
Four eggs, beaten in one at a time,
Two tablespoonsful of flour,
Rind of one large lemon,
One pint sweet milk,
(Juice of the lemon squeezed in.) One crust. This will make several pies.

Mince Meat.

Six pounds of meat boiled and beat in a mortar,
Six pounds of beef suet, chopped fine,
Two pounds of raisins,
Two pounds currants,
One pound citron,
Half dozen oranges,
Half dozen lemons, (grate the peel of each, remove the seed, and use the pulp and juice, sweeten to the taste,)
One peck of tart cooking apples, chopped fine,
One quart cherry preserves,
One quart damson preserves,
One quart of quince,
Three quarts fine whisky.

Cracker Mince Pies.

Break four large soda crackers into one and a half pints boiling water—

One cupful and a half of butter,
Two cupsful and a half of sugar,
Two cupsful of raisins, cut fine,
Half a cupful of wine or whisky,
The juice and rind of one lemon.

Cloves, allspice and cinnamon to the taste, a few chopped apples. This is sufficient for four pies.

Peach Cobbler.

Take nice, finely flavored peaches, peel and stone

them, sweeten to the taste; put them into a nice baking pan, (tin is the best,) put a rich crust on the top and bake slowly; when done, remove the crust into a dish that will hold it, and if your peaches are well cooked, spread them nicely on the crust, (lay the top of the crust on the bottom of the dish.) Eat with sweetened cream.

Gooseberry Pie.

Stew the berries well, adding sugar and no water, as they throw out so much juice. Make a nice, rich pastry, and bake, sticking the crust to keep it from puffing; when cold, put in your berries, and have the whites of two eggs beaten with sugar and spread on the top; set in the oven to slightly brown. Any fruit pie may be made in the same way. No fruit pie should be made to stand over night, as the crust becomes soggy and unfit for use.

Lemon Pie.

Make your crust and line your pie plate; then take a teacupful of white or a light brown sugar and spread it evenly over the crust; grate off the rind of one lemon, peel off the white skin, and the slice the lemon with a very sharp knife, to have the slices thin; lay them piece by piece over the sugar in the crust; then take your dredge box and shake about one tablespoonful of flour over it, and then put the grated rind of the lemon and about half a teacupful of cold water.

Put on upper crust and bake slowly. This pie is as cheap a pie as can well be made, and if made and baked right, there is none better. If cooked too fast the juice runs out, and the pie is too dry. Try it.

Lemon Pie.

(MRS. BUNN.)

The grated rind and the juice of two lemons,
Half pound white sugar,
Quarter pound butter,
Eight eggs, beat the whites separately.

Lastly add nearly one pint rich cream. Make three pies. One crust.

Potato Pie.

Scald one quart of milk, grate in four large potatoes while the milk is hot; when cold add four eggs well beaten, and four ounces of butter; spice and sweeten to taste; lay in paste. Bake half an hour.

Lemon Pie.

(MRS. HUNT.)

Two eggs, leave out the white of one,
One teacupful white sugar,
One lemon,

Grate the rind and use the juice, and cream enough to make it fill the crust, or a small piece of butter and milk, if you have no cream; this makes one pie.

Take the remaining white, beaten stiff, with two tablespoonsful white sugar, and when the pie is baked spread this over the top smoothly, and return to the oven till lightly brown.

Mush Pie.

One pound well-cooked mush
Half a pound butter,
One pound brown sugar,
Six eggs,
The juice of a lemon.

Beat the butter well into the hot mush; beat the sugar and yelks of the eggs well together; then add the mush and butter, then the juice and grated rind of the lemon; lastly the white of the eggs, which must be well-beaten.

Silver Pie.

(W. S. HURST.)

Peel and grate one large white potato into a deep plate, add the juice and grated rind of—

One lemon,
The white of one egg, well beaten,
One teacupful white sugar,
A teacupful of cold water.

Pour this into a nice under crust. When done have ready the well-beaten whites of three eggs, half a teacupful of white sugar, a few drops of rose water; put this over the pie and return it to the oven to brown. When ready for the table lay lumps of currant jelly on the top; have it made just before dinner.

Lemon Pie.

(MRS. LEWIS.)

Grate the rind of three lemons, take off the thick white skin, cut the lemons in very thin slices, take out the seed, add—

Three large cupsful of fine white sugar,
Two eggs,
Half a cupful of water,
Two tablespoonsful flour.

Mix well, and make two pies with two crusts; to be eaten warm.

Mince Pie.

(MRS. VAN NESS.)

Seven pounds meat,
Ten pounds apples,
Two pounds suet,
Two pounds raisins,
Two pounds currants,
One pound citron,
Three lemons,
Brandy and spices to the taste.

Cream Pie.

One teacupful of cream, one teacupful of sugar, two tablespoonsful flour rubbed smoothly in a little of the cream, a lump of butter the size of an egg; one crust, and strips of crust across it.

Golden Pie.

Take one lemon, grate the rind and squeeze the pulp into a bowl, to which add—

    One teacupful white sugar,
    One teacupful new milk,
    One tablespoonful corn starch,
    The yelks of three eggs, well-beaten.

Pour these ingredients into a nice paste crust to bake slowly; beat the whites of three eggs stiff, and when the pie is just done, pour it over the pie evenly, and return it to the oven to sfiffen, not to brown.

Cream Pie.

Take the yelks of four eggs, beat light with a large tablespoonful sifted flour, one pint of cream and a teacupful of sugar. When baked, add the whites of the eggs beaten stiff, with three tablespoonsful sugar; spread over the top after the pie is baked, and return to the oven till lightly brown.

Egg Mince Pies.

Boil six eggs hard, shred them small; shred double the quantity of suet; then put currants washed and picked one pound, or more, if the eggs are large; the peel of one lemon shred very fine, and the juice, six spoonsful of sweet wine, mace, nutmeg, sugar, a very little salt; orange, lemon, and citron, candied. Make a light paste for them.

Molasses Pie.

    The yelks of four eggs, beaten very light,
    One large spoonful flour,
    One pint molasses,
    Two tablespoonsful strong vinegar,
    Two tablespoonsful ginger.

Bake, then add the whites of the eggs, well-beaten, with three spoonsful sugar; return to the oven to brown.

Mince Pie.

(MRS. VAN DUSEN.)

    Three pounds beef,
    Two pounds suet,
    Six pounds apples, (that will cook well,)
    Three pounds raisins,
    Three pounds currants,
    Three pounds sugar,
    Two pounds citron,
    Three oranges,
    Two quarts brandy,
    Two quarts wine,
    Two quarts cider,
    One ounce rose water,
    One tablespoonful ground ginger.

Cinnamon, allspice, cloves and mace, salt and pepper to the taste.

Delicate Pie.

The grated rind and juice of one lemon,
One teacupful white sugar,
The yelks of three eggs,
Two tablespoonsful of flour,
Two-thirds of cupful of water.

Take the whites of the eggs and three tablespoonsful of sugar, and beat to a stiff froth and turn it over the pie when it is baked; set it in oven to brown. One crust.

Cream Pie.

(MRS. HURST.)

For the crust use—
One cupful and a half flour,
One cupful white sugar,
Half cupful sweet milk,
Two eggs,
Half teaspoonful soda,
One teaspoonful cream tartar,
One tablespoonful butter,
Flavor to snit the taste.

Bake this in two jelly cake pans, and let it get cold, and use one for the upper crust and one for the under crust. For the cream for the pies take:
Half cupful white sugar,
One-third cupful flour,

Half pint sweet milk,
One egg.

Let the milk boil; beat the eggs and sugar together; take a little milk and wet the flour to a smooth paste, and stir into the sugar and egg; then stir all into the milk, and let it boil tolerably thick and spread on to one of the crusts previously baked, and then put the other crust on. Eaten warm for dinner, or eaten cold for supper.

Lemon Pie.

(MATE ELLIOTT.)

Three Eggs,
One tablespoonful butter,
Half cupful milk,
One cupful sugar,
One lemon, grate the rind.

Mix the grated lemon with sugar and butter; then add the yelks, then the milk, then lemon juice, last the whites, well-beaten; mix well. This makes two pies.

Corn Starch Pie.

(CARRIE HURST.)

Three eggs,
Six tablespoonsful white sugar,
One tablespoonful corn starch,
One pint sweet milk.

Bake the crust first; beat the yelks and three tablespoonsful white sugar together; stir in the corn starch;

make custard of the milk, eggs, sugar and corn starch; flavor and pour on the crust; whip the whites and the other three spoonsful of sugar, and spread over the pie after it is baked, and return to the oven to slightly brown.

Piecrust Glaze.

In making pies which have a juicy mixture, the juice soaks into the crust, making it soggy and unfit to eat; to prevent this, take an egg well-beaten, and wet the crust of the pie with it just before putting in the fruit. For pies which have an upper crust, wet the top with the same before baking. This is also nice for biscuit or ginger cakes, and with a little sugar added, is very nice for rusk.

Transparent Pie.

To one pie take the yelks of three eggs, three tablespoonsful of sugar, and a tablespoonful and a half of butter; beat well together; flavor to suit the taste. Make a rich puff paste and line the pie plate. Only one crust is required.

Stewart Pie, (Splendid.)

Two teacupsful brown sugar,
One-half cupful butter,
One teacupful cream or new milk,
Four eggs, beat the yelks light.

Add the sugar, then your milk and flavoring, then the half cupful melted butter; beat the whites to a stiff paste; stir in and beat it well. This makes two pies.

Summer Mince Pie.

Four crackers broken up fine and dissolved in water; then mix two eggs, well beaten; add—
    One cupful raisins, cut fine,
    One cupful citron,
    One cupful butter,
    One cupful vinegar,
    Two cupsful sugar,
    One cupful molasses,
    Six apples, cut fine,
    Add cinnamon and brandy to the taste.
This will make six pies.

Mince Pies without Meat.

Of the best apples six pounds, pared, cored, and minced; of fresh suet, and raisins stoned, each three pounds, likewise minced; to these add of mace and cinnamon a quarter of an ounce each, and eight cloves, in finest powder; three pounds of the finest powder sugar, three-quarters of an ounce of suet, the rinds of four and juice of two lemons, half a pint of cider, the same of brandy, if you like. Mix well, and put into a deep pan. Have ready washed and dried four pounds of currants, and add as you make the pies, with candied fruit.

Lemon Mince Pie.

Squeeze a large lemon, boil the outside till tender enough to beat to a mash, add to it three large apples chopped, and four ounces of suet, half a pound of currants, four ounces of sugar; put the juice of the lemon, and candied fruit as for other pies. Make a short crust, and fill the patty pans as usual.

Lemon Pie.

Three lemons,
One quart milk,
One heaping tablespoonful flour,
One tablespoonful melted butter,
Four eggs,
One teacupful sugar.

Rub your lemon on a grater, then roll till soft, then squeeze the juice out. Make a frosting for the top of the whites of the eggs and white sugar. This will make three pies.

Lemon Pie.

Two lemons,
Two teacupsful sugar,
One teacupful milk,
Two tablespoonsful corn starch,
Yelks of six eggs,
Two tablespoonsful melted butter.

Beat the whites of the eggs with six tablespoonsful sugar, and pour over after the pie is baked. This makes two pies.

—15

Mince Pie.

Four pounds chopped beef,
Four pounds chopped suet,
Four pounds chopped raisins,
Four pounds chopped currants,
Seven pounds chopped apples,
One pound chopped citron,
Two pounds sugar,
One ounce nutmeg,
One quart madeira wine or pint brandy,
One pint of golden syrup,
A little salt.

Apple Custard Pie.

Peel and boil sour apples till soft, and not much water left in them, then rub through a colander if necessary. Beat two eggs, half a cupful sugar and a large table spoonful butter for each pie; flavor with nutmeg. If the apples are very sour, add more sugar.

Georgetown, Kentucky Pie.

Break five large soda crackers into one and a half pints boiling water—

One teacupful and a half butter,
Two teacupsful and half sugar,
One teacupful cut raisins,
Half teacupful wine or whisky,
The juice and rind of one lemon,
Spices to the taste.

One large apple chopped fine will improve the pies. This makes four pies.

Lemon Pie.

Three eggs,
One cupful sugar,
One teaspoonful butter,
One cupful flour,
Juice of one lemon,
Whites of two eggs,
Two-thirds cupful sugar to make frosting for the top.

When the pie is done, put the frosting on the top, and return to the oven to brown.

Strawberries Stewed for Tarts.

Make a syrup of one pound of sugar and a teacupful of water; add a little white of eggs; let it boil, and skim it until only a foam rises; then put in a quart of berries free from stems and hulls; let them boil till they look clear and the syrup is quite thick. Finish with fine puff paste.

Lemon Pie.

One lemon, four eggs, seven tablespoonsful sugar mixed with yelks; grate the rind, and mix juice, rind, sugar and yelks together. Beat the whites stiff with sugar, and spread over the top. Bake in a good crust. No top crust.

Pie Plant Short Cake.

Make a short cake in the usual way, with sour milk or cream and soda, or with sweet milk and soda and cream tartar; many prefer this way to the rich pie crust short cake; bake in long pans; split them open, butter and spread your fruit between, or, as many prefer, have your fruit ready, and serve at the table. Any fruit will answer. Always steam fruits of this kind, they are much nicer than if they come in contact with the fire.

Cheap Lemon Pies.

Take one large lemon, squeeze out the juice, chop the peel very fine; take—

    One teacupful sugar,
    One teacupful molasses,
    Three teacupsful water,
    One cupful sifted flour,
    One egg.

One or two good cooking apples, stewed or grated, and sweetened to suit the taste, boil the peel till soft; then put in the flour, which must be wetted and rubbed smooth; boil till it thickens; then add the juice and other ingredients. This will make four medium sized pies with two crusts.

Apple Trifle, (A Supper Dish.)

    Ten good-sized apples,
    The rind of half a lemon,

Six ounces of pounded sugar,
Half-pint milk,
Half-pint cream,
Two eggs,
Whipped cream.

Peel, core, and cut the apples into thin slices, and put them into a saucepan with two tablespoonsful of water, the sugar, and minced lemon rind. Boil all together until quite tender, and pulp the apples through a sieve; if they should not be quite sweet enough, add a little more sugar, and put them at the bottom of the dish to form a thick layer. Stir together the milk, cream, and eggs, with a little sugar, over the fire, and let the mixture thicken, but do not allow it to reach the boiling point. When thick, take it off the fire; let it cool a little, then pour it over the apples. Whip some cream with sugar, lemon peel, etc., the same as for other trifles; heap it high over the custard, and the dish is ready for table. It may be garnished as fancy dictates with strips of bright apple jelly, slices of citron, etc.

Cream Pie.

Three pints of new milk,
Eight eggs,
Half a cupful butter,
Two tablespoonsful flour,
One cupful sugar.

Beat the butter and flour together, and the sugar and eggs. Let the milk get warm by setting it in warm water on the stove; a small pail is nice to put the milk in; set this in a kettle of boiling water, then add the butter and flour, stir a few minutes; then add the sugar and eggs, stir until a little thick; then flavor with vanilla, this is the only kind of flavoring for these pies; remove from the fire. Have a crust made as follows:

   One teacupful of water,
   One teacupful of lard,
   A little salt.

Mix this soft enough to roll out for pies; have but one crust. When the pies are baked, have the whites beaten stiff with a little white sugar, and spread on the top and let it brown lightly. This makes splendid pies.

CAKES.

General Directions for Cake Making.

As a general thing there has been more cake wasted by carelessness in mixing than from any other cause, unless it is the want of *patience* to *beat* it as it should be. Some have an idea, that to have the proper materials and throw them into a pan and give them a stir or two, is all that is required. But such is not the case. The same rule holds good in most cakes. The butter and sugar should *always* be beaten together till they are perfectly light. The whites should be beaten perfectly stiff. Your cream tartar or baking powder, just as your receipt calls for it, should *always* be mixed well in the flour. Add a little flour to the butter and sugar before putting in the milk; dissolve the soda in the milk; then add the flour and whites alternately. Beat very little after the whites are put in the pan, and bake immediately. Nice white butter makes the whitest cake.

A Fine Icing for Cake.

Beat up the whites of five eggs to a froth, and put to them a pound of double-refined sugar, powdered and sifted, and three spoonsful of orange flower water or lemon juice. Keep beating it all the time the cake is in the oven, and the moment it comes out, ice over the top with a spoon.

Black Cake.

(MRS. DR. JOEL PRICE, KY.)

One pound and a quarter of very light dough, made with potato yeast,
Six eggs,
Three-quarters of a pound butter,
One pound sugar,
Two pounds raisins,
Two pounds currants, thoroughly washed and slowly dried in a slow oven,
One pound of citron, cut fine,
One glass blackberry jelly,
One tablespoonful cloves,
One nutmeg,
Two tablespoonsful cinnamon,
One teasoonful soda,
One wine glass of whisky or brandy,
One glass of madeira wine.

Work the butter into the dough; have the eggs and sugar well-beaten together, and add to the dough in small quantities at a time; flour the fruit, add it gradually. Cut a paper to fit the bottom of the mould, grease it well; pour the whole into the mould. Let it rise one hour, bake three hours. Let it stand in the mould after it has been baked for several hours.

Currant Cake.

Two cupsful sugar,
One cupful butter,
Four even cupsful of flour,
One cupful of currants,
One cupful sweet milk,
Four eggs,
One teaspoonful soda,
Two teaspoonsful cream tartar.

Custard Cake.

Two cupsful sugar,
Nine tablespoonsful melted butter,
Two-thirds of a cupful sweet milk,
Three cupsful flour,
Six eggs,
Half teaspoonful soda,
Two teaspoonsful cream tartar.

White Cake.

One pound powdered sugar,
One pound flour,
Half pound butter,
Whites of sixteen eggs,

One teaspoonful soda,
Three teaspoonsful cream tartar.

Beat the butter and sugar to a cream, and stir a little flour with it. Beat well.

Cream Cake.

Five eggs,
Three cupsful sugar,
Four cupsful flour,
One cupful butter,
One cupful cream,
One teaspoonful soda.

Mix the sugar and butter, then add the rest.

Cold Icing.

One egg, eight large teaspoonsful of white sugar; beat well and hard; add tartaric acid to whiten; flavor to the taste.

Ice Cream Cake.

Two cupsful white sugar,
One cupful butter,
Three cupsful flour,
Half cupful sweet milk,
Whites of eight eggs,
One teaspoonful cream tartar,
Half teaspoonful soda.

Beat the butter and sugar together, then the whites of the eggs, well-beaten; stir in the flour, and cream of tartar, well-mixed, and lastly the milk with the soda dissolved in it. Butter shallow pans, spread evenly on the bottom half an inch thick; bake quickly to a delicate light brown.

Receipt for Icing.

Put three cupsful white sugar in a saucepan with one cupful of water, let it boil to a clear, thick syrup; then pour in boiling hot over the whites of three eggs, stirring it very hard; add half teaspoonful of pulverized citric acid; flavor with vanilla; spread over the cake warm. If it gets cold, warm it by steam.

Soft Ginger Cake.

(MRS. JUDGE VAN DOERSTON'S.)

One pint molasses,
Three eggs,
One teacupful sour milk,
Butter the size of an egg.
One tablespoonful soda stirred into the molasses; flour enough to make a soft dough; ginger to the taste.

Doughnuts.

One pint flour, lump of butter the size of a walnut rubbed into it, half cupful sugar, one-third of a teaspoonful soda, one egg, enough buttermilk to make it a proper consistency; make in twists, or roll and cut in cakes, and fry in hot lard.

Citron Cake.

Eight whites of eggs,
Three teacupsful flour,
Half teacupful sweet milk,
Two teacupsful powdered white sugar,
Three-quarters of teacupful butter,
Half teaspoonful soda,
Two teaspoonsful cream tartar,
One pound best citron.

Cut the citron in very thin slices, beat whites to a stiff froth; beat butter and sugar together; add a little flour with cream tartar, well-mixed; then the milk, in which the soda has been well dissolved; then add the whites, and last stir in the citron; mix well. Bake in long or square baking tins. Such cakes, and the gold cake, made with the yelks of eggs, are always better baked in shallow pans, and with a little icing on the top looks much nicer when cut for the table.

Cottage Cake.

One cupful and a half sugar,
Half cupful butter,
Two eggs,
One scant teaspoon soda, dissolved in one cupful milk,
Two teaspoonsful cream tartar rubbed in flour enough to make this thick as pound cake,
Juice and rind of a lemon.

This is good to be eaten fresh, but will not keep long.

Delicious Cake.

Two cupsful white sugar,
One cupful butter,
One cupful milk,
Three eggs,
Half teaspoonful soda,
Scant teaspoonful cream tartar,
Three cupsful flour.

Stir butter and sugar together and add the beaten yelks of the eggs, then the beaten whites; dissolve the soda in the milk, rub cream tartar in the flour, and add the last thing.

Tipsy Cake.

Make any nice sponge cake; bake it in one or more oval pans, as may be needed, (if for an evening company, of course one would not be enough;) let it be baked a delicate light brown; when cold, put it into any nice platter or large glass dish that will hold it nicely. Pour over it madeira wine till it is perfectly saturated; have ready blanched almonds, sufficient to stick over the top of the cakes. Make a nice, rich, boiled custard and pour it around the edges of the dishes or dish in which your cake has been placed, reserving enough custard to add to each dish of the cake as you serve it up. According to my own taste, I think that about three or four whites of eggs to each cake, well-beaten, and four tablespoonful powdered sugar beaten in it, and spread over the top, is a great improvement. It can be set in the oven to slightly brown before putting the custard around the edges.

Silver Cake.

Half teacupful butter,
One cupful and a half sugar,
Two cupsful and a half flour,
The whites of eight eggs.

Dissolve half a teaspoonful soda in one tablespoonful water, one teaspoonful cream tartar. Beat butter and sugar well together. Beat the whites stiff.

Ginger Snaps.

Two teacupsful brown sugar,
Two teacupsful best sugar house molasses,
One teacupful butter,
One teacupful sour milk,
One teaspoonful soda.

Work in flour enough to make it stiff, and roll in thin cakes. Bake to a nice brown.

Drop Cakes.

The yelks, after making a large, or even small white cake, make very nice drop cakes. Take—

Seven or eight yelks
Two coffeecupsful brown sugar,

One coffeecupful butter,
One coffeecupful sweet milk,
One teaspoonful soda,
Two teaspoonsful cream tartar.

Flour enough to make them drop nicely in a well-greased pan. Beat well together before putting in the milk; drop them and give them room to spread. They can be baked in the tins that are now made for muffins. Flavor to suit the taste.

Fruit Cake.

Four eggs,
One cupful brown sugar,
One cupful butter,
One cupful cold strong coffee,
Two teaspoonsful cream tartar,
One teaspoonful soda,
One pound citron,
One pound currants,
One pound raisins,
Four cupsful flour.

Beat butter and sugar well together, then add eggs, and beat well before adding coffee, in which the soda must be dissolved; mix cream tartar in flour; lastly mix in the fruit. Try with a straw before taking from the stove.

Spice Cake.

Three Eggs,

One cupful of brown sugar,
Half cupful sweet milk,
Half cupful butter,
Two teaspoonsful cream tartar,
One teaspoonful soda,
One teaspoonful cinnamon,
One teaspoonful cloves,
One teaspoonful allspice,
A little lemon.

This is to be mixed as other cakes are, sugar and butter together, then add the other ingredients. Great care should be given to the beating of cake, the more it is beaten the better it is, of course. Let the beating all be done before the cream tartar and soda are put in. It should then be gently stirred, and put in to bake immediately.

Sponge Gingerbread.

One cupful of sour milk,
One cupful molasses,
Half cupful butter,
Two eggs,
One tablespoonful ginger.

Flour to make it as thick as pound cake. Put the butter, molasses and ginger together, and make them quite warm; then add the milk, flour and yeast powder, or baking powder, as it is more generally called.

Ginger Snaps.

One cupful molasses,
Half cupful brown sugar,
Half cupful butter,
Half cupful warm milk, the butter melted in it,
Two tablespoonsful baking powder.
The dough should be stiff, roll out and cut in cakes

Rolled Jelly Cake.

Three eggs,
One china teacupful sugar,
One china teacupful flour.
Beat the yelks of the eggs till light, then add the sugar, continue beating some time; then add the whites, beaten to a stiff froth, then flour, very little at the time; bake in a long pan well-greased. When done, turn out on bread board, then cover the top well with jelly, and roll up while warm, and slice as needed.

Macaroons.

Blanch four ounces of almonds, and pound; whisk the whites of four eggs to a froth, then mix it, and a pound of sugar, sifted, with the almonds, to a paste; and laying a sheet of wafer paper on a tin, put it on in different little cakes, the shape of macaroons.

Tea Cakes.

Rub fine four ounces of butter into eight ounces of flour; mix eight ounces of currants, and six of fine
—16

sugar, the yelks of two and white of one egg. Roll the paste the thickness of a cracker, and cut with a wine glass. You may beat the other white, and wash over them; and either dust sugar, or not, as you like.

Black Cake.

Half pound butter,
Half pound sugar,
Half pound flour,
Six eggs,
One pound and a half raisins,
One pound and a half currants,
Half pound citron,
Half teaspoonful soda,
Half teaspoonful mace,
Half teaspoonful cinnamon,
Half teaspoonful cloves,
Half teaspoonful allspice,
One teaspoonful nutmeg,
One cupful molasses,
Half gill brandy.

Bake slowly three hours. This makes three loaves.

Pudding.

One cupful milk,
One cupful molasses,
Half cupful butter,
Three and a half cupsful flour,
One glass brandy,

One teaspoonful each of all kinds of spice,
One teaspoonful saleratus.
Steam three hours.

Doughnuts.

One cupful sugar,
Two eggs,
Small spoonful butter,
One cupful and a half milk,
Two teaspoonsful cream tartar,
One teaspoonful soda.
Mix with flour and roll out stiff. Flavor to taste.

Silver Cake.

Half cupful butter,
One cupful and a half sugar, beat well together,
Whites of eight eggs, beaten to a froth,
Two and a half cupsful flour.
Dissolve one-half teaspoonful soda in one tablespoonful water,
One teaspoonful cream tartar.
For gold cake take the yelks of the eggs and mix the same as above.

Cream Tea Cakes.

One pound flour,
Pint sour cream,
Two-thirds of a cupful butter,

Half teaspoonful saleratus dissolved in a litttle warm water.

Mix lightly. Flour your hands well and make out in small cakes, the size of an egg. Lay close in a buttered pan, and bake in a quick oven.

Fruit Cake.

One cupful of butter,
One cupful sugar,
One cupful molasses,
Three cupsful flour,
Four eggs,
Half pound currants,
Half pound raisins,
Quarter pound citron,
Quarter teaspoonful saleratus,
One teaspoonful each of all kinds of spice.

This cake will keep a year.

Cocoanut Cake.

One cupful sugar,
One cupful flour,
Three eggs,
Three tablespoonsful sweet milk,
One teaspoonful cream tartar mixed in the flour,
Half teaspoonful soda dissolved in the milk,
Ten teaspoonsful sugar to two eggs.

One cocoanut, and mix two-thirds of it with the frosting and spread over the cake; then add the rest of the cocoanut. Bake the cake as for jelly cake.

Coffee Cake.

One-third cupful butter,
One cupful molasses,
Half cupful brown sugar,
Half cupful cold strong coffee,
Two eggs,
One teaspoonful each of cinnamon, cloves and soda.

Delicate Cake.

One cupful butter,
Two cupsful sugar,
Half cupful sweet milk,
Three cupsful flour,
Half teaspoonful soda,
One teaspoonful cream tartar,
Whites of ten eggs.

Railroad Cake.

(MRS. W. A. TURNEY.)

Sixteen eggs,
One pound sugar,
One pound flour,
Half pound butter.

Beat the whites to a stiff froth, add yelks; then

sugar, melted butter, then add flour; stir as little as possible.

Sponge Cake.

Eleven ounces flour,
Seventeen ounces sugar,
Twelve eggs.

Beat the whites and yelks separately.

Cocoanut Pound Cake.

One pound sugar,
One pound flour,
Twelve ounces butter,
Ten eggs,
One grated cocoanut.

Beat the butter till creamy, add sugar; then cocoanut, then flour.

Sponge Cake.

Two tumblersful of sugar,
Two tumblersful of flour,
Ten eggs, well beaten,
Add the flour last.

Chocolate Puffs.

The whites of two eggs,
Half pound sugar,
One ounce and a half chocolate,

Two tablespoonsful corn starch, with the chocolate pulverized.

Beat the eggs to a stiff froth, add the sugar; then add chocolate; drop sugar on paper; then drop the puffs on, and dust sugar over them. Bake in a quick oven.

Cocoanut Cake.

One cupful butter,
Two and half cupsful sugar,
Four cupsful flour,
One cupful sweet milk,
One teaspoonful soda,
Two teaspoonsful cream tartar,
Whites of seven eggs,
One grated cocoanut.

Ginger Snaps.

Three cupsful molasses,
One cupful sugar,
Quarter cupful butter,
Four spoonsful ginger,
One spoonful cinnamon,
One spoonful cayenne pepper.

Jumbles.

One pound of nice sugar into two pounds of flour; beat four eggs with three-quarters of a pound of butter, very light, and bake quickly.

Fruit Cake.

Ten eggs,
Two tumblersful and a half sugar,
Three tumblersful flour,
Three-quarters pound butter,
Two pounds currants,
Two pounds raisins,
Half pound citron.
Last, the whites well-beaten.

White Sponge Cake.

One cupful and a half sugar,
One cupful flour,
One teaspoonful cream tartar,
The whites of ten eggs.

White Cake.

One cupful butter,
Four cupsful sugar,
Six cupsful flour,
Whites of fourteen eggs, beaten to a stiff froth.
One teaspoonful soda dissolved in one teacupful of sweet milk, and two teaspoonsful of cream tartar mixed in flour. Flavor to taste and bake in a moderate oven.

White Mountain Cake.

The whites of six eggs,
Two-thirds cupful butter,

One cupful sweet milk,
Two cupsful sugar,
Three cupsful flour,
One teaspoonful soda,
Two teaspoonsful cream tartar or baking powder.
Make a thin icing, (and stir in grated cocoanut, if you prefer it,) and put on the cake as in jelly cake.

Almond Icing for Wedding Cake.

Beat the whites of three eggs to a stiff froth; beat a pound of blanched almonds very fine in a mortar with rose water, (a few only at a time,) mix them with eggs lightly together; put in by degrees one pound of powdered loaf sugar; spread the icing smoothly on the cake. It must be well-beaten.

Pork Cake.

One pound of pickled pork chopped as fine as can be,
Two pounds currants,
Two pounds raisins,
One pound citron,
Two teacupsful brown sugar,
One teacupful molasses,
One tablespoonful cloves,
One teaspoonful cinnamon,
One tablespoonful allspice,
One nutmeg,

One tablespoonful soda,
One wine glassful brandy or whisky,

Four pints of flour; put three in the cake, and put the other on the fruit, and rub it over to prevent settling at the bottom. Mix as for other cake. Bake three hours. Pour over the pork after it is chopped one pint of boiling water, and when cool put in the other ingredients into the water and pork. This makes a splendid large cake that will keep well. No butter or eggs. Try it.

Fruit Cake.

Fourteen eggs,
One pound and a half butter,
One pound and a half brown sugar,
One pound and a half flour,
Three pounds raisins,
Three pounds currants,
One pound citron,
One coffeecupful syrup,
One wine glassful brandy,
One tablespoonful each of cinnamon, allspice, cloves and nutmeg.

Almond Macaroons.

Three-quarters pound sweet almonds, one-quarter pound bittter almonds; blanch and pound to a smooth paste, in a mortar, a few at a time. Beat to a stiff froth the whites of six eggs, and beat into these, by degrees, one pound white sugar; mix in the almonds gradually, stir well, and form into small cakes and bake on buttered paper, being careful not to let the cakes touch other. Bake in a quick oven to a light brown.

Feather Cake.

One teacupful sugar,
One teacupful sweet milk,
Two teacupsful flour,
One tablespoonful butter,
One egg,
Half teaspoonful soda,
One teaspoonful cream tartar,
Flavor with nutmeg.

Cup Cake.

One teacupful butter,
Two teacupsful sugar,
Three teacupsful flour,
Four eggs,
One teacupful sour milk,
One small teaspoonful soda.

White Cake.

The whites of six eggs,
Two-thirds teacupful butter,
Two teacupsful white sugar,
Three teacupsful flour,
One teacupful sweet milk,

One teaspoonful soda,
Two teaspoonsful cream tartar,
Flavor with peach water.

Golden cake is made with the yelks, and in the same proportion as the above white cake.

Sponge Cake.

One teacupful sugar,
One teacupful flour,
Three eggs,
Half teaspoonful soda,
One teaspoonful cream tartar,
One tablespoonful warm water.
Bake quickly.

Jumbles.

One pound butter,
Two pounds flour,
Two pounds sugar,
Eight eggs,
One teaspoonful soda,
One cupful sour milk.

Rose Cake.

(MRS. DR. GRISSUM'S, KY.

One pound flour,
One pound white sugar,
Three-quarters pound butter,
The whites of fourteen eggs, well beaten.

Beat the butter and sugar to a cream, then stir in the whites and flour alternately until thoroughly mixed. Take one teaspoonful cochineal in a tablespoonful of cold water, and beat till dissolved; strain it in a half teacupful of the batter, cover the bottom of the pan with the white; then mix in as in the marble cake. Flavor with rose. The cochineal must be prepared thus:

One-third cochineal,
One-third alum,
One-third cream tartar.

They must be pulverized well together at the drug store.

Cocoanut Jumbles.

Two eggs,
Three teacupsful white sugar,
One teacupful butter,
One teacupful sour cream,
One scant teaspoonful soda,
Five teacupsful flour,
One large cocoanut grated.

Roll in sugar and drop in the pan. Add the nut last.

Mountain Cake.

(MRS. BUNN.)

Three teacupsful white sugar beaten up with five eggs and a scant cupful of butter,

Four and half cupsful flour,
One cupful sweet milk,
Half teaspoonful soda,
One teaspoonful cream tartar.

Put ordinary icing between it. It is nice to have every alternate layer of nice fair jelly.

Lady Cake.
(MRS. DR. RYAN.)

Whites of eight eggs,
Two teacupsful white sugar,
One teacupful butter,
Four teacupsful flour,
Half teacupful sweet milk,
Half teaspoonful soda,
Two teaspoonsful cream tartar,
Flavor with peach and rose.

Fruit Cake.
(MRS. W. S. HURST.)

Ten eggs,
One pound brown sugar,
One pound flour,
Three pounds raisins,
Two pounds currants,
One pound citron,
Cloves, cinnamon, allspice, nutmeg, wine and brandy to the taste,
One large cupful molasses.

Beat well, as in all cakes.

Almond Cake.

Whites of seventeen eggs,
Three-quarters of a pound butter,
One pound white sugar,
One pound flour.

Beat the whites stiff, add the sugar and butter together and beat well, add flour and whites alternately. Use extract of almond or blanched almonds, and rub in rose water.

Pound Cake.

One pound sugar,
One pound flour,
Three-quarters of a pound butter.

Beat the butter and sugar well together, add the yelks of ten eggs; beat the whites stiff, and add with the flour. Bake one hour.

White Cake.

(MRS. WM. S. HURST.)

Whites of ten eggs,
Two coffeecupsful white sugar,
One coffeecupful butter,
Four coffeecupsful flour,
One coffeecupful sweet milk,
One teaspoonful soda,
Two teaspoonsful cream tartar,
Flavor to suit the taste.

Cup Cake.

Five eggs,
Three teacupsful sugar,
One teacupful butter,
Five teacupsful flour,
One teacupful sour milk,
One small teaspoonful soda.

This is very nice made with currants, and it makes an excellent jelly cake.

Sponge Cake.

Ten eggs,
One pound white sugar,
Half pound flour,

Beat the yelks and the sugar to a cream, the whites stiff, and add alternate with the flour. Flavor with lemon. Bake quickly; add a quarter of a teaspoonful of tartaric acid.

Fruit Cake.

(MRS. WM. S. HURST.)

Use the ten yelks left from the above white cake—
Two coffeecupsful brown sugar,
One coffeecupful butter,
One coffeecupful sweet milk,
One teaspoonful soda,
Two teaspoonsful cream tartar,
Four coffeecupsful flour, brown the flour, if preferred, black,

Two pounds raisins,
One pound currants,
Half pound citron.

Cream Sponge Cake.

One teacupful white sugar.
One teacupful flour,
Half teacupful cream,
Two eggs.

Union Cake.

One teacupful butter,
Two teacupsful white sugar,
Three teacupsful flour,
One teacupful sweet milk,
One teacupful corn starch,
Three eggs,
One teaspoonful soda,
Two teaspoonsful cream tartar.

Harrison Cake.

(MRS. MATE ELLIOTT.)

Three eggs,
One teacupful and a half butter,
One teacupful and a half brown sugar,
Two teacupsful molasses,
Five teacupsful flour,
Two pounds raisins,
One pound currants,

One pound citron,
One teacupful sour milk,
One teaspoonful soda,
Two tablespoonsful each of cinnamon and cloves,
Two grated nutmegs.
Bake two hours, if all baked in one pan.

Delicate Cake.

(MRS P. B. PRICE.)

Stir to a cream one pound powdered white sugar and seven ounces butter; beat the whites of sixteen eggs stiff; stir in one pound sifted flour. Flavor to the taste. Bake immediately.

Marble Cake.

(MRS. DR. RYAN.)

WHITE PART.

The whites of eight eggs,
One teacupful sweet milk,
Three teacupsful white sugar,
One teacupful butter,
Four teacupsful and a half flour,
One teaspoonful soda,
Two teaspoonsful cream tartar.

DARK PART.

The yelks of the eight eggs, and one whole egg,
One teacupful sweet milk,
Three teacupsful brown sugar,

One teacupful molasses,
One teacupful butter,
Five teacupsful flour.
One teaspoonful soda,
Two teaspoonsful cream tartar,
One tablespoonful each of cinnamon, cloves, allspice and nutmeg.

Put enough of the white in the pan to cover the bottom; then put in the spice and white alternately till all is in the pan. Bake two hours. This is one of the most delicious cakes I have ever tasted. It will keep almost as well as fruit cake.

Fancy Cake.

Beat the yelks of four eggs into a half pound of sugar; add a little less than half pound flour; beat fifteen minutes, then add one teaspoonful rose water and the whites of the eggs beaten stiff. Bake in small cakes and put sugar plums on top.

Aunty's Cake.

Eight whites of eggs,
Three teacupsful flour,
Half teacupful sweet milk,
Two teacupsful white sugar,
Three-quarters of a teacupful butter,
Half teaspoonful soda,
One teaspoonful cream tartar.

Cocoanut Cake.

(MRS. DR. RYAN.)

One teacupful butter,
Two teacupsful and a half sugar,
Four teacupsful flour,
One teacupful sweet milk,
One teaspoonful soda,
Two teaspoonsful cream tartar,
Whites of seven eggs,
One grated cocoanut.

Bake in shallow tins. Make frosting, and grate into it another cocoanut to put between the cakes. Use a very little extract lemon in both cake and cocoanut.

Sponge Cake.

(MARIA WATSON.)

Thirteen eggs, beaten separate,
One pound sugar beaten with the yelks,
Half pound flour stirred in lightly the last thing,
Flavor with lemon.

Snow Cake.

(MRS. WM. A. TURNEY.)

The whites of ten eggs,
One tumbler and a half powdered sugar,
One tumbler and two tablespoonsful flour,
A scant teaspoonful cream tartar.

White Cake.

The whites of ten eggs,
Two coffeecupsful white sugar,
One coffeecupful butter,
One coffeecupful sweet milk,
Four coffeecupsful flour,
One teaspoonful soda,
Two teaspoonsful cream tartar,
Flavor to suit the taste.

Ambrosial Cake.

(ELLA MYERS.)

Make any rich white cake; bake in jelly cake pans, using the following:

Two coffeecupsful white sugar,
Yelks of six eggs,
Whites of four eggs,
Four lemons.

Grate the rind of two lemons; one-quarter pound butter. Put in a pan and stew over a slow fire until it becomes thick.

Sponge Cake.

(ELLA MYERS.)

One pint powdered sugar,
One pint flour,
Eight eggs, beaten separately, the yelks for half an hour,
Flavor with lemon. Bake one hour.

Silver Cake.

Three-quarters teacupful butter,
Two teacupsful sugar,
Four teacupsful flour,
One teacupful sweet milk,
One teaspoonful soda,
Two teaspoonsful cream tartar,
The whites of five eggs,
Flavor to taste.

Peach is good for the silver, and lemon or nutmeg for the gold.

Gold Cake.

Two teacupsful sugar,
Three-fourths teacupful butter,
Four teacupsful flour,
One teacupful sweet milk,
One teaspoonful soda,
Two teaspoonsful cream tartar,
Yelks of five eggs,
Flavor to taste.

Starch Cake.

The whites of seven eggs,
One teacupful butter,
Two teacupsful white sugar,
Three teacupsful flour,
One teacupful corn starch,

One teacupful sweet milk,
One teaspoonful soda,
Two teaspoonsful cream tartar,

Corn Starch Cake, (No. 2.)

The whites of sixteen eggs,
One pound white sugar,
Three-quarters pound butter.

Beat the sugar and butter well together; beat the whites stiff; one pound of corn starch, one teaspoonful baking powder; beat lightly after adding the whites.

Milwaukee Cake.

Half teacupful butter,
Two teacupsful sugar,
Three teacupsful flour,
Three eggs,
One teacupful sour milk,
Half teaspoonful soda, or one teacupful water, three teaspoonsful baking powder,
Flavor with lemon.

Tipsy Cake, (Sponge,)

Cut a small cake in slices, put them into a flat glass dish, pour some wine and a little jamaica over the cake; let it soak a few hours; put into a dish and serve with some custard round. It may be decorated with a few blanched almonds or whipped cream and fruit.

Chocolate Macaroons.

Scrape fine half a pound baker's cocoa; beat stiff the whites of four eggs, and into this stir one pound powdered sugar and the scraped cocoa, adding a very little flour. Form the mixture into small, thick cakes, and lay them not too close on a buttered tin, and bake a few minutes. Sift sugar on them while warm.

Chocolate Cake.

Beat the whites of two eggs with a quarter of a pound powdered sugar into a frothy cream; add the juice of half a lemon and six ounces of finely grated chocolate. Drop this mixture in spoonsful on a flat tin, and bake them slowly.

Little Plum Cake, to Keep Long.

Dry one pound of flour, and mix with six ounces of finely powdered sugar; beat six ounces of butter to a cream, and add to three eggs, well-beaten; half a pound of currants washed and nicely dried, and the flour and sugar; beat all for some time, then dredge flour on tin plates and drop the batter on them the size of a walnut. If properly mixed, it will be a stiff paste. Bake in a brisk oven.

Lemon Drops.

Grate three large lemons, with a large piece of

double-refined sugar; then scrape the sugar into a plate, add half a teaspoonful of flour, mix well, and beat it into a light paste with the white of an egg. Drop it upon white paper, and put them into a moderate oven on a tin plate.

Lemon Cake.

(MRS. RAPP, JACKSONVILLE.)

Six eggs,
Six ounces flour,
Eight ounces sugar.

(FILLING FOR CAKE.)

Three ounces butter,
Four eggs,
Four lemons,
Three-fourths of a cupful sugar,
Grated rind of two lemons.

Mix all together; then put in a pan and let it come to a boil. Be careful not to burn. Spread on cakes like jelly.

Golden Cake.

One teacupful of butter,
Two teacupsful sugar,
Three teacupsful flour,
Eight eggs, the yelks,
Half teacupful milk,
One teaspoonful cream tartar,
Half teaspoonful soda.

Mix the flour and cream tartar together. Flavor with nutmeg.

Jane's Cream Cake.

One pint water,
Half pound butter,
Three-quarters of a pound flour,
Ten eggs.

Boil the water, melt the butter in it; stir in the flour dry while the water is boiling. When cool, add one teaspoonful soda and the eggs well-beaten. Drop the mixture on buttered tins with a spoon, and bake twenty minutes.

(INSIDE MIXTURE.)

One cupful flour,
Two cupsful sugar,
One quart milk,
Four eggs.

Beat flour, eggs and sugar together, and stir into the boiling milk; when scalded enough add lemon and vanilla. When the cakes are cold open and fill with this mixture.

Cocoanut Cake.

One coffeecupful butter,
Three coffeecupsful sugar,
One coffeecupful sweet milk,
Four coffeecupsful and a half flour,
Four eggs, the whites beaten to a stiff froth.
One teaspoonful soda,

Two teaspoonsful cream tartar,
One grated cocoanut.   (Excellent.)

Cookies.

(MAGGIE LAMB.)

Seven eggs,
Two coffeecupsful sugar,
Flour enough to make a soft dough,
Three teaspoonsful baking powder,
No milk or water,
Two coffeecupsful butter.   (Splendid.)

Cookies.

Two eggs,
One teacupful loaf sugar,
One teacupful butter,
Two tablespoonsful buttermilk,
One teaspoonful soda.
Flour enough to roll out thin.   Spice to the taste.

Plum Cake.

One pound flour,
One-quarter pound butter,
One-quarter pound sugar,
One-quarter pound currants,
Three eggs,
Half pint milk,

One teaspoonful soda,
Two teaspoonsful cream tartar,
Spices to suit the taste.

The above is excellent. These cakes are always baked in small pans.

Excellent Cookies.

Two teacupsful sugar,
One teacupful butter,
One teacupful lard,
One teacupful sweet milk,
Three-quarters of a pound corn starch,
Three-quarters of a pound flour,
One teaspoonful soda,
Two teaspoonsful cream tartar.

Roll very soft.

Jumbles.

One coffeecupful sugar, after it is sifted,
One scant coffeecupful butter,
Two coffeecupsful flour,
Two eggs,
Flavor with lemon.

Coffee Cake.

One cupful butter,
One cupful of made strong coffee,
Two cupsful brown sugar,
Three cupsful flour,

One cupful raisins,
One cupful currants,
Two teaspoonsful cinnamon,
Two teaspoonsful cloves,
One teaspoonful soda.

Sponge Cake.

Take five eggs, half a pound powdered sugar, break the egg upon the sugar, and beat with a steel fork for half an hour. Take the weight of two eggs and a half in the shell of flour; after you have beaten the eggs and sugar the time specified, grate in the rind of a lemon, the juice may be added at pleasure; stir in the flour, and immediately pour it into a tin lined with buttered paper, and put it instantly into a moderate oven.

Marble Cake.

FOR THE WHITE.

Two cupsful sugar,
One cupful butter,
One cupful sour milk,
Three cupsful flour,
Whites of seven eggs,
One teaspoonful soda.

FOR THE BLACK.

Two cupsful brown sugar,
One cupful butter,
One cupful sour milk,
Three cupsful flour,

One cupful molasses,
Yelks seven eggs,
One teaspoonful soda,
Spice to taste.

Mix each cake separately; paper the bottom of your pan and grease well, then cover the bottom with some of the dark cake, and then add white and dark alternately till all is in the pan. Bake an hour and a half.

Molasses Cup Cake.

One coffeecupful molasses,
One coffeecupful sugar,
One coffeecupful sour milk or cream,
One coffeecupful of mixed butter and lard,
Four coffeecupsful flour,
One coffeecupful chopped raisins,
One coffeecupful currants,
Four eggs,
One teaspoonful soda,
A pinch of salt,
One teaspoonful cloves,
One tablespoonful ginger,
One nutmeg.

Water Cookies.

Two teacupsful sugar,
One teacupful butter,
One teacupful cold water,
Half teaspoonful soda,

One teaspoonful cream tartar,
Flour enough to roll,
Ginger to taste.

Soft Ginger Cake.

Half teacupful butter,
Half teacupful brown sugar,
Half teacupful molasses,
One teacupful and a half flour,
Half teacupful sour milk,
One teaspoonful soda,
One tablespoonful ginger,
Two eggs.

Soft Ginger Cake.

Two teacupsful molasses,
One teacupful sugar,
One teacupful mixed butter and lard,
Four teacupsful and a half flour,
One teacupful sour milk or water,
One teaspoonful soda,
Or with water, four teaspoonsful baking powder,
Two tablespoonsful ginger,
One teaspoonful cloves.

Soft Ginger Bread.

One teacupful butter,
Two teacupsful sugar,

One teacupful molasses,
Five teacupsful flour,
One teacupful sour milk,
One teaspoonful soda,
Three eggs,
One tablespoonful and a half ginger,
Cinnamon and allspice to the taste.

Ginger Snaps.

(BEN. WATSON'S.)

Half pound butter,
Half pound sugar,
One pint New Orleans molasses,
One ounce ginger.

Flour enough to make very stiff dough; work smooth and roll thin, cut with a small cutter. Bake dark brown.

Sponge Ginger Bread.

Melt a piece of butter the size of a hen's egg,
One pint New Orleans molasses,
One tablespoonful ginger,
One quart flour.

Dissolve a tablespoonful of saleratus in half a pint sour milk, strain and mix; add flour enough to enable you to roll about an inch thick, and bake in a quick oven.

Ginger Cakes.

(MRS. DR. RYAN.)

Two coffeecupsful molasses,
One coffeecupful lard,
One tablespoonful ginger,
One tablespoonful mustard,
One tablespoonful soda,
Flour enough to make very soft.
Roll thin and bake quickly.

Soft Ginger Bread.

One coffeecupful butter,
One pint molasses,
One tablespoonful ginger,
One pint flour,
Two eggs,
Two tablespoonsful saleratus,
Half pint sour milk.
Flour to make as stiff batter as pound cake.

Jumbles.

Three teacupsful sugar,
Two teacupsful butter,
Three eggs,
Four tablespoonsful sour cream,
One teaspoonful soda.
Roll thin, sprinkle with coffee sugar thickly on the top before placing in the oven.

Soft Ginger Bread.

(JANE ILES.)

One pint New Orleans molasses,
Two tablespoonsful butter,
Three pints and a half flour,
Two tablespoonsful ginger,
Half pint sour milk,
One tablespoonful soda.

Raised Cake without Eggs.

Stir together a coffeecupful of light sugar and half a cupful of butter; add a pint of warm water, half a cupful of yeast, and flour enough to make as thick as ordinary fruit cake; rise over night; when very light, add a little mace, cinnamon, allspice and nutmeg, one cupful chopped raisins. Put in the pan, let rise until light, then bake.

Ginger Snaps.

One egg,
One teacupful sugar,
Piece of butter the size of an egg,
Quarter of a teaspoonful soda dissolved in warm water,
One spoonful ginger,
Flour to roll.

Low's Ginger Snaps.

One pint molasses,
One cupful lard,

Half cupful sugar,
One teaspoonful soda dissolved in warm water,
Cinnamon and ginger to taste.
Mix them stiff, pound them, roll thin, and bake

Almond Cake.

One coffeecupful butter,
Two coffeecupsful white sugar,
Four coffeecupsful flour,
One coffeecupful cream or rich milk,
Twelve whites of eggs,
One teaspoonful cream tartar,
Half teaspoonful soda,
One teaspoonful extract of almond,
Two pounds of almonds in the shell.

Blanch the almonds and slice very thin, and rub on a little flour before putting them in the cake. Mix as for other cakes; stir, but not beat, after all is in.

Cocoanut Jumbles, No. 1.

Three eggs,
Three cupsful sugar,
One cupful butter,
One cupful cream,
One teaspoonful soda,
One large or two small cocoanuts grated,
Five cupsful and a half flour.

Roll them out in sugar.

Cocoanut Jumbles, No. 2.

One cupful sugar,
One egg,
A piece of butter the size of two eggs,
Two tablespoonsful sour cream,
Half teaspoonful soda.

One teaspoonful cream tartar, if sweet milk is used, and flour enough to make the dough stiff enough to roll out in sugar. Half package of prepared cocoanut or one whole one grated.

Almond Icing.

If it is wished to ice a cake, as is done for bride cake, a layer of almonds must be first spread over the cake according to the following receipt: Take the whites of three fresh eggs, and beat them to a stiff froth; bruise one pound of jordan almonds very fine with rose water enough to prevent their oiling in a mortar, and mix them with the whites of eggs very lightly together; mix in by degrees one pound of powdered sugar, when the cake is taken from the oven lay this mixture on very smoothly; let it dry gradually, and when dry enough proceed to sugar ice it.

Sugar Ice.

Beat two pounds of double-refined sugar and two ounces of fine starch, sift through a gauze sieve; then beat the whites of five eggs till they are stiff, adding the sugar by degrees; when all the sugar has been put in, continue to beat it half an hour longer; then lay it over the almond icing and spread it very even with a bread knife. If it is put on as soon as the cake comes out of the oven, it will be hard by the time the cake is cold.

Tea or Coffee Cake.

Four eggs,
Two cupsful nice brown sugar,
One cupful butter, or half lard,
Three teacupsful sour milk,
One teaspoonful soda,
Half a nutmeg grated.

Put the eggs and sugar into a suitable pan and beat well together, add butter, and beat all well; put in the nutmeg; now stir in flour, to make it of such a consistency that it will not run from the spoon when it is lifted up. Any one preferring any other flavor can suit their own taste. This can be baked in little cakes or in square baking pans.

Pork Cake without Butter, Eggs or Milk.

A most delightful cake is made by the use of pork, (fat pickled pork.) It must be tasted to be appreciated, and another advantage is, you can make enough some leisure day to last through the season. I have eaten it three or four months after it was baked, and it was very nice and moist. Take nice fat pickled pork, free from any lean or rind, and chopped to look almost like lard, of this after it is chopped, one pound; pour half a pint boiling water on it; raisins stoned and chopped two pounds; citron, shaved into shreds half a pound; currants, washed and dried one pound; brown sugar, two cupsful (teacupsful measure;) molasses, one cupful; soda, one teaspoonful, rubbed fine and put into the molasses. Mix them all together and stir in sifted flour to the consistency of any other fruit or pound cake. Put in such spices as are suited to the taste. Cinnamon, cloves and allspice, are usually put into fruit cake, but in making any cake that requires flavor or spices, persons are not required to adhere strictly to the receipt if it does not suit the taste. Paper and grease a pan well and bake slowly. The best rule for baking cake is to watch it closely and try it with a straw; if nothing adheres to the straw, and your judgment tells you it has been in long enough, take it out of the oven. Be careful not to take a fruit cake out of the pan while it is too hot. You can put in as much fruit or as little as you like. It is intended for a cheap cake, and for those who do not feel able to always have the richer fruit cakes.

Cider Cake.

Six cupsful flour,
Three cupsful sugar, white or brown,
One cupful butter,

Four eggs,
One cupful cider,
One teaspoonful soda,
One grated nutmeg.

Mix as other cakes. Put soda in the cider. Bake in a quick oven.

Roll Jelly Cake.

One cupful and a half nice brown sugar,
Three eggs,
One cupful sweet milk,
Two cupsful flour, or a very little more,
One teaspoonful soda,
One teaspoonful and a half cream tartar,
Flavor to suit the taste, lemon is nice.

Beat the sugar and eggs together till light; mix the cream tartar and soda into the milk, stirring in the flavor also; now mix in the flour, remembering to bake soon, spreading thin upon a long tin pan well-greased. As soon as it is done, take it out on your bread board; spread jelly upon the top of it, and spread it all over nicely and roll up, slicing only as it is to be used.

Dried Apple Cake.

Very fine. Try it.

One coffeecupful dried apples soaked over night. In the morning drain, chop fine, and cook slowly in one coffeecupful syrup.

CAKE.

One coffee cupful brown sugar,

One-third of a coffeecupful butter,
Two coffeecupsful flour,
One coffeecupful sour milk,
One egg,
One teaspoonful soda,
Spice to the taste.

White Fruit Cake.

The whites of ten eggs,
Two coffeecupsful powdered white sugar,
One coffeecupful butter,
Four coffeecupsful flour,
One coffeecupful sweet milk,
One teaspoonful soda,
Two teaspoonsful cream tartar,
Flavor with rose and peach water,
Two pounds raisins well stoned and chopped,
Two pounds currants well washed and dried,
One pound citron sliced thin.

Beat butter and sugar together till it is light; mix cream tartar in the flour, and stir in a little flour before putting in the milk; then add flour and whites (which must be well-beaten) alternately, stir well together, and add fruit till all is in. Have ready a pan sufficiently large. It is well, in all cakes, to have the bottom of the pan covered with a well-greased paper. This will take about two hours to bake. Do not have your oven too hot, but keep a steady and regular heat. If it should require it, put a thick brown paper on the top to prevent its getting too brown.

Icing for Cake.

To the white of an egg, one quarter pound powdered sugar. Beat the egg stiff, and add by degrees the sugar. Flavor with lemon juice. This makes it whiter and smoother, and improves it much.

Ginger Pound Cake.

Eight eggs,
Four cupsful brown sugar,
Nine cupsful flour,
Three cupsful and half butter,
One cupful and a half rich sour cream,
Two cupsful ginger,
Two teaspoonsful soda,
Four teacupsful molasses.

Beat the eggs very light, add the sugar to them; cream the butter with the flour; warm the cream with the soda; then mix all together alternately with the ginger and molasses, and then beat very hard. Bake either in little pans or in a large cake pan.

Crullers.

Four eggs,
Six tablespoonsful white sugar,
Four tablespoonsful melted butter,
Four tablespoonsful sweet milk,
Half teaspoonful soda,

Mix soft and fry in hot lard.

Cookies.

Two cupsful sugar,
Four cupsful flour,
One egg,
One cupful cream,
A little soda,
One cupful butter.

Pork Cake.

(CLARA'S.)

Half teacupful fat salt pork (pickled) chopped very fine,
One teacupful brown sugar,
One teacupful molasses,
One teacupful milk,
One teacupful raisins or currants,
One teaspoonful soda,
Two eggs,
Cinnamon, nutmeg and allspice to the taste.

Sponge Cake.

(MRS. RYAN.)

Twelve eggs,
Sixteen ounces flour,
One pound powdered white sugar.

Heat the flour; beat the yelks and sugar well together; beat the whites very stiff; add the whites and flour alternate; flavor with either lemon or almond, one-fourth of a teaspoonful tartartic acid, which must be put in last. Do not beat after you begin to stir in the whites. If this is baked in shallow tins, after it is put into the pans have ready some blanched almonds sliced very thin, and sprinkle on the top.

Crullers.

Half cupful butter,
One cupful milk,
One cupful sugar,
Cinnamon and nutmeg to taste.

Flour enough to make a dough stiff enough to roll out in cakes. Fry in lard.

Doughnuts.

One cupful sugar,
One cupful sour milk,
Two eggs,
Five dessertspoonsful melted butter.
One teaspoonful soda,
One teaspoonful cream tartar,
Salt, cinnamon and nutmeg to taste.
Fry in hot lard.

Snow Cake, (Very Fine.)

Half pound butter,
Half pound powdered sugar,
One pound arrowroot,
The whites of six eggs.

Beat the butter to a cream, add arrowroot and sugar,

gradually, beating all the time; beat the whites separately, and when stiff add to the mixture; flavor to suit taste, and beat all together twenty minutes. Bake in shallow tins or in small tins in moderate oven.

Cream Jelly Cake.

  Three cupsful flour,
  Two cupsful white sugar,
  One cupful butter,
  Half cupful sweet milk,
  Four eggs,
  Half teaspoonful baking powder.
Bake in jelly tins.

CREAM FOR THE ABOVE.

  Grate two lemons, add the juice,
  One cupful sugar,
  Half cupful butter,
  Yelks of three eggs,
Stir constantly over the fire till it jellies; when cold spread between the cakes.

White Sponge Cake.

  Whites of ten eggs,
  One cupful and a half powdered white sugar,
  One cupful flour,
  One teaspoonsful cream tartar.
Mix cream tartar, sugar and flour together, beat well; stir in (after they are beaten stiff) very gently.

Newport Cake.

(MRS. ABLE.)

Two tablespoonsful sugar,
Piece of butter the size of an egg,
Two eggs, beaten separately,
One cupful and a half sweet milk,
One teaspoonful soda,
Two teaspoonsful cream tartar,
Three cupsful flour.

Bake fifteen minutes. (Cheap and good.)

Crullers.

One pint sour milk,
One cupful sugar,
Two eggs,
Two teaspoonsful salt,
One teaspoonful soda.

Cocoanut Cookies.

Three cupsful white sugar,
Three eggs,
One cupful sour milk,
One teaspoonful soda.

As much flour as will make it a soft dough. Then add a box of cocoanut, (or one grated cocoanut,) and a tablespoonful of grated nutmeg. Have the dough as soft as you can well roll it, and about an inch thick; cut and bake a light brown.

Ammonia Cake.

Three eggs,
Three-quarters pound sugar,
Half pound butter,
Half teacupful sweet cream,
Half teaspoonful ammonia,
One small teaspoonful soda,
One lemon.

Flour enough to make a dough. Roll thin.

White Cake.

One cupful butter,
Two cupsful and a half sugar,
Four cupsful flour,
One cupful sweet milk,
Whites of seven eggs,
Two teaspoonsful baking powder.

Bake on shallow tins.

Ginger Cake.

(MRS. PERKINS.)

Three tablespoonsful ginger,
Half of a nutmeg,
One teaspoonful cloves,
One teaspoonful cinnamon,
One tablespoonful soda,
One pint molasses,
One teacupful brown sugar,
One teacupful butter or sweet lard,

One teacupful sour cream or milk,
Four eggs, well-beaten.
Flour enough to make a stiff batter.

Ginger Snaps.

One cupful butter,
One cupful sugar,
Two cupsful molasses,
Ginger and spice to the taste.
Flour enough to roll out.

Soft Ginger Bread.

One cupful butter,
One cupful sugar,
Two cupsful molasses,
One cupful sour milk,
Five cupsful flour,
Four eggs,
Two tablespoonful ginger,
One teaspoonful soda,
One teaspoonsful cream tartar.

Snow Cake.

One cupful and a half powdered sugar,
One cupful flour,
The whites of eight eggs,
One teaspoonful cream tartar mixed in the flour.
Flavor to suit the taste.

Cocoanut Macaroons.

Beat to a stiff froth the whites of six eggs, and then beat into it very hard a pound of powdered white sugar; mix with it a pound of grated cocoanut to a stiff paste. Flour your hands and make it up into little balls. Lay them on sheets of buttered white paper, and bake them in a brisk oven, first grating white sugar over each. They will be done in a few minutes.

Orange Cake.

(MRS. J. BUNN.)

Make cake as for jelly cake, put together with icing; take the grated rind, all the inside pulp and juice of one large orange; then thicken with sugar. When a little dry frost all over with the frosting.

Ice Cream Cake.

(MRS. J. BUNN.)

One cupful butter, beat to a cream,
Two cupsful sugar,
One cupful milk,
One cupful corn starch,
Two cupsful flour,
Whites of seven eggs,
Two teaspoonsful cream tartar,
Two-thirds teaspoonful soda.
Bake quickly.

Sponge Cake.

Twelve eggs,
One pound sugar,
Ten ounces of flour,
One fresh lemon.
Put the flour in last.

Sponge Cake.

Weigh the eggs, and then weigh as much sugar as the eggs weigh; take half as much flour and two ounces more, two teaspoonsful cream tartar, one of soda, dissolve in a little water; wet the sugar with a little milk; beat the whites and put them in last.

Cream Cake.
(MRS. DAVIS.)

One cupful boiling water, one tablespoonful butter, while the water and butter are boiling, stir in one cupful flour; it will make a thick and smooth paste. After it is taken off the fire, add four eggs, and beat the mixture as hard as possible until very smooth. Drop into buttered tins in small cakes, and smooth over them the white of an egg beaten to a frost. Bake ten minutes in a very hot oven. For the filling of these cakes—

One sheet of isinglass,
One-third of a cupful hot water,
Two cupsful milk,
The yelk of one egg,
Sweeten and flavor to the taste.

—19

Strain the mixture and let it stand till it congeals; then put a spoonful into each cake.

Railroad Cake.

(MRS. DAVIS.)

One cupful sugar,
Four tablespoonsful melted butter,
Half cupful milk,
Three eggs,
One and a half cupsful flour,
Three teaspoonsful baking powder,
Flavor to suit the taste.

Common Crullers or Twist Cakes.

Mix well together half a pint of sour milk or buttermilk, two teacupsful sugar, one teacupful of butter, and three eggs well-beaten; add to this a teaspoonful of saleratus dissolved in hot water, a teaspoonful of salt, half a nutmeg grated, and a teaspoonful of powdered cinnamon; sift in flour enough to make a smooth dough; roll it out not quite a quarter of an inch thick; cut in small oblong pieces; divide one end in three or four parts like fingers, and twist or plait them over each other. Fry them in boiling lard. These cakes may be cut in strips, and the ends joined, to make a ring, or in any other shape.

Soft Crullers.

Sift three-quarters of a pound of flour, and powder

half a pound of loaf sugar; heat a pint of water in a round bottomed saucepan, and when quite warm, mix the flour with it gradually; set half a pound of fresh butter over the fire in a small vessel, and when it begins to melt, stir it gradually into the flour and water; then add by degrees the powdered sugar and half a grated nutmeg. Take the saucepan off the fire, and beat the contents with a wooden paddle or spatula till they are thoroughly mixed; then beat six eggs very light, and stir them gradually into the mixture. Beat the whole very hard till it becomes a thick batter. Flour a pasteboard very well, and lay out the batter upon it in rings, (the best way is to pass it through a screw funnel.) Have ready, on the fire, a pot of boiling lard of the very best quality; put in the crullers, removing them from the board by carefully taking them up, one at a time, on a broad-bladed knife. Boil but few at a time. They must be of a fine brown. Lift them out on a perforated skimmer, draining the lard from them back into the pot; lay them on a large dish, and sift powdered white sugar over them.

Cocoanut Jumbles.

Cut the meat of a large cocoanut in slices and grate them. Beat up the whites of five eggs and the yelks of three, and mix with them a few drops of the essence of lemon. Mix the grated cocoanut with a small portion of flour, roll it lightly on a floured pasteboard, cut it into rings with a tumbler, the edge of which is floured. Butter the pans into which the cakes are to be laid, and after sifting a little loaf sugar over the cakes; bake them in a quick oven. When they begin to brown they are done.

Rice Cake.

Take eight yelks and four whites of eggs, and beat to a foam; add six ounces of powdered sugar, and the peel of one lemon grated; then stir in half a pound of ground rice, and beat all together for half an hour. Put it into a buttered tin, and bake twenty minutes. This cake is recommended as very easy of digestion.

Corn Starch Cake.

One cupful sugar,
Butter the size of an egg,
Two eggs,
Two tablespoonsful milk,
One teaspoonsful cream tartar,
Half teaspoonful soda,
One cupful and two tablespoonsful corn starch,
Makes twelve cakes.

Tea Cakes.

Five cupsful flour,
Two cupsful sugar,
One cupful of butter or sweet lard,
One egg,
One teaspoonful soda,
One small cupful sour milk.

White Cake.

Two pounds powdered white sugar,
One pound butter,
One pound and three-quarters flour,
The whites of twenty-four eggs.

Beat the butter to a cream, then add the sugar, and beat them well together; add flour and the whites alternately. This should be very carefully watched while baking, paper should be kept over the the top to keep it from getting too brown. The beauty of any white cake is to have it thoroughly, and at the same time, delicately baked.

Almond Pound Cake.

One pound powdered white sugar,
Half pound butter,
One teacupful sweet milk,
One pound flour,
One teaspoonful soda, dissolved in hot water,
One teaspoonful essence of lemon,
Half pound of blanched almonds pounded small,
Four eggs.

Swiss Cream.

Four tablespoonsful white sugar,
One teaspoonful corn starch,
The whites of five eggs,

Put the cream on to boil, then let it cool, and then add the whites and boil again, stirring all the time.

Cookies.

(MRS. GOODELL.)

Two cupsful butter,
Two cupsful sugar,
Seven eggs,
Caraway seed.
Enough flour to roll out.

Doughnuts.

One cupful butter and lard,
One cupful sugar,
One cupful boiling water,
Flour enough to make a thick sponge,
One cupful yeast.

Let it stand over night. Then add—

One cupful sugar,
Three eggs,
Flour enough to make a dough, not too stiff.

Let it rise till quite light; then roll them out, cut and boil them in hot lard to a light brown, dipping them as you take them out in powdered sugar and cinnamon.

Crullers.

One cupful sugar,
Three eggs,
Butter the size of an egg,
Flour enough to roll out.

Cut and fry in hot lard.

Citron Marble Cake.

Mix up any nice white cake.
One pound almonds, blanched and sliced,
Half pound citron, sliced very thin,
Color one-third of the batter pink.

Put part of the white batter in your pan, then a little of the pink thrown in carelessly; then part of the almonds, then a part of the citron, then white and pink, and alternating each till all is in the mould. Have your oven the proper heat before putting it into the stove; watch it well; if it begins to brown too quickly, put a paper over it to keep it from browning too much.

Orange Paste.

Whites of two eggs,
Two-thirds of a cupful pulverized sugar,
The juice of two oranges and grated rind of one.

The eggs must be beaten up very light and stiff, then add the sugar and orange; spread on instead of jelly when the cakes are cold.

Imperial Cake.

(MRS. HODGES.)

Ten eggs,
One pound powdered sugar,
One pound flour,
One pound butter,

Two pounds almonds blanched, and sliced thin, and rubbed in a little flour,

One pounds raisins stoned and chopped.

Beat butter and sugar together to a cream, whites beaten stiff, and added with the flour alternately; one tumbler of good brandy; flavor with extract of almond; put in the raisins and almonds and stir well after they are in, but do not beat. Bake just like fruit cake, but not so long, about two hours and a half.

Irish Cake.

One pound sifted sugar,

One pound butter, beat to a cream,

One pound and a quarter flour,

One pound currants,

Three eggs, beat the whites to a froth,

Quarter of a pound blanched sweet almonds cut small,

A small glassful of brandy,

One nutmeg or one lemon.

Beat the cake one hour, or till it is very light; leave out the currants and almonds till you are ready to put it in the pan; put paper in the bottom of the pan.

Jumbles.

(MRS. MASTERS.)

One pound a half flour,

Three-quarters of a pound white sugar,

Three-quarters of a pound butter,

Three eggs,
Quarter teaspoonful soda in one tablespoonful of water.

Sift and weigh the flour, put it into your pan; take your hand and make a hole in the centre, pushing the flour to the sides of the pan; put in your butter and sugar; beat your eggs well together and pour in with the butter and sugar; then add your soda and water, and mix well, using all the pound and a half of flour; when mixed, take a piece of the dough and roll it in a round roll with your hands, and then cut them into lengths and join the ends together, making a cake with a hole in the centre. These cakes can be made as large or as small as you wish. Flavor with grated nutmeg.

Doughnuts.

Make just as you would for soda biscuits, only add
Two eggs,
Two cupsful sugar,
Cinnamon and nutmeg.

Roll, cut, and fry a light brown in hot lard.

Splendid Cookies.

(MRS. WILSON.)

Two pounds flour,
Two pounds sugar,
One coffeecupful butter, which is ten ounces,
Six eggs,

Five teaspoonsful baking powder,
Flavor to suit the taste.

Beat sugar and butter together, then add eggs, and beat all well together; put baking powder in flour, mix well. The dough will be soft; break off a small portion of the dough, flour your bread board, and with your two hands roll the piece of dough into a round long roll; then take a sharp knife, flour it, and cut the cakes off in inch pieces; they will be small, but will spread in the pan; it is the nicest way for all cookies, as the rolling the dough with a rolling pin destroys the lightness of almost any dough. By the addition of one grated cocoanut, you will will have splendid cocoanut macaroons.

PUDDINGS.

DIRECTIONS IN REGARD TO PUDDINGS.

In making bags for puddings that are to be boiled, the muslin should be close to keep out the water. It should always be dipped in water (cold) and wrung out, then thoroughly floured on the inside; turn it and put in your pudding, leaving sufficient room for the pudding to swell. Suet and Indian meal puddings require more room than others. Always put an old plate of some kind in the bottom of the pot to prevent sticking and burning. Have the pot well filled with boiling water, as cold would ruin the pudding. Keep the pot well filled, and if water must be added, use boiling water. Do not let it stop boiling, as it is an injury to the pudding. Turn the pudding over after it has been in a few minutes; always keep the pot covered. Dip the bag in cold water a moment before turning the pudding out. Be sure all eggs used are fresh, generally beat the whites and yelks separately. Do not put eggs into hot milk. All butter used in cooking should be sweet and good. In boiling custards, always set the vessel in another containing boiling water, it prevents sticking and burning.

Fruit and other materials used in puddings should always be, if possible, prepared before the time of using. In families where they can get such things in quantities, it will be found a great convenience to make a business of preparing currants and raisins at least. Take three or four pounds of dried currants, put them into a sieve, and set that into a large clean tin or other pan, and pour over the currants sufficient warm (not hot) water to cover them; let them remain ten or fifteen minutes, then take your hands and rub them well to remove all dirt and sand. Pour off that water and add more. Let the currants remain in the sieve, continue pouring on clean water till your fruit is clean, which will be seen by the color of the water. The use of the sieve is of great assistance, as it prevents the loss of fruit, and all the dirt is sure to be washed away, leaving the fruit cleaner than could be made in any other way. When clean, take the sieve from the water; shake it well, and and let it set till the water has all dropped off; then wipe in a clean cloth and put them in a large dripping pan, set them in the stove oven; watch them closely, stirring till the water is dried out and they appear fresh and full; then take them out; let them get cold, and put them away in either glass or earthen jars. In this way they can be used with less trouble. It takes but a very short time to prepare them, and is of great assistance, as they are always ready on short notice.

Raisins should, if possible, be stemmed and put away in tin boxes. Every housekeeper knows, no doubt, the inconvenience of having to wait to wash and clean currants, and stem and stone raisins, especially if the pudding or fruit cake is needed the same day. In a short winter day it is almost impossible to get them prepared in time, especially if the pudding is to take three hours to boil or steam, or the cake three or four hours to bake; hence the necessity of taking one spare hour in the morning and preparing the fruits ready for the "time of need." If once tried it will never be abandoned I am sure. I give this as my own way of preparation. All spices should kept on hand in such quantities as economy shall direct. Each bottle or box should be labelled and kept covered or corked tight. Cream tartar, soda, tartaric acid, and indeed all such things, should be carefully labelled to prevent mistakes. By using these precautions time and inconvenience will both be saved.

Brandy or Wine Sauce.

To a quarter of a pound of butter put a quarter of a pound of sugar and a gill of brandy or wine; grate half a nutmeg into it; make it hot and serve, or it may be beaten well together and used cold.

Lemon Sauce.

Make as directed for the above sauce, using the lemon juice instead of the wine or brandy.

Cold Sauce.

Four ounces butter,
Six ounces sugar,
White of one egg whipped,
One glass of wine,
Cream, butter and sugar together.
Add the lemon essence, then the white of egg.

Sauce for Pudding.

Half pound sugar,
Quarter pound butter,
Two eggs well beaten together.

Set the vessel in boiling water till it boils about two minutes. In making butter and sugar sauce, stir in a little lemon essence before putting in anything else. It makes it very light.

Sauce for Boiled Rice.

Beat the yelks of three eggs into sugar enough to make it sweet; add a teacupful of cream and the grated rind and juice of two lemons. When lemon cannot be had use dried lemon peel and a little tartaric acid. This is a nice sauce for other puddings, especially for corn starch puddings.

Pudding Sauce.

One cupful brown or white sugar,
One egg,
A piece of butter the size of an egg.

Beat all together to a cream, add half a wine glass of boiling water. Flavor to suit the taste.

Liquid Sauce.

Six tablespoonsful sugar,
Ten tablespoonsful water,
Four tablespoonsful butter,
Two tablespoonsful wine.

Heat the water and sugar very hot; stir in the butter till it is melted. Be careful and not let it boil. Flavor to suit the taste.

Butter and Sugar Sauce.

This is made by beating to a cream two cupsful white sugar and half a cupful of sweet butter. For plain batter puddings it may be thinned with a few spoonsful boiling water. Flavor to suit the taste. Nutmeg is very nice, though lemon juice or wine may be used.

Pudding Sauce.

One cupful brown sugar,
Two tablespoonsful of cream,
One ounce butter.

Stir the butter and sugar thoroughly; then add a little of the cream at a time to keep them from separating; add wine to the taste in the same manner, (not quite a wineglassful.) Let the mixture melt; it will be a white froth when done. Enough for five persons.

Brandy Sauce.

Heat over steam half apint of brandy; beat together to a cream two cupsful of sugar, and half a cupful of butter and two well-beaten eggs stirred into it; then add the brandy, mixing thoroughly. Keep hot till needed.

Wine Sauce.

Wine sauce may be made in the same proportion as the above, using a cupful of wine; heat over steam, but do not stir while melting.

Wine Sauce.

Piece of butter size of an egg,
One cupful powdered sugar, stirred till very high,
Three-fourths of a cupful boiling water,
One wineglassful of wine turned on to the sugar and butter, and stir briskly.

Mrs. R.'s Pudding Sauce.

Two eggs,
Two cupsful sugar,
One cupful butter,
One glassful of wine.

Beat all well together till creamy, and set over the fire a few minutes to scald through once, or set it in the tea kettle top to heat through.

Sweet Sauce.

Work a teacupful of sugar into a teacupful of butter with a teaspoonful of flour and half a nutmeg, grated; when it is a smooth paste, stir gradually into it half a pint of boiling water; set it over the fire for ten minutes, stir it all the time. This sauce is nice with almost any kind of puddings or dumplings; wine or brandy can be added, that is a matter of choice.

Chinese Fun.

(MRS. E. B. PEASE.)

One cupful of chopped suet,
Three cupsful flour,
One cupful molasses,
One cupful sour milk,
One teaspoonful soda in the milk,
A little salt,
One cupful raisins,
One teaspoonful each of ginger, cloves and cinnamon.

Steam three hours if all in one pan; if in small cups, steam two hours.

Rich Lemon Sauce.

Boil a nice large lemon in plenty of water, until you can run a straw through it, then cut it in slices. and each slice into quarters; put to them and the juice a teacupful of sugar, the same of butter, with a large teaspoonful of flour worked into it; put all together and stir in gradually half a pint of boiling water; grate half a nutmeg; put this over the fire ten minutes, stirring all the time.

Cheap Dessert.

Cook one teacupful of rice; when done to a jelly add a tablespoonful of currant jelly and half a teacupful of fruit juice; boil a few minutes; mould, and eat with cream and white sugar.

Potato Pudding.

One quart soft mashed potatoes,
Half a pound melted butter,
Six eggs, beat light.

Mix the butter with half a pound sugar; stir in the eggs, adding half a pound currants or raisins; put in a thick cloth and boil half an hour. To be eaten with wine sauce.

Brown Pudding.

Three cupsful flour,
One cupful molasses,
One cupful raisins,
Three-quarters of a cupful suet,
One cupful sour milk,
One teaspoonful soda,
One teaspoonful salt.

To steam three hours.

A Baked Indian Pudding.

Cut up a quarter of a pound of butter in a pint of molasses, and warm them together till the butter is melted; boil one quart of milk, and while scalding hot pour it over a pint of sifted corn meal, and stir in the molasses and butter, and let it steep for an hour covered over; take off the cover and let it cool; when cool beat six eggs, and into it add a tablespoonful of mixed cinnamon and nutmeg and the grated peel of a lemon; stir the whole very hard, and put it into a buttered dish and bake it two hours. Serve with any kind of sauce.

German Puffs.

Sift half a pound of flour; cut up into a quart of rich milk half a pound of fresh butter, set near the fire till melted; beat eight eggs very light and stir gradually into the milk and butter alternately with the flour; add a grated nutmeg and a teaspoonful of cinnamon; mix the whole to a fine smooth batter; butter some large cups and fill them a little more than half full; set them immediately in a quick oven, and bake a quarter of an hour; when done, turn them out into a dish and grate sugar over them. Serve with sauce.

Steam Pudding.

(MISS CARRIE HURST.)

Three pints sweet milk,
Three eggs,

    One teaspoonful soda,
    Two teaspoonsful cream tartar,
    Flour enough to make a little stiffer than batter pudding,
    A very little salt,
    Currants or raisins if you like.

Fill the cups half full; put them in a steamer and steam half an hour; eat with sauce: make with equal quantities of sugar and butter, with nutmeg and brandy.

Florentine Pudding.

(SALLIE FOREMAN.)

    One quart sweet milk,
    Five tablespoonsful white sugar,
    Three tablespoonsful corn starch,
    Three eggs.

Mix the corn starch and three spoonsful of the sugar and the yelks of the eggs and the milk; put on and boil until thick; then take off and put in a baking dish; after it is slightly browned, take the whites of the three eggs and the other two spoonsful of sugar and beat well and put on the top, and bake a light brown. Flavor to suit the taste; eat with cream.

German Pudding.

    Two eggs,
    One cupful sugar,
    One cupful milk,

Three cupsful flour,
Two teaspoonsful cream tartar,
One teaspoonful soda.
Bake and serve with sauce.

Batter Pudding.

(MRS. DR. GRISSOM, KY.)

Two tablesoonpsful of flour to one egg, and milk to make as thin as possible; of course you can make this as large as you want, but this is the proportion; beat all together, add a little salt.

Batter Pudding.

Nine eggs,
Ten tablespoonsful flour,
One quart milk.

Pound Pudding, (Steamboat.)

One pound white sugar and three-quarters of a pound butter, beat together; add five eggs, continue beating; add half a pound of flour; then add the other five eggs, one at a time, still beating them slowly together; add the other half pound flour; put the whole into a mould with a tight cover and steam, instead of baking, for one hour, fast, or one hour and a half, slowly. By adding beef suet instead of butter, with raisins, currants and citron, it makes an excellent plum pudding. The sauce is made by taking a little good butter and an equal quantity of sugar beat together. Flavor to suit the taste.

Chocolate Custard, (Very Nice.)

One-quarter pound Baker's prepared cocoa to one quart milk. Mix the milk and scraped chocolate to a thick paste. Boil one-quarter of an hour; while warm stir in three tablespoonsful of sugar, and set it away to cool. Beat eight eggs well and stir into this mixture. Bake in cups, and serve with a macaroon on top of each cup.

Almond Custard, (Rich.)

Boil in half a pint of milk one handful of bitter almonds, blanched and broken up. When highly flavored, strain this milk and set it aside. Boil one quart of milk by itself; when cold, add eight well-beaten eggs, the flavored milk and half a pint of powdered sugar; stir well. Bake in cups, and when cold serve with macaroons laid on each cup.

Pandoudy.

(MRS. CRAVEN.)

Pare, core and slice thin some sour, juicy apples; butter a deep dish, and put in a layer of apples; sweeten with brown sugar, and flavor with lemon peel; strew over a layer of bread crumbs and bits of butter; repeat this till the dish is full, finishing with a layer of bread crumbs. Bake till the apples are soft. A little cider improves this very much. To be eaten with sweetened cream.

Tapioca Pudding.

Three tablespoonsful of tapioca soaked in cold water till it is swelled enough; then add one quart of milk, and put it in a double kettle, or in a pitcher, and set into boiling water, and when the tapioca is sufficiently tender add the yelks of three eggs, a small teacupful of sugar, a little salt; stir this into the boiling milk; flavor with vanilla; then pour half in a dish; add the whites of the eggs beaten to a froth; then pour the remainder on the top. You can make it in the morning, as it is to be eaten cold, and is very nice.

Rice Pudding.

One pound washed rice to one quart rich milk,
One-quarter pound sugar,
One teaspoonful powdered cinnamon.
A little salt.

Bake two hours. A little cream added is an improvement.

Plum Pudding.

Pick and stone half a pound of raisins, wash and dry the same quantity of currants; chop, not too fine, three-quarters of a pound of beef suet, put in a convenient basin with six ounces of sugar, two ounces of candied peel sliced, three ounces of flour, three ounces of bread crumbs, a little grated nutmeg, four eggs, a gill of water, or perhaps a little more, to form a nice consistence; butter a mould, put a piece of white paper over the top and round the sides; tie it in a cloth, boil for four hours in plenty of water; when done, remove the cloth, turn it out of the mould, take the paper off the sides and top, and serve with sweet sauce round. It may also be boiled in a cloth.

Lemon Drops.

Grate three large lemons with a large piece of double-refined sugar; then scrape the sugar into a plate, add half a teaspoonful of flour, mix well, and beat into a light paste with the white of an egg; drop it upon white paper, and put them in a moderate oven on a tin plate.

Batter Pudding.

Eight eggs,
Eight tablespoonsful flour,
One quart milk.
Steam it for two hours.   Sauce.

Tapioca Pudding.

Soak a teacupful of tapioca in three and a half cupsful of boiling water and two spoonsful of white sugar; keep it in a warm place for three hours; fill a two quart pudding dish three-fourths full of rich, ripe tart apples, peeled and quartered; pour the tapioca over the apples, and add half a teacupful of cold milk to brown the tapioca. Bake an hour.

Sago Pudding.

Pick over and wash a teacupful of sago, pour on nearly a quart of boiling water; add a half teacupful sugar, and a little milk if preferred, brown; when cold, pour it over the apples, or mix the two together in a pudding dish and bake an hour.

Blanc Mange and Fruit Pudding.

Boil for a few moments six spoonsful of dissolved corn starch in a quart of boiling water; pour it immediately over a quart of ripe peaches, previously peeled and quartered and placed in a dish with sugar sprinkled over them. To be eaten cold. Instead of peaches, mellow pears, apples or stewed quinces, ripe plums, cherries, marmalade or jam may be used. Instead of corn starch, five spoonsful of fine flour, or, still better, graham flour, with, or without, an egg, may be substituted.

Sponge Pudding.

One-quarter of a pound of flour, the same of sugar; boil with one quart of milk to a thick batter; after it is boiled add one-quarter of pound butter to it, mix well; then divide twelve eggs, mix the yelks in the batter; beat the whites to a stiff froth; then mix the whole together. Put it in a pan, and set the pan in which you bake it in another pan with some water, and bake it in a hot oven. To be eaten with liquid sauce.

Snow Pudding (Splendid.)

Half ounce of gelatine,
One pint of boiling water,
Three-quarters of pound white sugar,
The juice of two lemons.

After it is thoroughly dissolved, strain as soon as it begins to thicken, add the well-beaten whites of two eggs; beat it for half an hour and set it on the ice after putting it in a mould. Make a rich custard; flavor with lemon rind grated. Send to the table in the middle of the custard.

Rice Pudding.

Wash thoroughly a teacupful of best rice; add half a cupful of white sugar, a quart of water and the same of milk. Bake slowly four hours, stirring occasionally, except the last hour. A cupful of raisins is an improvement.

Sweet Potato Custard.

One pound potatoes mashed and sifted fine,
Half pound sugar,
A small cupful of cream,
One-fourth pound butter,
Four eggs,
Nutmeg and lemon to suit the taste.

If you have no cream put half a pound of butter. This makes two large custards.

Lemon Pudding.

Take four ounces of butter, melt and pour it on four ounces of powdered loaf sugar; add the juice of a large lemon with the rind, grated, and the yelks of six eggs. Line the dish with paste, bake it half an hour.

Eve's Pudding.

Grate three-fourths of a pound of stale bread and mix it with three-fourths of a pound fine suet, the same quantity of chopped apples and dried currants, five eggs, and the rind of a lemon; put it into a mould and boil it three hours; serve it with sweet sauce.

Farina Pudding.

Sprinkle two-thirds of a teacupful of farina slowly into a quart of boiling water; add half a teacupful of white sugar and a cupful of milk; mix thoroughly and pour into a pudding dish, in which a quart and a half of nice tart apples, peeled and quartered, have been put, or mix the apples and farina together. Two teacupsful of pitted raisins, previously stewed, may be substituted for the apples. Bake one hour.

Apple Custard.

Peel, quarter and bake rich, tart apples, or stew them slowly in a very little water, fill a pudding dish two-thirds full. When cold pour over a custard by stirring into a quart of boiling milk a tablespoonful of flour; wet with a little milk two spoonsful of white sugar and two eggs. Flavor with lemon. Bake in a quick oven. To be eaten cold.

Rice and Apple Pudding.

Pick over and wash a teacupful of best rice, steam it until tender in two cupsful of cold water; spread it over a quart or three pints of good ripe apples, quartered; pour over one or two cupsful milk if preferred, or omit the milk, and add a little water to the apples. Half a cupful of white sugar may be added at the table, if preferred.

Cream Pudding.

Beat up the yelks of four eggs and two whites,
One pint of cream,
Two ounces of clarified butter,
One spoonful flour,
A little grated nutmeg,
Salt and sugar.

Beat till smooth. Bake it in buttered cups or paste.

An Excellent Pudding.

One pint and a half of milk,
Two eggs,
One small tablespoonful flour.

Mix the flour with cold milk to the consistence of thick cream; boil the rest of the milk and pour boiling hot upon the flour, stirring all the time; add a saltspoonful of salt; sugar to your taste, and when cool, two eggs well-beaten. Have ready a buttered dish, pour the whole into it; grate lemon peel or nutmeg over it, and bake thirty-five or forty minutes. It should be out of the oven fifteen minutes before serving. It is delicious to eat cold with jam, tart, or fruit pie.

Plain Boiled Pudding.

Two teacupsful sweet milk,
One cupful sour cream,
Two well-beaten eggs,
A small teaspoonful soda,
A little salt,
Flour enough to make a batter about as for griddle cakes,
One teacupful fruit, raisins or currants.

Pour the whole into a mould with a close cover and boil two hours. Serve with sauce to suit the taste.

Orange Pudding.

Make a light paste and roll it to the extent you require it. Take your oranges, slice them with the rinds on, removing carefully the pips or seeds from the pulp. Place a layer of fruit, well sugared, within one side of the paste and turn it over the fruit, and repeat the same course until the whole of the slices are disposed of. Fold the paste up at each end, so as to secure the syrup. Boil it in a pudding cloth. It constitutes, in some families, a nursery luxury.

Apple Cream.

Peel and core five large apples, boil in a little water till soft enough to press through a sieve; sweeten, and beat with them the beaten whites of three eggs. Serve it with cream poured around it.

Cranberry Roll.

Stew a quart of cranberries in just enough water to keep them from burning; make it very sweet; strain it through a colander, and set it away to cool; when quite cold make a paste as for apple pudding, spread the cranberries about an inch thick; roll it up in a floured cloth, and tie it close at the ends. Boil it two hours, and serve it with sweet sauce. Stewed apples, or any other kind of fruit may be made in the same way.

Bread Pudding.

Take white light bread, cut in thin slices; put into a pudding dish a layer of any sort of preserves, then a slice of bread, and repeat until the mould is almost full Pour over all a pint of warm milk, in which four beaten eggs have been mixed; cover the mould with a piece of linen, place it in a saucepan with a little boiling water. Let it boil twenty minutes, and serve with pudding sauce.

Apple and Paste Pudding in Basin.

Make one pound of paste, roll it a quarter of an inch

thick, lay some in a bowl; fill it with apples cut in quarters, add two cloves, two ounces of sugar, a little butter; put another piece of paste on the top, and join the edge nicely; tie it in a cloth and boil. It can be served up either in the basin or turned out. Do not open the top to put more sugar in, as it spoils the flavor and makes it heavy. All fruit puddings may be done the same way.

Lemon Cream.
(MRS. DR. GIBSON.)

Pare four lemons thin, soak the rinds twelve hours in half a pint of cold water; then add the juice of the lemons and half a pint more of cold water; beat to a froth the whites of eight eggs, yelks of three; strain lemon juice and water, mix it with the eggs; set the whole on a few coals; sweeten it with powdered white sugar; stir till it grows thick; take it from the fire, stir till cold. Serve in glasses.

Meringue Rice Pudding.

Take a teacupful of rice to one pint of water, when the rice is boiled dry add one pint of milk, a piece of butter the size of an egg, and five eggs. Beat the yelks and grated rind of a lemon, and mix with the rice. Butter a dish, pour in the mixture, and bake lightly. Beat the whites to a stiff froth; add a cup of sugar and the juice of a lemon. When the pudding is nearly done, spread on this frosting, and bake in a slow oven till the top is light brown.

Light Dough Dumplings.

One pound of raised dough, make it into small balls the size of eggs; boil in plenty of water, and serve with butter and sugar, or with sauce. Two ounces of chopped suet added to the above, or, to vary the flavor, add a few currants, a little sugar, grated nutmeg or lemon peel.

Charlotte Russe.

One pint cream, well-beaten; a gill and a half of wine, four eggs, yelks and whites beaten separately. Beat five tablespoonsful sugar with the yelks, half a pint of milk, and half an ounce isinglass or gelatine simmered together till the gelatine is dissolved. Then mix with this, first the yelks, then the whites of the eggs, then the cream, and set it aside to stiffen a little. When it is cool, pour it into a mould which you have previously lined with sponge cake, and when it is stiff, put it on a plate and grate sugar over the top.

Snow Cream.

(MRS. HARRIMAN.)

One quart cream,
Whites of three eggs cut into a stiff froth,
Four spoonsful sweet wine,
Sugar to your taste,
Flavor with lemon or vanilla.

Whip it to a stiff froth with a whisk; fast as the

froth foams, take it off and lay it in dishes; it will not return to the liquid state even if kept several days.

Potato Pudding.

Six large potatoes boiled and mashed,
A piece of butter the size of an egg,
A little salt.

Roll out with a little flour, make a layer of this crust, then a layer of apples. Steam one hour.

Pudding Sauce.

Two eggs,
Two cupsful sugar,
One cupful butter,
One glass of wine.

Beat all well together till creamy, and set over the fire a few minutes to scald through once, or set it in the tea kettle top to heat through.

Velvet Cream.

To a pint of cream put a very little sugar; keep stirring it over the fire till the sugar is dissolved; then take it off, but keep on stirring it till it is milk warm, after which pour it through a fine colander into a dish containing three spoonsful of lemon or orange juice, a little grated peel and fruit marmalade chopped fine, two spoonsful white wine. This should be prepared the evening before it is wanted.

—21

Transparent Pudding.

Beat eight eggs very well; put them into a stewpan with half a pound of sugar pounded fine, the same quantity of butter, and some grated nutmeg; set it on the fire and keep stirring it till it thickens, then set it in a basin to cool; put a rich puff-paste round the edge of the dish; pour in your pudding and bake it in a moderate oven. It will beat light and clear. You may add candied orange, or citron, if preferred.

Apple Roll, or Apple Pudding.

Make a paste with one-fourth of a pound of butter to one pound of flour mixed with water, not very stiff. Peel and slice rather thick tart apples; roll the paste very thin, as the bottom crust of a pie; spread the apples on a crust, so as to cover it; dredge on a little flour; roll it as tight as possible, cut the ends even and put it in the steamer, or wrap it in a thick cloth and boil it, which will take one hour steady cooking. Serve with butter and sugar; cut in thin slices from the end when serving.

Soda Pudding.

(MRS. N. V. HUNT.)

One pint sifted flour,
One cupful sugar,
One cupful sweet milk,
One teaspoonful soda,

Two teaspoonsful cream tartar,
One egg,
Two tablespoonsful melted butter, mixed while warm.

Bake twenty minutes. Served with wine sauce.

Soufflee Pudding.

Two ounces sugar,
Four ounces flour,
Two ounces fresh butter, melted,
Yelks of three eggs, well-beaten, also the whites, beaten separately.
A tablespoonful of orange juice.

Beat the whole together; strain it into a pie dish, which must be filled only half full, and bake in a quick, sharp oven for half an hour.

Orange Marmalade Pudding.

Quarter of a pound marmalade, chopped fine,
Two ounces of butter, melted or creamed,
Two ounces white sugar, sifted,
Two eggs, well-beaten and strained,
One pint of milk.

Beat all these ingredients together with the milk; then crumble sponge cake into it; line a dish, at the edge only, with puff paste, and bake an hour.

Nursery Pudding.

Slice some white bread without crust, pour scalding

milk upon it; let it stand till well soaked; then beat well with four eggs, a little sugar and grated nutmeg. Bake in small cups half filled.

Bread and Butter Pudding.

Line the edge of a dish with paste; put thin slices of bread and butter at the bottom of it, and a layer of currants on them, and so fill the dish; then pour over some new milk mixed with three eggs and flavoring. Let it stand to soak a couple of hours, and then bake.

Brown Charlotte Pudding.

Butter a pudding mould well, and line it with thin slices of bread and butter; these slices must be cut neatly, and the crust at the edges removed; take some good baking apples and cut them as for dumplings; fill the mould with them, putting in between the quarters some slices of candied lemon peel, a little grated nutmeg and some sugar. Cover it with bread on which there is plenty of butter; put a small plate on the top of the mould, and bake three hours.

Plum Pudding (Plain.)

Half a pound of beef suet, chopped fine,
One pound stoned raisins, rubbed in flour,
Half a pint grated bread crumbs,
One heaped tablespoonful of flour.

Half-pint boiling milk,
Four eggs.
Mix all well together and steam three hours.   Sauce.

Molasses Pudding.

Sift a large quart of Indian meal, simmer over the fire one quart of milk, and stir into it while hot one pint West Indian molasses; mix into this, while warm, the Indian meal; add one large spoonful ground ginger, one teaspoonful ground cinnamon; beat this thoroughly, as the lightness of the pudding depends on it. If the batter seems too thin, add a little meal; if too thick, a little more molasses. Steam it for three hoars.   Sauce.

Bread Pudding.

Crumble enough stale bread to fill a bowl; boil one pint of milk with a stick of cinnamon in it; pour the boiling milk over the bread, three tablespoonsful sugar, two tablespoonsful butter, four well-beaten eggs, added when the mixture is lukewarm; juice and grated rind of a lemon, raisins, or not, as you prefer. Bake three-quarters of an hour.   Sauce.

Cracker Fruit Pudding.

Six crackers, powdered fine,
One quart boiling milk,
One tablespoonful flour,
One cupful brown sugar,

Six eggs,
Raisins and spices to taste.
To be eaten with sauce.

Suet Pudding.

One coffee cupful chopped suet,
One coffeecupful raisins,
One coffeecupful molasses,
One coffeecupful water,
One teaspoonful soda,
Flour enough to make a thick batter,
Cloves and cinnamon to taste.

Roly Poly.

Make a crust like soda biscuit; that is, put a piece of butter the size of an egg to one quart of flour, two teaspoonsful cream tartar, and one even-full teaspoon soda; milk enough to make a paste that will roll out. Into this when rolled out, put any sort of fruit, fresh or preserved; fold the paste together, so the fruit will not run out, and steam one hour. Sauce.

Charlotte Russe.

(M'FERSON.)

Half gallon cream,
One pound white sugar,
One ounce gelatine,
Half pint madeira wine,
Flavor with vanilla.

Soak the gelatine in part of the cream; dissolve sugar and gelatine in one pint of cream and bring to a boil; strain when cool enough, but not congealed; add to balance of cream, which must be previously beat up to a light froth; then beat all together until quite light, and set off to congeal according to fancy. The cream should be set on ice several hours before you wish to use it, as it whips much easier.

A Boiled English Plum Pudding.

 One pound currants,
 One pound stoned raisins, dredged with flour,
 Half pound beef suet, chopped fine,
 One pound bread crumbs,
 Quarter of a pound citron,
 Eight eggs,
 A teaspoonful salt,
 Half pint milk,
 One gill of wine,
 A heaping coffeecupful of sugar,
 Mace and nutmeg to your taste.

Eaten with sauce of butter, sugar and wine. It requires six or seven hours to boil, and must be turned over several times. In these puddings cut the whites to a stiff froth.

Suet Pudding.

(MOLLIE WOHLGEMUTH.)

 Half pound beef suet,
 Half teaspoonful salt,

Half pound pared and chopped apples,
Half pound sugar,
Half pound flour,
Half pound stoned raisins dredged with flour,
Five eggs,
A grated nutmeg,
A glassful of brandy.

Lemon Apple Dumpling.

Nine tablespoonsful of apples, either stewed or grated,
One lemon, grated peel, pulp and juice,
Too-thirds of a cupful butter,
Three eggs,
Sugar to taste.

Mix and bake with or without upper crust.

English Plum Pudding.

Quarter pound suet, chopped fine,
Half pound bread crumbs,
Half pound stoned raisins, wet and dredged with flour,
Half pound currants,
Half pound sugar,
Three ounces citron,
Milk and six eggs.

Pour enough scalded milk on the bread crumbs to swell them; when cold, add the other ingredients; if it is too stiff, thin it with milk; if too thin, add more bread crumbs; then add two grated nutmegs, a tablespoonful of mace and cinnamon, half a gill of brandy and one teaspoonful of salt. Boil two hours.

The Queen of Puddings.

One pint bread crumbs,
One quart milk,
One teacupful white sugar,
Yelks of four eggs,
Grated rind of one lemon.

Beat yelks, sugar and lemon together, and stir in the crumbs; bake till a light brown color. When the pudding is done, beat the whites of these four eggs to a stiff froth with four tablespoonsful sugar. Spread currant jelly over the top of the pudding, then spread over this the beaten whites of eggs, and set it in the oven long enough to brown it. Serve cold.

Sallie's Meringue Pudding.

Put a teacupful of rice to one pint of water. When the water is boiled out, add one pint of milk, a piece of butter size of an egg, and yelks of three eggs. Beat yelks into the grated rind of one lemon and mix with the rice. Butter a pudding dish, and pour in the mixture and bake lightly. Beat the whites of the eggs with one teacupful of sugar, and the juice of one lemon. When the pudding is nearly done, spread on the frosting, and bake it a light brown in a slow oven.

Apple Potato Pudding.

Six large potatoes boiled and mashed fine,
Add a little salt,
A piece of butter the size of an egg.

Roll this out with a little flour, enough to make a good pastry crust. This is for the outside of the dumpling, instead of the ordinary pastry. Into this crust put peeled and chopped apples. Roll up like any apple dumpling and steam one hour. Eat hot with liquid sauce.

A Welsh Pudding.

Let half a pound of fine butter melt gently; beat with it the yelks of eight and whites of four eggs; mix in six ounces of loaf sugar and the rind of a lemon grated. Put a paste into a dish for turning out, and pour the above in, and nicely bake it.

Baked Fruit Pudding.

One coffeecupful raisins, chopped fine,
Four apples, chopped fine,
One coffeecupful sugar,
One coffeecupful flour,
One coffeecupful sweet milk,
Half coffeecupful butter,
Two eggs,
Nutmeg to taste.

Bake one hour. To be eaten with butter and sugar sauce.

Christmas Plum Pudding.

Pick and stone half a pound Malaga raisins, wash and dry the same quantity of currants; chop, not too fine, three-quarters of a pound of beef suet, put it in a convenient basin, with six ounces of sugar, two ounces candied peel sliced, three ounces of flour, three ounces of bread crumbs, a little grated nutmeg, four eggs, a gill of water, or perhaps a little more, to form a nice consistence; butter a mould, put a piece of white paper over the top and round the sides, tie it in a cloth; boil for four hours in plenty of water; when done, remove the cloth, turn it out of the mould, take the paper off the sides and top, and serve with sweet sauce round; it may also be boiled in a cloth.

Steam Pudding.

Slice a nice dish of bread in squares; then put a layer of fruit and bread; make a nice custard and pour over the whole and steam it.

Jersey Pudding.

Two quarts of milk,
One cupful rice,
One cupful sugar,
One teaspoonful salt.

Wash the rice and add it to the milk cold, and bake. The secret of having it nice consists in its being taken out of the oven before the milk is all dried away. It should be creamy in consistency, and when cool it is better than a pudding made with eggs, as there is no watery whey. Essence of lemon or raisins are an improvement; add a lump of butter. Bake slowly about an hour and a half.

Steam Pudding.

Dry bread, as much as you may think necessary, soaked enough to crumb easy—
    One teacupful currants,
    One teacupful chopped suet,
    One teacupful and a half brown sugar,
    Four eggs,
    Spices to the taste.
Steam three hours. Serve with brandy sauce.

Sago Pudding.

    One quart milk,
    One cupful sago,
    Eight apples, sliced thin,
    Two slices of bread grated,
    Flavor with lemon.
Mix well together and bake.

Suet Pudding.

    Three-quarters of a pound suet,
    Half a loaf of bread, grated,
    Six eggs,
    One cupful sour milk,

Half pound raisins, chopped,
Half pound currants,
One cupful molasses,
Half pound brown sugar,

Steam three hours. Serve with sauce.

Suet Pudding.

Half pound suet,
Six eggs,
Two cupsful sour milk,
One cupful and a half molasses,
Two cupsful brown sugar,
Four pints flour,
Flavor with nutmeg.

Steam an hour and a half; have the water boiling before you put it on.

Lemon Pudding.

(MRS. DR. PRICE, FRANKFORT, KY.)

Seven eggs,
Three teacupsful sugar,
Three lemons.

Take half the whites to beat separately for an icing, which is made with one cupful of white sugar. Beat the yelks and sugar together until light; squeeze the juice from the lemons into it, and grate the yellow off the peel; add the largest part of a nutmeg, beat all together. Beat the whites to a stiff froth and stir in. Make a rich paste, roll thin, and pour one-third into each pan. Bake till thoroughly cooked, then pour the icing over each one, and brown it nicely.

Kentucky Pudding.

 Four eggs,
 One teacupful sugar,
 One quart sweat milk, boiled,
 One pint light bread crumbs,
 One teacupful butter.

Bake and let it get cold; then spread jelly over it. Make a meringue of—

 The whites of four eggs,
 Four tablespoonsful of sugar,
 Juice of one lemon.

Pour this on the top of the jelly, and set it into the oven and let it bake a light brown. To be eaten cold.

Nameless Pudding.

 One cupful butter,
 Three cupsful sugar,
 Five cupsful flour,
 One cupful milk,
 Two teaspoonsful cream tartar,
 One teaspoonful soda,
 Five eggs,
 One wine glassful of brandy,
 Half a grated nutmeg.

Rub the butter, sugar, flour and cream tartar together well; then add the milk and yelks of eggs;

beat it ten minutes; then add the soda dissolved in boiling water and the whites of the eggs. Bake an hour in a moderate oven.

Boiled Pudding.

Half a cupful chopped beef suet,
One cupful raisins,
Two cupsful flour,
One cupful milk,
One cupful molasses,
One teaspoonful soda.

Tie in a floured bag and boil hard two hours. Serve with rich sauce.

Meringue Rice Pudding.

Take a teacupful of rice to one pint of water; when the rice is boiled dry add one pint milk, a piece of butter the size of an egg, and five eggs. Beat the yelks and grated rind of a lemon and mix with the rice. Butter a dish, pour in the mixture, and bake lightly. Beat the whites to a stiff froth; add a cupful of sugar and the juice of a lemon. When the pudding is nearly done, spread on this frosting, and bake in a slow oven till the top is light brown.

Potato Pudding.

Six large potatoes boiled and mashed,
A piece of butter the size of an egg,
A little salt.

Roll out with a little flour; make a layer of this crust; then a layer of apples. Steam one hour.

Pumpkin Pudding.

Take one pint of pumpkin that has been stewed soft and pressed through a colander; melt in half a pint of warm milk a quarter of a pound of butter and the same quantity of sugar, stirring them well together; one pint of rich cream will be better than milk and butter; beat eight eggs very light, and add them gradually to the other ingredients alternately with the pumpkin; then stir in a wineglassful of rose water and two glassesful of wine, mixed together, a large teaspoonful of powdered mace and cinnamon mixed, and a grated nutmeg. Having stirred the whole very hard, put it into a buttered dish, and bake it three-quarters of an hour.

Fig Pudding.

Procure one pound of good figs, and chop them very fine, and also a quarter pound of suet, likewise chopped as fine as possible; dust them both with a little flour as you proceed—it helps to bind the pudding together; then take one pound of fine bread crumbs, and not quite a quarter pound of sugar; beat two eggs in a teacupful of milk, and mix all well together. Boil four hours. If you choose, serve it with wine or brandy sauce, and ornament it with blanched almonds. Simply cooked, however, it is better where there are children, with whom it is generally a favorite. We forgot to say, flavor with a little allspice or nutmeg, as you like; but add the spice before the milk and eggs.

Jelly Pudding.

(MRS. PRICE, KY.)

One glassful of jelly,
Three eggs, well-beaten,
The white of one egg,
One tablespoonful butter.

Beat until very light. Bake this with a paste. Make a meringue of the whites; spread over the top, and let it lightly brown.

Canary Pudding.

Fill a pudding dish half full of bread crumbs; pour over it one quart milk; beat the yelks of seven eggs well, stir into them nearly a pint of milk; beat the whites of three eggs and stir into it, pour this over the bread crumbs. Bake this. Of the four remaining whites make an icing, pour over the pudding after it is baked; replace in the stove to brown a light brown. Serve hot, with sauce either boiled or cold.

Macaroni Pudding.

Three-quarters of a pound of macaroni, boil it till quite soft,
Half a pound of sugar,

Quarter of a pound of currants,
Juice of one lemon.

Bake till browned. A simple mode of cooking macaroni, or tapioca, is to sweeten and boil till soft; add the juice of a lemon, and turn into a mould till cool.

Cream Pudding.

Beat up four eggs a little, strain them; add a teacupful of fine white sugar, the rind and juice of a lemon, and a pint of cream. Line a pudding dish with puff paste; put in the above. Bake half an hour.

Corn Meal Pudding.

(MRS. FITZSIMMONS.)

One quart sweet milk,
One teaspoonful soda,
One teaspoonful cream tartar,
Three tablespoonsful chopped suet,
Twelve tablespoonsful corn meal,
One cupful molasses,
Ginger and spice to suit the taste.

Heat the milk and scald the meal; if the milk is sour; mix it all cold, and omit the cream tartar. Boiled sauce.

Cottage Pudding.

(MRS. FITZSIMMONS.)

Five tablespoonsful flour,

Five eggs,
One pint sweet milk,
One small teaspoonful baking powder.
Butter and sugar sauce. Bake in a quick oven.

Raisin Pudding.

Soak two ounces of raisins in enough brandy to cover them; take
Half pound flour,
Half pound chopped suet,
A dessertspoonful of ground ginger,
Two eggs,
Four ounces white sugar.

Enough milk to make it a pretty light paste. Add the raisins and brandy; put it into a cloth or basin; boil it for two hours, and serve with what pudding sauce you please.

Orange Pudding.

(MRS. PRICE, KY.)

Slice sponge cake thin; peel and slice oranges, freeing them of the seed; sprinkle sugar over them a short time before using them. Lay in a pie plate alternate layers of cake and oranges. Make a meringue and put over the top, and set it in the oven to brown. For sauce—
Two teacupsful white sugar,
A piece of butter the size of an egg,

Enough water to dissolve the sugar,
A few strips of orange peel.
Let it boil to a thick syrup.

Frozen Pudding.

(MRS. DR. PRICE, KY.)

Line the freezer with sliced sponge cake; then place a layer of sponge cake spread with cherry or any acid preserves, repeating till the freezer is half full. Pour upon this a custard made of—

Two quarts rich cream,
The yelks of five eggs,
One pint white sugar.

Boil well, stirring constantly until it thickens Flavor with vanilla. Let it cool, and pour in the freezer over the cake, and freeze well. Before using place a cloth wrung out of hot water around the freezer for a few moments, and it will turn out the shape of the freezer.

Almond Pudding.

A large teacupful of finely chopped beef suet,
One teacupful milk,
Four ounces bread crumbs,
Four ounces well-cleaned currants,
Two ounces almonds,
Half-pound well-stoned raisins,
Three well-beaten eggs, and the whites of two others,

Sugar to taste,
Nutmeg and cinnamon,
A small glass Jamaica rum.

Butter a shape and place part of the raisins neatly in rows; blanch the almonds, reserve the half of them to be placed in rows between the raisins, just before serving. Mix all the other ingredients well together. Put in the shape and boil three hours.

Citron Pudding.

Beat the yelks of three eggs with two tablespoonsful of flour; when light, add one pint boiling milk, and a quarter of a pound citron, cut fine; put in buttered cups and bake half an hour in a quick oven; turn them out and serve with liquid sauce.

Blanc Mange.

Boil a pint of cream and a quart of milk together; clarify an ounce and a half of isinglass and stir it into the cream; make it sweet with white sugar, and flavor with lemon, rose or vanilla. Let it boil up once, stirring it well. Have ready some earthen or any kind of moulds, dipped in cold water. When cold, turn them out and serve with sweetened cream. Jelly is very nice to eat with blanc mange.

Ribbon Blanc Mange.

Make the same as the above receipt. Have one mould filled with white, and the other filled with pink.

Use the same coloring as for the white and pink cake; then, when cold, turn them out and cut an inch thick of the white, then of the pink, and put one on the other; the two moulds, of course, will make two dishes. This is very pretty for an evening company.

Dried Peach Dumplings.

Cook dried peaches till very tender, sweeten while cooking. When done, and cold, flavor to suit the taste. Mash them fine with the hand, and spread on a nice crust. Roll and steam.

Dried Apple Dumplings

Are made in the same manner.

Egg Sauce for Puddings.

(MRS. N. V. HUNT.)

One cupful sugar,
Half cupful butter,
One glassful sherry wine,
One egg, beat white and yelk separately.

Then beat all together and set it over a boiling tea-kettle. Do not stir it after it has been set on the tea-kettle. Let it heat through.

Green Apple Dumplings.

Make a dough as you would for soda biscuit, roll into pieces large enough to hold an apple, after it has been peeled and cored; roll an apple in each piece, and secure the crust with flour, that it will not burst open; grease a steamer well and put your dumplings in and set them over a pot of boiling water. Be sure, in boiling or steaming anything, to always have a kettle kept full of boiling water to add as the other boils away. Cold water will check the steam and make the dumplings heavy.

Suet Pudding.

One cupful chopped suet,
One cupful molasses,
One pint fruit,
One cupful sweet milk,
One teaspoonful soda mixed in molasses,
Four cupsful flour,
Spice to suit the taste.

Steam three hours. Any kind of sauce.

Poor Man's Pudding.

One pint sweet milk,
Four eggs,
Two tablespoonsful flour,
A little salt.

Potato Pudding.

One pound sugar,
Half a pound butter,
Three-quarters of a pound mashed potatoes,

Nine eggs,
Spices to the taste,
Half pint cream.

Pudding.

Four cupsful bread, after it is soaked in milk,
Sugar to the taste,
One tablespoonful butter,
One pint of fruit of any kind,
Three eggs,
One handful of flour.

Boil two hours. No soda.

Meringues.

Whites of three eggs,
One coffeecupful of coffee sugar,
Flavor with lemon.

Drop on buttered paper or tins. Set in the stove and slightly brown.

French Pudding.

Break three eggs into a bowl without separating them; add one teacupful powdered sugar, and beat them light; add half a cupful flour with one teaspoonful and half baking powder, and a little water. Spread on jelly or sweetmeats of any kind when cool, and over this the whites of two eggs beaten up with two tablespoonsful of sugar and a little lemon.

Tapioca Pudding.

Pare and core six large apples, fill them with sugar; pour over them one teacupful of tapioca, previously soaked in cold water for two hours; season with lemon or cinnamon; add more sugar and a little pinch of salt; place the apples in a dish and fill around them with water. Bake one hour. Eat with cream.

Cocoanut Pudding.

Half pound sugar,
Half pound butter,
Half a cocoanut,
Six eggs, whites only,
Two tablespoonsful brandy.

Pare off the brown skin of the nut, wash and grate it. Cream the butter and sugar; whip the eggs stiff; then stir, but not beat, the whole together. Bake slowly.

Marlborough Pudding.

Six large tart apples,
One teacupful white sugar,
One teacupful butter or thick sweet cream,
Six eggs,
The grated peel of one lemon and the juice of the same.

Grate the apples after paring and coring them; stir sugar and butter as for cake; then add the other ingredients, and bake in a rich paste; some prefer nutmeg to lemon, in such cases the taste must be consulted. It is much better to grate, than to stew apples for this and all puddings and pies.

Transparent Pudding.

One tumblerful of sugar,
One tumblerful butter,
Eight eggs, omitting the whites of five.

Mix sugar and butter, then stir in the eggs. The above receipt, with the addition of one grated lemon is an excellent lemon pudding; or, with jelly, is jelly pudding.

Potato Pudding.

One pound sugar,
Half pound butter,
Three-quarters of a pound mashed potatoes,
Nine eggs,
Spice to suit the taste,
Half pint cream.

Beat sugar and butter to a cream, add yelks of eggs, then beat all together till very light; add potatoes and mix well; then whites beaten stiff, and then cream. Bake or steam.

Potato Pudding.

(MRS. DR. PRICE, KY.)

One pound of potatoes, after they are pressed through a sieve,

Half pound butter,
Eight eggs,
One nutmeg.

Beat the butter and potatoes together; the yelks of the eggs and sugar together; add in small quantiites of the potato and butter; then add the whites, well-beaten, and a wineglassful of whisky; flavored with orange peel. Make a rich paste. Place in a deep pudding dish and bake. Serve hot, with citron, or other kind of preserves, if liked, or with any of the pudding sauces preferred.

Boiled Loaf.

Pour a quart of boiling milk over four little rolls of bread; cover them up, turning them occasionally till saturated with the milk; flour a pudding cloth and tie them tight, and boil an hour; be careful in turning them out. Eat with hot sauce. A nice pudding for children.

Tapioca for Puddings

(MRS. BURK.)

Should be put into a moderate oven and let dry thoroughly. Then grind in a coffee mill, the mill can be cleaned by grinding corn meal through it. This makes a cheap and nutricious dessert, and is very nice cold for tea, eaten with cream. Take belleflower or other good cooking apples, peel and core them, place them in a pudding pan, and take three or four tablespoonsful of the ground tapioca, soaked first in water and sweetened; pour this over the apples with sufficient water to cover them. Bake slowly. Take the apples out and place them in the dish in which they are to be served, and then pour the tapioca over them.

Souffle Pudding.

Boil one pound of nice prunes in enough water to cover them; when soft, sweeten them a little; pour them in a pudding dish. Prepare a maringue of whites of eggs beaten with sugar, and spread over them. Set in the stove and brown lightly.

Sutherland Pudding.

Ten eggs,
One quart of milk,
Five tablespoonsful of flour.

Beat the whites and yelks separately; stir the flour into the yelks of the eggs; then add one-half of the milk; then a little salt, then the whites of the eggs and the remainder of the milk. Bake half an hour.

Cottage Pudding, (Eaten Cold.)

(MRS. GRAY.)

One pint bread crumbs, grated,
One teacupful sugar,
One quart sweet milk,
One tablespoonful butter,

Four yelks of eggs,
Flavor with lemon.

Then bake and let it cool a little. Have the four whites beaten stiff with seven tablespoonsful of sugar; spread this nicely over the top, and drop fruit or jelly on the top of that and return to the oven for a few moments.

Rod Grod, (A Danish Receipt.)

It is made of fruit juice, arrowroot and cream. Take—

Three pounds and a half of currant juice,
Three pints of water,
A good quantity of sugar,
A flavoring of almond or cinnamon, one ounce or one ounce and a half.

Boil this mixture; when in begins to boil add a pound and a quarter of ground rice or one pound of sago; boil a quarter of an hour, stirring very often; pour out into moulds and leave to cool. Then turn out and eat with cream and sugar. The juice of other fruits may be used.

Cocoanut Pudding.

Stir one pound of white sugar and a quarter of a pound butter to a cream; take the yelks of twelve eggs and the whites of six, and when beaten separately and light, add them to the butter and sugar, and then put in one pound of grated cocoanut; lastly put in four tablespoonsful of rose water, four of cream and the juice of two lemons. Bake in puff paste and put the other six whites, beaten with sugar, over the top and let it it brown a very delicate brown.

Gooseberry Cream.

Take a quart of gooseberries and boil them very quick in enough water to cover them; stir in half an ounce of good butter, and when they become soft, pulp them through a sieve; sweeten the pulp while it is hot, and then yelks of four eggs. Serve in a dish or in glasses.

To Make a Hen's Nest.

Get large fine eggs, make a hole at one end and empty out the egg; fill the shells with blanc mange; when stiff and cold take off the shells; pare the yellow rind from six lemons, boil them in water till tender, then cut them in strips to resemble straw, and preserve them in sugar. Fill a small deep dish half full of nice jelly; when it is set, put the strips of lemon peel on in the form of a nest, and lay the eggs in it. This makes a beautiful dish for an evening company.

A Trifle.

Place half a pound of maccaroons or Naples biscuits at the bottom of a large glass bowl. Pour on them as much white wine as will cover and dissolve them. Make a rich custard flavored with bitter almonds or peach leaves, and pour on the maccaroons; the custard may be either baked or boiled. Then add a layer of marmalade or jam. Take a quart of cream, mix with it a quarter of a pound of sugar and half a pint of white wine, and whip it with rods to a stiff froth, laying the froth (as you proceed) on an inverted sieve, with a dish under it to catch the cream that drips through; which must be saved and whipped over again. Instead of rods you may use a little tin churn. Pile the frothed cream upon the marmalade in a high pyramid. To ornament it, take preserved watermelon rinds that has been cut into leaves or flowers, split them nicely to make them thinner and lighter. Place a circle or wreath of them round the heap of frothed cream, interspersing them with spots of stiff red currant jelly. Stick on the top of pyramid a sprig of real flowers.

PICKLES.

GENERAL DIRECTIONS FOR PICKLING.

There seems to be such a diversity of opinion in regard to the use of brass or bell-metal in pickling, that one will have to be governed by their own judgment and experience a good deal. I have always used brass kettles myself, and have never had to suffer from any bad effects by so doing. The kettles must be well and thoroughly cleaned each time before using, and never, (as many direct,) should they be cleaned with salt and vinegar, but with good wood ashes and soap, or bath-brick, and always kept bright. Vinegar should be of the best cider vinegar. Use glass or good stone jars in putting away pickles. Always see that while in the vinegar, the pickles are well covered. Sliced, or chopped pickles of any kind, should always have a plate or saucer put down into the jar to keep them from spoiling on the top, thus causing many to lose the entire jar of pickles. In greening pickles, keep them closely covered, that the steam may assist in giving them a good color. A little alum helps to make them crisp. Too much boiling takes away the strength of the vinegar. Cucumbers, melons, and all such pickles as require to be put in brine, should, when taken out of it, be washed nicely and then put into a clean vessel to freshen. The smaller pickles, and such as are required for mangos, must be each gathered in its season, salted (a day and night are sufficient) and dropped into vinegar till time to make and fill the mangos. Great care should be taken to have them well selected and both young and tender. Chopped and sliced pickles must be cut or chopped over night and hung in a basket in which a clean cloth has been placed in the bottom. Let them drain all night, then empty them and spice and mix according to the various directions in each receipt. The water must be entirely squeezed out of the chopped pickle. After it has drained all night, take what you can well hold in your hands and squeeze them as dry as you can. Your pickles will be all the better for the trouble. If the water or juice that is in them after it is chopped is let remain, it will certainly spoil the pickle, by weakening the vinegar. The grated cucumber must be done in the same manner. Tomato pickles are very insipid unless they are highly seasoned. The curry powder receipt, being a mixture of all kinds of spices, well-pounded together and sifted, is a splendid addition to the sliced and chopped tomato pickles—one tablespoonful of it to the gallon of pickles.

To Pickle Cauliflower.

Make a strong brine, and after picking over your cauliflower and breaking it in such shaped pieces as you like, put it in the brine and let it remain twenty four hours. Then take them out and heat the brine, and pour it on the pickles scalding hot. Let them remain in the brine till next day. Drain off the brine and pour on spiced vinegar; scaldt he spices in the vinegar, but pour it over the pickles cold.

Martinoes.

Gather them when they are young and tender. Have a weak brine, and after wiping your pickles one by one, drop them into this brine and let them remain eight or ten days, or make a stronger brine and let them remain till they are salt enough to keep. Then wash and wipe them dry, and pour spiced vinegar over them. These are a most delicious pickle, and persons who are fond of the walnut pickle will not fail to like these. They grow wild, but can be cultivated, and are worth trying.

A Fine Cabbage Pickle.

Cut two heads of cabbage fine, on a slaw cutter or with a knife; put in a chopping bowl and chop fine; take six green peppers, two handsful of salt, one pound of black mustard seed; mix well together. Pack in a jar and pour cold cider vinegar over. Some like a little celery seed mixed with it.

Grape Pickle.

Grapes made into sweet pickles are very fine. They can be made by any of the sweet pickle receipts in this book. Those having an abundance of grapes will do well to try them. They are very fine.

Pickled Peaches.

Have a tub of cold water setting near, and one with boiling water with ashes in it; fill a large skimmer with peaches and dip them in the ley water; than throw them in the cold water, and with a flannel or rough cloth rub off the down. Stick four or five cloves in each peach and put them in jars. Have some boiling vinegar with sugar, cinnamon, allspice and nutmeg; pour over the peaches. Let them set 24 hours, then heat again, and let them remain another 24 hours; then put the vinegar on and let it come to a boil, and add the peaches; let all come to a boil together; take out, put in jars and tie closely.

Peach Mangoes.

Select large, fine flavored peaches, dip them in soda water, to remove the down from them, and with the blade of a sharp knife cut out the seed, leaving the peach as whole as possible; then have some cabbage (the white hard part of the head) chopped fine, and a very little onion and a few bits of red pepper pod. Spice with mace, cloves, allspice, white mustard seed, (whole,) two nasturtiums in each peach. Fill your peaches, and pour vinegar that has been boiled with spices in it; keep them well under the vinegar, by putting a plate or saucer in the jar.

Nasturtiums.

Soak them for a few days in salt and water, as you collect them, changing the water every few days; then pour off the brine, wipe them and drop them in cold vinegar. These are very fine to flavor mangoes, especially the peach mango.

Sweet Cherry Pickle.
(MRS. ILES.)

Five pints cherries, one pint vinegar, two pints sugar; spiced with cloves, allspice, cinnamon and a little pepper. Boil all together one hour.

Spiced Peach Pickles.
(MRS. HURST.)

Three pounds sugar, three pints vinegar, spiced and boiled to a syrup. For a gallon jar of peaches—grate three nutmegs, one tablespoonful of cloves, one tablespoonful allspice and two tablespoonsful cinnamon. Put in a portion of the peaches, and scald in the syrup till tender; take them out, put them into the jar, and put more into the syrup, and so on till you have enough to fill the jar; then pour the syrup over the peaches. Do not have too hot a fire, or the syrup will boil away too fast.

Watermelon Rind Pickle.

Prepare the rinds as you would for preserving; let them remain in soda water all night. Take one quart cider vinegar and three pounds sugar, let it boil till quite thick syrup; then put in your fruit, let it boil till they are soft; put them in a jar and pour the syrup over boiling; seal them up. Put in a little mace, cinnamon and nutmeg, spices make them too dark.

Sliced Tomato Pickles.

Take the smoothest large green tomatoes after the first good frost, slice them very thin with one-quarter onions; put a clean cloth in a basket and put them in it, and hang it up and let it drip all night; in the morning, put them into a large clean pan, and with the hands mix them up with cloves, allspice, mace, black pepper, and garlic peeled and sliced thin. When well-mixed add curry powder till it has a yellow look; then put it into your jar; pour over it enough of the best cider vinegar to cover it well. It will soon be ready for use.

Chopped Mixed Pickles.

Take a white, hard head of cabbage, green tomatoes, green peppers, celery and onions, chop very fine separately, then mix well; put cloves, plenty of ground pepper, allspice, mace, garlic, red pepper pods and mustard seed; put in a jar and pour boiling vinegar over them.

Red Cabbage Pickle.

Take the small, deep red cabbage, cut with a slaw cutter very fine; add a very little salt over night; boil a few spices in vinegar, put it over the cabbage cold.

Cucumber Pickles.

Make a weak brine of salt and water, boil and pour over the cucumbers three mornings in succession; fourth morning pour it off, and scald vinegar and pour over three mornings in succession; seventh morning scald new vinegar, adding spice, and pour on. In this way pickles may be made at any time they are fresh gathered, and will be perfectly green.

To Pickle Oysters.

Wash four dozen of the largest oysters you can get in their own liquor, wipe them dry, strain the liquor off, adding to it a dessertspoonful of pepper, two blades of mace, a tablespoonful of salt, if the liquor be not very salt, and seven of vinegar. Simmer the oysters a few minutes in the liquor; then put them in small jars and boil the pickle up, skim it, and, when cold, pour over the oysters; cover close.

Pickled Butternuts.

Gather them the last week in June. Make and skim a brine of salt and water, strong enough to bear up an egg when it is cold; pour it on the nuts, and let them lie in it twelve days. Drain them, lay them in a jar, and pour over them the best of cider vinegar, which has been previously boiled with pepper corns, cloves, allspice, white mustard seed, ginger, mace and horse radish. This vinegar must be cold when poured on; cover close, and keep one year before using. Walnuts are pickled in the same way, and the vinegar may be used as catsup, for it is very nice.

Pickled Mangoes.

Select young nutmeg melons, not too large, cut them in the side; make a strong brine and let them stay nine days, or longer as required. When you are ready, take them out, and let them freshen in cold well water all night. Have ready, for the filling, young beans, silver onions, radish pods, gherkins, small green peppers, small green tomatoes, cloves, allspice, mace, garlic, black pepper, white and black mustard seed. The beans small. Pickles and such things are hard to procure at one time. It is well to get them as they come in season, and throw them in a strong brine over night or longer; then green them and put the best vinegar on them. Put them in a good sized jar, and as you get the other things, they can be greened and added. When all is ready take them out of the vinegar; first green the melons to be filled, and try to have them all alike. Put a little sugar in the vinegar while it is boiling, enough to make it a pleasant sweet. Add plenty of pepper and spices.

Chow-Chow.

Three heads of cabbage, twenty-five peppers, half pint of white mustard seed and grated horse radish. Cut the cabbage fine, chop the peppers, and put them in a jar, then the cabbage, then a little salt, and sprinkle a little horse radish and mustard seed over the whole, and so on till all the ingredients are in the jar. Fill with cold vinegar. To every quart of vinegar dissolve two ounces of brown sugar.

Pickled Onions.

In the month of September, choose the small white round onions, take off the skin, have ready a very nice tin stewpan of boiling water, throw in as many onions as will cover the top; as soon as they look clear on the outside, take them up as quick as possible, and lay them on a clear cloth; cover them close with another, and scald some more, and so on. Let them lie to be cold, then put them in a jar, or glass, or wide-mouth bottles, and pour over them the best vinegar, just hot, but not boiling. When cold, cover them. Should the outer skin shrivel, peel it off. They must look quite clear.

Pickled Plums.

To every quart of plums allow one-half pound of sugar and one pint of best cider vinegar. Melt the sugar in the vinegar, and put spices of all sorts in a fine muslin bag, and boil up with the sugar and vinegar. When the sugar and spiced vinegar boils up, put in the plums and give them one good boil. If you wish to keep the plums whole, pick them with a needle.

To Pickle Cucumbers and Onions Sliced.

Cut them in slices, and sprinkle salt over them. Next day drain them for five or six hours; then put them into a stone jar, pour boiling vinegar over them, and keep them in a warm place. The slices should be thick. Repeat the boiling vinegar, and stop them up again instantly; and so on till green; the last time put in pepper. Keep in small stone jars.

Pickled Eggs.

Boil them twelve minutes, and throw them into cold water to make the shells come off easily. Boil some red beets very soft, peel and mash fine, and put them with salt, pepper, cloves and nutmegs, into vinegar enough to cover the eggs. Put the eggs in a jar, and pour the mixture over them.

Tomato Pickle.

Eight pounds skinned tomatoes and four of brown sugar. Put them in a preserving kettle, and stir often to prevent burning. Boil to the thickness of molasses, then add one quart of good cider vinegar, one teaspoonful mace, one teaspoonful cloves, and boil five minutes longer.

To Pickle Tomatoes.

Always use those which are thoroughly ripe The small round ones are decidedly the best. Do not prick them, as most receipt books direct. Let them lie in strong brine three or four days, then put them down in layers in your jars, mixing with them small onions and pieces of horseradish; then pour on the vinegar (cold,) which should be first spiced as for peppers; let there be a spice bag to throw into every pot. Cover them carefully, and set them by in the cellar for a full month before using.

East India Pickles.

Have ready a white cabbage sliced and the stalks removed; a cauliflower cut into neat branches, leaving out the stalk; sliced cucumbers, sliced carrots, sliced beets, all nicked around the edges; button onions, string beans, radish pods, cherries, green grapes, nasturtium, capsicum, bell pepper, etc. Sprinkle all these with salt; then put them into a large earthen jar and pour scalding salt and water over them. Let them lie in the brine for four days, turning them every day. Take them out, wash each piece separately in vinegar and wipe them on a dry cloth; let them dry thoroughly. To every two quarts vinegar (best cider) put an ounce and a half of white ginger root scraped and sliced, the same of long peppers, two ounces of peeled shallots or little button onions, half an ounce peeled garlic, an ounce turmeric and two ounces mustard seed or ground mustard. Let all these ingredients, mixed with the vinegar, infuse in a close jar, setting in a warm place by the fire. Then, after the vegetables have been dried from the brine, put them all into one large stone jar and strain the pickle over them. Cork tight.

Two quarts vinegar, one ounce and a half white ginger root scraped and sliced, one ounce and a half long peppers, two ounces peeled button (silver) onions, half ounce peeled garlic, one ounce turmeric and two ounce white mustard seed.

Pickle.

Green tomatoes, cabbage and cucumbers, one pint of each; half pint onions, all chopped fine; salt well and stand over night; strain through a sieve, and add pepper, horseradish, white mustard seed and half pint sugar. Mix well, fill your jar, and cover with vinegar.

Buck and Breck, (Splendid.)

One peck green tomatoes, half peck ripe tomatoes, twelve onions, twelve peppers, (six red and six green,) one large head cabbage; chop them all fine; salt heavily; let them drain all night; add two tablespoonsful allspice, one tablespoonful ground black pepper and one tablespoonful mace. Put on one quart vinegar and three pounds brown sugar. When boiled, put in your drained tomatoes, then skin and slice the ripe tomatoes and put in.

Boil three hours. When done put in jars and add cold vinegar. Stir often while boiling.

Pickled Peaches.

Seven pounds peaches, three and a half pounds sugar, one quart of vinegar, and spices to the taste. Make them whole, and peel them or not, just as you prefer. Scald the vinegar and sugar with the spices and pour on the peaches while hot.

Chopped Pickle.

One large head of cabbage, three of celery and twelve onions, chop fine; salt well and stand twenty-four hours; drain and cover with vinegar, remain twelve hours; drain, and add four red peppers and two green ones, one-quarter of a pound mustard seed and two tablespoonpsful mixed mustard, one tablespoonful allspice, one tablespoonful back pepper, half tablespoonful cloves, half a cupful sweet oil and a teacupful brown sugar. Mix all well, and cover with vinegar.

Onion Pickles.

Peel white onions, (medium or small sized,) lay them in fresh water all night; in the morning place in a jar alternate layers of onions, celery seed, ginger, cloves, allspice and red pepper; add to the vinegar a little turmeric, sugar and salt; beat it, and pour over the onions while hot. In a few days pour off the vinegar; heat it again, and pour over the pickles. When perfectly cold they will be fit for use.

Sweet Pickle.

To one pound vinegar add six pounds of sugar; add cinnamon, a few cloves, allspice and a little mace, boil well together; have your fruit in a stone jar, strain the syrup over it while hot, let it remain until next day; pour off the syrup, place it over the fire; as soon as it commences to boil put in your fruit and boil till it is tender. This pickle will answer for peaches, pears, apples, watermelon rind, or any pickle that can be made sweet.

Gherkins.

These make a very nice pickle, and if gathered when young make a nice filling for mangoes. They should be gathered when young and tender, and left in the brine till they become yellow; then scald vinegar, with spices to suit the taste, and when cold pour it over the pickles.

Mushrooms.

Be careful in the selections of mushrooms, that they are perfectly fresh, throw a little salt on them, and remove the skin from the top; scald them in salt water for only a few moments; then pour off the water, and pour on spiced vinegar. If you wish them to keep well, cork tight.

Catsup, (Tomato Catsup.)

Take very ripe tomatoes, wash and mash them up well, adding a very little salt; put in a clean tub or wooden vessel, and let it stand covered all night. In the morning, put them in a large brass kettle and let them cook well; then take off and strain through a sieve; boil down till quite thick; about half an hour before taking from the stove, put in considerable red pepper pods, cloves, allspice and cinnamon, tied in a thin cloth. Have ready about one dozen large onions sliced fine, and fresh peppers and spices tied in a thin cloth, (to prevent further straining;) put the onion and spices so tied up into a large earthen vessel, and let it stand covered twenty-four hours; then make as thin as you like with the best cider vinegar. Bottle, cork and seal; add a little garlic, if you like the flavor.

Pepper Catsup.

Take fifty pods of large red bell peppers, seed and all; add one pint of vinegar and boil till you can mash the pulp through a sieve; add to the pulp another pint of vinegar, two tablespoonsful sugar, cloves, mace, spice, onions and salt. Put it into a kettle and boil to the proper consistency. Some omit the spices.

Tomato Catsup.

(MRS. JUDGE BREESE.)

Slice and boil the tomatoes well, (not strained;) a quarter of an ounce each of mace, nutmeg and cloves, one handful scraped horseradish, two pods red pepper, salt to the taste; boil this away to three quarts and then strain; adding one pint of wine and half a pint of vinegar. Bottle and leave the bottle open a day or two. Then cork and seal.

Tomato Catsup.

(MRS. HARRIMAN.)

One gallon tomatoes, four tablespoonsful salt, four tablespoonsful cloves, one tablespoonful mace, one tablespoonful cayenne pepper, two tablespoonsful allspice, eight tablespoonsful black mustard seed, eight whole peppers, five garlics, two quarts cider vinegar, one pound brown sugar. Boil away one half, strain and bottle.

Chopped Catsup.

To one gallon chopped tomatoes put three-quarters of a gallon chopped cabbage, two pints of onions chopped fine and three-quarters of a pint green peppers chopped. Let them stand one night with salt over them and drip; add cloves, allspice, horseradish grated, fine celery, mustard seed and garlic.

Pickled Peaches.

Seven pounds peaches, three or four pounds brown sugar, one quart vinegar, two tablespoonsful whole cloves, two tablespoonsful allspice, one tablespoonful mace. Boil together and pour over the peaches. Let them stand twenty-four hours, and repeat the boiling three or four times.

Yellow Pickle.

One pound horseradish dried and sliced, one pound skinned garlic, twelve ounces ginger, two ounces cloves, one large cupful black pepper, half pound mustard seed, half a cupful ground mustard, two tablespoonsful celery seed, one ounce nutmeg; put all these spices in two gallons vinegar. Take hard, white cabbage, halve or quarter them, and boil in salt and water till you can run a straw into them; then dry them on a cloth, turning often. One day will dry them, if the sun is bright. Put them in plain vinegar for three weeks, then put them in the spiced vinegar, which must be put in a three gallon jar. To pickle onions, pour over them boiling salt and water, and let them stand in it twenty-four hours. Dry them one or two days and put into spiced vinegar. Two pounds brown sugar added to this pickle improves it greatly.

Chow-Chow.

Three heads of cabbage, twenty-five peppers, half a pint of white mustard seed and grated horseradish; cut the cabbage fine, chop the peppers, and then put in the jar a layer of cabbage, then a layer of peppers, then a little salt, and sprinkle a little horseradish and mustard seed over the whole, and so on until the ingredients are all in the jar; then fill the jar with cold vinegar, to every quart of which dissolve two ounces of brown sugar.

Pickled Plums.

One peck plums, seven pounds sugar, half-pint vinegar; dissolve together sugar and vinegar, add the plums; boil three hours, stirring it all the time, and take out the stones while boiling; add two tablespoonsful allspice, two of ground cloves.

Virginia Damson Pickles.

To five pounds damsons allow five pounds sugar and two and a half pints vinegar. Take the vinegar and put to it two ounces mace, one ounce cinnamon, and one ounce cloves. Let it come to a boil and pour over the fruit and sugar; cover close. Turn off and scald the syrup for six successive days; the seventh day let fruit, spices, and all come to a boil. It will keep for years.

Walnut Catsup.

Take walnuts fit for pickling, beat them well in a mortar till they are pulped; then squeeze out the juice, and let it settle a day; pour off the clear. To a pint of juice put one pound of anchovies with one ounce of shallots; stir it on the fire till the anchovies are dissolved; strain it off clear. To every quart put a quarter of an ounce mace, a quarter of an ounce of cloves, a quarter of an ounce of jamaica pepper, and half a pint of white wine vinegar; boil the whole together a quarter of an hour, then bottle it. It will keep three years. A tablespoonful is sufficient for half a pint of melted butter. One hundred walnuts will produce one quart of juice.

Universal Sauce.

Two gallons of vinegar, quarter of a pound of cayenne pods bruised, thirty-two cloves or garlic; mix the above, and let it stand five days; then strain it; add three pints of walnut juice and three pints of indian soy. Bottle it for use.

Tomato Catsup.

One peck of tomatoes, two teaspoonsful salt, one and a half ground pepper, two spoonsful ground cloves, one spoonful ground allspice, one spoonful red pepper, and one tablespoonful ground ginger. Boil down thick, and add good cider vinegar. The tomatoes should be first cooked, and then run through a sieve to remove the skins and seed. If onion and a little garlic is sliced thin and the catsup poured over them while it is hot, it will improve the flavor.

Sweet Tomato Pickles.

One pint of sugar to one quart of vinegar, one teaspoonful cinnamon, and one teaspoonful cloves; slice green tomatoes over night, and salt between each layer until all are in. Lay a clean white cloth in a basket before putting the tomatoes in; let them drain over night to remove the bitter water from them. Put them in a clean kettle, and pour the sugar and vinegar over, and cook them till tender. Those who like the chow-chow or mustard pickles that are sold in the stores, can have just as good by adding ground mustard. Sliced onions are very nice mixed with the green tomatoes. But as onions are disagreeable to many persons, they can be used or not.

Salad Dressing.

One teaspoonful mixed mustard, one teaspoonful white sugar, two tablespoonsful salad oil, four tablespoonsful milk, two tablespoonsful vinegar, cayenne and salt to the taste. Put the mixed mustard into a salad bowl with the sugar, and add the oil drop by drop, carefully stirring and mixing all these ingredients together. Proceed in this manner with the milk and vinegar, which must be added very gradually, or the sauce will curdle. Put in the seasoning, when the mixture will be ready for use. If this dressing is properly made it will have a soft, creamy appearance, and will be found very delicious with crab or cold fried fish, as well as with salad. In mixing salad dressings the ingredients cannot be added too gradually or stirred too much.

Onion Pickles.

In November take dried onions, small and round, peel them and throw them in salt water; let them remain there a few days, drain them; put them in a jar and pour vinegar over them that has been boiled with cloves, allspice, cinnamon and mace in it. Some think a better way is to scald the onions, (not cook them,) and throw a little milk in the water, it keeps them white.

Cabbage Salad.

Rub together six tablespoonsful sweet cream and one tablespoonful mustard; butter can be used instead of cream. Set in a kettle of boiling water, and add two eggs, well-beaten. Then pour in, gradually, nine tablespoonsful of vinegar. Pour this over nicely cut cabbage while it is hot; add salt, pepper and sugar, and more vinegar, if the mixture is not thin enough. This should be constantly stirred. It should be of the consistency of thick cream.

Tomato Catsup.

To every gallon of the pulp, after it has been cooked and strained, three even tablespoonsful of salt, two tablespoonsful black pepper, one tablespoonful ground cinnamon, two tablespoonsful mustard, one tablespoonful allspice, one teaspoonful cloves, one teaspoonful ground ginger, two tablespoonsful sugar, one teaspoonful cayenne pepper and one quart cider vinegar.

Boil all together until sufficiently thick. Bottle while hot, and keep in a cool place.

Ripe Cucumber Pickles.

Pare seven pounds cucumbers and cut in slices lengthwise. Soak two or three days in salt and water, after scraping out the inside; then cook them in weak vinegar with a spoonful of alum until tender. Boil three pounds sugar, three pints vinegar and half a cupful spices of different kinds in a bag. Pour over the pickles while hot.

Peach Pickles.

Beat together cinnamon, cloves, allspice and race ginger; add a little turmeric. Wash firm freestone peaches and wipe them dry, cut in halves, remove the seed, then sprinkle a small quantity of the mixed spices in each half, and fill them with white mustard seed and a few celery seed; put them together and tie them; place them in a jar with slices of onions, cinnamon, race ginger, allspice, cloves, celery seed and cayenne pepper. Stir into a half gallon of vinegar one pound of sugar, a half pint of salt, and enough turmeric to color the peaches. Pour over the peaches cold.

Pepper Mangoes.

Select white cabbage heads, chop them fine; add salt, celery seed, white mustard seed, ground ginger, turmeric, and mix the whole with a little pure olive oil. Seed and fill the peppers; after washing and wiping them, sew the side of them with a white thread; then place in a jar alternate layers of peppers, allspice, sliced onions, ginger and cloves. Stir into one gallon of vinegar half a pound of sugar, one pint of salt and half an ounce of turmeric. Pour over the peppers cold. In about six weeks pour off the vinegar and replace it with salt, sugar and turmeric, as the first will probably have lost all the flavor.

Cabbage Pickle.

Quarter nice large cabbage heads; place in a tray or tub alternate layers of cabbage and salt, let them remain all night; next day cover them just as they stand with boiling water; let them remain until cold enough to press the water out with a towel. Place in a jar alternate layers of cabbage, allspice, cloves, white mustard seed, ginger, celery seed, cayenne pepper, (green and red,) and sliced onion. Add to the vinegar, sugar and salt, (if the cabbage should not be salt enough;) have the turmeric in a bag and rub out in the vinegar; pour the vinegar over the cabbage.

Plum Catsup.

(MRS. DR. RYAN.)

One gallon of plums, with a very little water; stand them on the top of the stove till they are cooked perfectly soft; then set the kettle off and let it cool enough to be rubbed through the sieve, letting the juice and pulp both pass through the sieve; when all is well rubbed through, put it again in the kettle and set it on the stove, adding two and a half pounds brown sugar to three quarts of the pulp; let them boil together about an hour and a half, then add a pint of best cider vinegar, and spice to suit the taste—allspice, cloves and cinnamon, about two tablespoonsful of each to that quantity. When done, bottle and cork tight, seal the corks over it, it is safer.

Damson Sweet Pickle.

Four pounds damsons, one pint cider vinegar, one pound sugar, one ounce cloves, one ounce mace, two ounces cinnamon and two ounces allspice. Boil the vinegar with sugar and spices, and pour over the fruit while hot. This will have to be repeated several times.

Melon Sweet Pickle.

Three pounds rind of melon, two pints best vinegar and one pound and a half sugar. Soak the rind one week in brine, then soak it in clear water till the salt is out; scald in alum water; then throw it in cold water several hours; boil the vinegar, sugar and spices, and scald the melon till it is clear. Use the same spices as for any other sweet pickle.

Chow-Chow.

One gallon unpeeled cucumbers, half a gallon cabbage, half a dozen onions and half a dozen green peppers. Chop fine, salt separately; let it stand to drain in a basket twenty-fours. Mix, scald in old vinegar; strain, and add sugar and spices as above, and cold vinegar.

Cucumber Catsup.

Slice and salt one gallon of cucumbers; let them stand two or three hours, then press out all the water in a coarse linen. Add four tablespoonsful of best table oil, two tablespoonsful white mustard seed, one tablespoonful ground mustard, one tablespoonful mace, two tablespoonsful black pepper, one-quarter of a teaspoonful of cayenne, one teaspoonful turmeric, one pint madeira wine, one cupful and a half loaf sugar. Mix this in a vessel and pour over the pickle cold.

Yellow Cabbage Pickle.

One gallon vinegar, quarter of a pound mustard seed, half a teacup ginger, one tablespoonful pepper, a handful of horse radish, one ounce turmeric, garlic and onions to the taste. Keep the cabbage in brine three days, then wash it off in fresh water and drain. Boil all together three minutes.

PRESERVES.

GENERAL DIRECTIONS FOR PRESERVING.

Perhaps the following few general hints on preserving, for the use of a young housewife, may not be unacceptable. Several of the directions may appear needless, but there may be some inexperienced persons to whom they may be beneficial:

Let everything used for the purpose be clean and dry, especially bottles.

Never place a preserving pan flat on the fire, as this will render the preserve liable to burn to, as it is called; that is to say, to adhere closely to the metal, and then to burn; it should always rest on a trivet, or the lower bar of the kitchen range.

After the sugar is added to them, stir the preserves gently at first, and more quickly towards the end, without quitting them until they are done; this precaution will prevent their being spoiled.

All preserves should be perfectly cleared from the scum as its rises.

Fruit which is to be preserved in syrup must first be blanched or boiled gently, until it is sufficiently softened to absorb the sugar; and a thin syrup must be poured on it at first, or it will shrivel instead of remaining plump and becoming clear. Thus, if its weight of sugar is to be allowed, and boiled to a syrup, with a pint of water to the pound, only half the weight must be taken at first, and this must not be boiled with the water more than fifteen or twenty minutes at the commencement of the process. A part of the remaining sugar must be added every time the syrup is reboiled, unless it should be otherwise directed in the receipt.

To preserve both the true flavor and the color of fruit in jams and jellies, boil them rapidly until they are well reduced, before the sugar is added, and quickly afterwards; but do not allow them to become so much thickened that the sugar will not dissolve in them easily, and throw up its scum. In some seasons the juice is so much richer than in others that this effect takes place almost before one is aware of it; but the drop which adheres to the skimmer, when it is held up, will show the state it has reached.

Never use tin, iron or pewter spoons or skimmers for preserves, as they will convert the color of red fruit into a dingy purple, and impart, besides, a very unpleasant flavor.

When cheap jams or jellies are required, make them at once with loaf sugar, but use that which is well refined always for preserves in general. It is a false economy to purchase an inferior kind, as there is great waste from it in the quantity of scum which it throws up.

Pans of copper or bell-metal are the proper utensils for preserving fruit. When used, they must be scoured bright with sand. Tinned pans turn and destroy the color of the fruit that is put into them. A stewpan made of iron, coated with earthenware, is very nice for preserving.

Canning Fruits.

In canning fruit the same rule will hold good in most fruits. In the first place they should be fresh gathered, peeled and let get scalding hot; they do not need to be cooked. The bottles or jars should be carefully cleaned and scalded, and should be kept hot while putting in the fruit, and then sealed or soldered as quickly as possible. There is some difference of opinion about the way of putting up fruit; some think that the fruit should be put cold in the cans or bottles, and the cans set in a vessel of cold water, and that set to boiling till the fruit has thoroughly scalded; others prefer the quicker way of scalding the fruit and putting it into the hot cans. Either way is good. I prefer the latter way for most fruits. When sugar is to be used, the proper proportion is: to each pound of fruit a quarter of a pound of sugar and half a pint of water. Do a kettle full, or as many pounds as can be attended to at a time, then fill your cans. Prepare more fruit, and weigh the sugar and measure the water, and let them scald thoroughly. They must be hot all through, or they will not keep. Peaches, pears, quinces and sweet fruit, can be put in tin without injury to their color; but cherries, blackberries, strawberries, plums, and all fruits containing acid, should be put in earthen or glass.

Peaches Canned Whole.

This is one of the nicest ways that peaches can be up put. They not only look nicer on the table, but retain more of their natural flavor, having the stones left in them. Select such as are finely flavored, peel them, and weigh as many as you can do at a time. To each pound of peaches put a quarter of a pound of white sugar and half a pint of water. Let your syrup come to a boil, and drop your fruit into it, and let them cook till they are very tender, but not cooked to pieces. Have your cans hot by pouring boiling water into them, fill and seal up immediately. It is well to lay a heavy weight on each can (if they are sealed with wax) till they become cold.

Plums.

There are several varieties of plums. The richest purple plum for preserving is the damson; there are of these large and small; the large are called sweet damsons, the small ones are very rich flavored. The great difficulty in preserving plums is that the skins crack and the fruit comes to pieces. The rule here laid down for preserving them obviates that difficulty. Purple gages, unless properly preserved, will turn to juice, and skins; and the large horse plum (as it is generally known) comes completely to pieces in ordinary modes of preserving; the one recommended herein will keep them whole, full and rich. Make a syrup of clean brown sugar; clarify it as directed in these receipts; when perfectly clear and boiling hot, pour it over the plums, having picked out all unsound ones and stems; let them remain in the syrup two days, then drain it off; make it boiling hot, skim it, and pour it over again; let them remain another day or two, then put them in a preserving kettle over the fire, and simmer gently until the syrup is reduced, and thick or rich. One pound of sugar for each pound of plums. Small damsons are very fine, preserved as cherries or any other ripe fruit; clarify the syrup, and when boiling hot put in the plums; let them boil very gently until they are cooked, and the syrup rich. Put them in pots or jars; the next day secure as directed.

Plums Without the Skins.

Pour boiling water over large egg or magnum bonum plums; cover them until it is cold, then pull off the skins. Make a syrup of a pound of sugar and a teacupful of water for each pound of fruit; make it boiling hot, and pour it over; let them remain for a day or two, then drain it off and boil again; skim it clear, and pour it hot over the plums; let them remain until the next day, then put them over the fire in the syrup; boil them very gently until clear; take them from the syrup with a skimmer into the pots or jars; boil the syrup until rich and thick; take off any scum which may arise, then let it cool and settle, and pour it over the plums. If brown sugar is used, which is quite as good except for green gages, clarify it as directed.

Peaches.

Take ripe freestone peaches; pare, stone and quarter them. To six pounds of the cut peaches allow three pounds of the best brown sugar. Strew the sugar among the peaches, and set them away in a covered vessel. Next morning, put the whole into a preserving kettle, and boil it slowly about an hour and three-quarters or two hours, skimming it well.

Pears.

Pare them very thin, and simmer in a thin syrup; let them lie a day or two. Make the syrup richer and simmer again. Repeat this till they are clear; then drain and dry them in the sun or a cool oven a little time; or they may be kept in the syrup and dried as wanted, which makes them richer.

Currants for Tarts.

Get your currants, when they are dry, and pick them; to every pound and a quarter of currants put a pound of sugar, into a preserving pan, with as much juice of currants as will dissolve it; when it boils, skim it, and put in your currants, and boil them till they are clear; put them into a jar, lay paper over, tie them down, and keep them in a dry place.

Pears for the Tea Table.

Take ripe pears and wipe them carefully; place a layer, stem upward, in a stone jar, sprinkle over sugar, then set in another layer of pears, and so on until the jar is filled. To every gallon put in a pint and a half water. Cover the top of the jar with pie crust, and set it in a slow oven for two hours.

Apple or Quince Jelly.

Pare, quarter and core the apples; put them in a saucepan with enough water to cover them; let them boil five minutes; put them in a bag, and let them drain until the next day. To one pint of juice put one pound of sugar, and boil it from fifteen to twenty minutes. Cranberry jelly may be made in the same way.

Strawberries.

To two pounds of fine large strawberries add two pounds of powdered sugar, and put them in a preserving kettle, over a slow fire, till the sugar is melted; then boil them precisely twenty minutes, as fast as possible; have ready a number of small jars, and put the fruit in boiling hot. Cork and seal the jars immediately, and keep them through the summer in a cold dry cellar. The jars must be heated before the hot fruit is poured in, otherwise they will break.

Raspberries.

These may be preserved wet, bottled, or made jam or marmalade of, the same as strawberries. Rasp berries are very good dried in the sun or in a warm oven. They are very delicious stewed for table or tarts.

Quince Jam.

Twelve ounces brown sugar to one pound of quince. Boil the fruit in as little water as possible, until the fruit will mash easily. Pour off the water, mash the fruit with a spoon, put in the sugar, and boil twenty minutes, stirring often.

Cranberry Jelly.

Wash and pick over the fruit, and boil till soft in water enough to cover it. Strain through a sieve, and weigh equal quantities of the pulp and sugar. Boil gently fifteen or twenty minutes, taking care it does not burn.

Peaches.

Take ripe, but not soft peaches. Pour boiling water over them to take off the skins, which will pull off easily. Weigh equal quantities of fruit and sugar, and put them together in an earthen pan over night. In the morning pour off the syrup, and boil a few minutes; set off the kettle and take off the scum. Put back the kettle on the fire; when the syrup boils up, put in the peaches. Boil them slowly three-quarters of an hour, take them out and put in jars. Boil the syrup fifteen minutes more, and pour over them.

Currant Jam, (Black, Red or White.)

Let the fruit be very ripe, pick it clean from the stalks, bruise it, and to every pound put three-quarters of a pound of loaf sugar; stir it well, and boil half an hour.

Currant Jelly, (Red or Black.)

Strip the fruit, put in a stone jar, and stew them in a saucepan of water, or by boiling it on the hot hearth; strain off the liquor, and to every pint weigh a pound of loaf sugar, put the latter in large lumps into it, in a stone vessel till nearly dissolved; then put in a preserving pan; simmer and skim as necessary. When it will jelly on a plate, put it in small jars or glasses.

Apple Jelly.

Boil your apples in water till they are quite to a mash; then put them through a flannel bag to drip. To every pint of the juice put one pound of sugar; boil till it jellies; season with lemon juice and peel to your taste a little before it is finished. I may as well add, that I can say from experience, that this jelly is excellent, and of a beautiful color.

Currant Jelly.

Pick fine red, but long ripe currants from the stems; bruise them, and strain the juice from a quart at a time through a thin muslin; wring it gently, to get all the liquid; put a pound of white sugar to each pound of juice; stir it until it is all dissolved; set it over a gentle fire; let it become hot, and boil for fifteen minutes; then try it by taking a spoonful into a saucer; when cold, if it is not quite firm enough, boil it for a few minutes longer.

Crab Apple Marmalade.

Boil the apples in a kettle until soft, with just water enough to cover them. Mash, and strain through a coarse sieve. Take a pound of apple to a pound of sugar; boil half an hour, and put into jars.

Apple Marmalade.

Take any kind of sour apples, pare and core them, cut them in small pieces, and to every pound of apples put three-fourths of a pound of sugar. Put them in a preserving pan and boil over a slow fire until they are reduced to a fine pulp. Then put them in jelly jars, and keep them in a cool place.

Crab Apple Jelly.

Boil the apples, with just water enough to cover them, until tender. Mash with a spoon, and strain out the juice. Take a pint of juice to a pound of sugar; boil thirty minutes, and strain through a hair sieve.

Apple in Jelly.

Pare and core some well-shaped apples; pippins or golden russets if you have them, but others will do; throw them into water as you do them; put them in a preserving pan, and with as little water as will only half cover them; let them coddle, and when the lower side is done, turn them. Observe that they do not lie too close when first put in. When sufficiently done, take them out on the dish they are to be served in, the stalk downward. Take the water and make a rich jelly of it with loaf sugar, boiling the thin rind and juice of a lemon. When come to a jelly, let it grow cold, and put it on and among the apples; cut the peel of the lemon in narrow strips, and put across the eye of the apple.

Apple Jam that Will Keep for Years.

Weigh equal quantities of brown sugar and good sour apples; pare, core, and chop them fine; make a good, clear syrup of the sugar. Add the apples, the juice and grated rind of three lemons, and a few pieces of white ginger. Boil it till the apple looks clear and yellow; this resembles foreign sweetmeats. On no account omit the ginger.

Quinces Whole.

Pare and put them into a saucepan, with the parings at the top; then fill it with hard water; cover it close; set it over a gentle fire till they turn reddish; let them stand till cold; put them into a clear, thick syrup; boil them for a few minutes; set them on one side till quite cold; boil them again in the same manner; the next day boil them until they look clear; if the syrup is not thick enough, boil it more; when cold, put brandied paper over them. The quinces may be halved or quartered.

Quince Jelly.

Take some sound, yellow quinces, which are not over ripe; peel them, cut them in quarters, and boil them in as much water as will cover them When they have been well-boiled, squeeze them through a linen cloth, clarify the juice in a filtering bag, weigh it, and put it with three-quarters of its weight of sugar in a brass kettle. Do not forget to put in a piece of cinnamon. Cook the whole together until it has become a jelly. Take it from the fire, and tie up in pots when it is cold.

Quince Marmalade.

To one gallon of quinces, three pounds of good loaf sugar. Pare the quinces and cut them in halves, scoop out the cores and the hard strip that unites the core with the string; put the cores and some of the parings in a saucepan with about a quart of water, put the halves of quinces in a steamer that fits the saucepan; boil them until the quinces are softened by the steam; then mash them with a wooden spoon, in a dish, and pour the water from the saucepan on them, which is now of a thick glutinous substance; put with the sugar in a stewpan or enamelled saucepan, and let them boil for about half an hour, keeping them well stirred.

To Clarify Sugar.

Put into a preserving pan as many pounds of sugar as you wish; to each pound of sugar put half a pint of water, and the white of an egg to every four pounds; stir it together until the sugar is dissolved; then set it over a gentle fire; stir it occasionally, and take off the scum as it rises. After a few boilings up, the sugar will rise so high as to run over the side of the pan; to prevent which, take it from the fire for a few minutes, when it will subside, and leave time for skimming. Repeat the skimming until a slight scum or foam only will rise; then take off the pan, lay a slightly wetted napkin over the basin, and then strain the sugar through it. Put the skimmings into a basin; when the sugar is clarified, rinse the skimmer and basin with a glass of cold water, and put it to the scum, and set it by for common purposes.

Brandy Peaches.

Drop the peaches in hot water, let them remain till the skin can be ripped off; make a thin syrup, and let it cover the fruit; boil the fruit till it can be pierced with a straw; take it out, make a very rich syrup, and add, after it is taken from the fire, and while it is still hot, an equal quantity of brandy. Pour this while it is still warm, over the peaches in the jar. They must be covered with it.

Pears.

Take six pounds of pears to four pounds of sugar; boil the parings in as much water as will cover them; strain it through a colander; lay some pears in the bottom of your kettle, put in some sugar, and so on alternately; then pour the liquor off the pear skins over; boil them until they begin to look transparent, then take them out, let the juice cool, and clarify it; put the pears in again, and add some ginger; boil till done; let the liquor boil after taking them out until it is reduced to a syrup.

Pears for the Table.

Peel three pounds of pears and place them in a stewpan; cover them with water, and let them stew two hours. Take them out and put them in a brown jar with three-fourths of a pound of loaf sugar and two tablespoonsful of the water they were stewed in to each pound. Add a little candied lemon, cut in small pieces, or a few cloves, if preferred. Place the cover on the jar, and stew them in an oven for two hours. Sometimes they require a little longer time. Golden syrup sufficient to cover them may be substituted for sugar and water.

Raspberry Jam.

Weigh the fruit, and add three-quarters of the weight of sugar; put the former into a preserving pan, boil, and break it; stir constantly, and let it boil very quickly; when the juice has boiled an hour, add the sugar and simmer half an hour. In this way the jam is superior in color and flavor to that which is made by putting the sugar in at first.

Currant Jelly.

Put your currants into a stone pot, and set them into a pot of water over the fire. Having strained the juice of these heated currants through a cloth, measure it, and to each pint allow a pound of sugar. Put your sugar into the oven in a shallow pan, and let it heat through, but be careful not to scorch it. Have your currant juice hot, and put in the sugar hot, and let both boil together four minutes. This is very nice, if carefully made.

Cantelope Rind.

Take one pound of rind, not quite mellow, and cut the outside carefully off; lay it in a bowl and sprinkle over it one teaspoonful of alum; cover it with boiling water, and let it stand all night; then dry it in a cloth, scald it in ginger tea, but do not boil it; then dry it again in a cloth; to one pound of rind allow one pound of sugar and half a pint of water. Boil it an hour.

Citron.

Cut the citron the round way of the citron; take off the rind, take out the seed; it should be cut about an inch thick, and can then be cut into any shape to suit the fancy; soak it in soda water two or three hours; then rinse it in clear, cold water; wipe it dry or let it drain till the water is all off. Allow a pound of white sugar to each pound of citron; do not add a great deal of water; let the syrup boil well and skim it; then put in your fruit. Be careful it does not cook dark, nor let it become too thick, or it will turn to sugar. Boil in a cup an ounce of the best race ginger, and add the water to the preserves while cooking. The ginger should be pounded to make it soft. Renew the water on the ginger till it is soft; then add the ginger to the preserves. This way of giving it the ginger taste is the cheapest, but candied ginger can be purchased at the confectioneries, which will be much nicer, and can be eaten as well as the citron. Two lemons should be added, slice them, leaving the rind on. The syrup can be cooked down, and makes a most splendid jelly.

Cherry.

I have no doubt that all housekeepers have had the same experience in regard to cherry preserves, and that is, that after being made for some time, they always become strong. To avoid this, squeeze out all the juice with the hand, (the juice can be used for cordial or "royal acid," a receipt in this book,) and then wash the cherries in two or three waters of good, cold well water. Take one pound of white sugar to each pound of cherries; add water enough to cook them. Do not put too much, or it will make them dark by long cooking. If you want cherry preserves that you can eat, and that will keep sweet as long as you have them, try this way, and you will never want to make them any other way.

Tomato.

Take tomatoes, not too large, (either red or yellow,) scald and skin them; add one pound of white sugar to every pound of tomatoes. Let them stand over night, then take out the tomatoes and boil the syrup, and skim it well. Add tomatoes and boil till done. Flavor with stick cinnamon.

Tomato Marmalade.

(MRS. DR. STEWART.)

To every pound of tomatoes one pound of sugar; peel the skin off and add sugar without any water, one ounce of ginger powdered, and juice of two lemons, rind grated, to every three pounds of fruit. Boil until a thick jam, and cover while hot.

Damson Sauce.

Twelve pounds ripe damsons, four pounds of cider vinegar and three pounds of sugar. Boil till the damsons are soft; take them out and mash them, and then put them back into the syrup and boil from a half to three-quarters of an hour, stirring them and watching them closely, that they do not stick to the kettle or burn.

For Canning Corn.

After the corn is first cut from the cob, boil it, and when cooked almost as much as for the table, to a large iron stove pot of the boiling corn, put one teaspoonful and a half tartaric acid. Use only glass jars, as nothing else will do. When you prepare it for the table in winter, after it boils use a small teaspoonful of soda to destroy the acid taste; then season with butter, pepper and salt. I have this receipt from a Kentucky lady, who says it is perfectly delightful, and will keep splendidly. She has tried it for years, and never fails.

MISCELLANEOUS.

Strawberry Ice Cream.

Take one pint strawberries, one pint cream, nearly half a pound of powdered white sugar and the juice of one lemon. Mash the fruit through a sieve or very fine with the hand; the sieve will remove the seed, if it is preferred. Mix with the other articles, and freeze. A little new milk added will make the whole freeze more quickly.

Raspberry ice cream is made in the same manner.

Italian Snow.

Two pounds white sugar, the juice of six lemons, two quarts water and twenty-four whites of eggs whipped to a stiff froth. Mix the water, juice and sugar well together, then add the eggs, stir all together, put into a freezer and stir till it freezes.

Itallienne Ice.

Boil two quarts rich cream; have ready fourteen ounces of ground mocha coffee; when boiling hot, pour the cream over the coffee; cover very tightly, and let it infuse for two hours. Then take ten eggs, very fresh, separate the whites from the yelks, whip lightly the whites; then pour the coffee and cream through a very fine sieve and stir in the whites, and add sugar to suit the taste. Put this on the fire for a few moments, then strain; when cold, put into a freezer and freeze.

Chocolate ices are made in about the same way. Grate half a pound best French chocolate into one quart milk or cream; let it boil till thick, add sugar; stir well. Let it get cold, and freeze.

Strawberry Water Ice.

Have fresh nice strawberries, rub them through a sieve; add the juice of one lemon. Make a strong, tolerably thick syrup, and when cold, add the strawberry juice and lemon. Freeze well.

Lemon Ice.

Lemon juice and water, each half a pint, and strong syrup one pint. The rind of the lemon should be rasped off before squeezing with the sugar. Mix the whole, strain after standing an hour, and freeze. Beat up with a little sugar the whites of three or four eggs, and as the ice is beginning to set, work this in with a wooden paddle or spoon, it will greatly improve the ice.

Orange water ice is made in the same way.

Pineapples

Chopped fine, sweetened delicately, and nice madeira wine poured over them and frozen, is delicious.

Peaches.

Nutmeg grated over peaches is a great improvement. Try it.

Ice Cream.

Take one gallon of rich cream, sweeten delicately, and flavor with vanilla or lemon. Set the cream in a tin bucket, and let it get ice cold; then whip to a stiff froth. Put it in the freezer and keep it well stirred, unless the "patent" freezer is used.

Lemon Syrup, (To Save the Lemon.)

When you have lemons that are likely to spoil or dry up, take the insides which are yet sound, squeeze out the juice, and to each pint put a pound and a half white sugar and a little of the peel; boil for a few minutes, strain and cork for use. This will not require any acid, and half a teaspoonful of soda to three-quarters of a glassful of water, with two or three tablespoonsful of syrup, will make a foaming glass.

Cream Soda, (This is Splendid.)

Coffee sugar four pounds, water three pints, three grated nutmegs, whites of ten eggs well-beaten, gum arabic one ounce, oil of lemon twenty drops, or extract equal to that amount. By using oils of other fruits, you can make as many flavors from this as you desire or prefer. Mix all well, and place over a gentle fire, and stir well about thirty minutes; remove from the fire, strain, and divide into two parts; into half put eight ounces supercarbonate of soda, and into the other half put six ounces tartaric acid; shake well, and when cold, they are ready to use. By pouring three or four spoonsful from both parts into separate glasses which are one third full of cold water, stir each and pour together, and you have as nice a glass of cream soda as was ever drank, which you can drink at your leisure, as the gum and eggs hold the gas.

Cheap Ice Cream.

Six quarts milk and Oswego corn starch half a pound; first dissolve the starch in one quart of the milk; then mix all together and just simmer a little, (not to boil;) sweeten and flavor to suit the taste, or make it as the following receipt: Irish moss one ounce and a half and milk one gallon. First soak the moss in a little cold water for an hour, and rinse well to clear it of sand; then steep it for an hour in the milk just at the boiling point, but not to boil; two or three whites of eggs, well-beaten, and added after it is cold is an improvement. Beat while freezing.

Wine Jelly.

For one package of gelatine or one ounce isinglass, pour one pint cold water, and let it stand ten minutes; then add one pint boiling water, one pound white sugar and whites and shells of two eggs. Then mix all with isinglass. Boil five minutes and strain through a flannel bag. Be sure not to squeeze it. Flavor with wine to the taste.

Splendid Ginger Pop.

Five gallons and a half water, quarter of a pound bruised ginger root, half an ounce tartaric acid, two pounds and a half white sugar, whites of three eggs, well beaten, one teaspoonful lemon oil and one gill yeast. Boil the root for thirty minutes in one gallon of the water, strain off, and put the oil in while hot. Mix, make over night, and in the morning skim and bottle, keeping out sediments.

Elderberry Wine.

Elderberry juice two quarts, water one quart and brown sugar three pounds. Jam the elderberries well, squeeze out the juice and measure it. If you rinse out the juice that remains in the squeezed berries, measure it or the water you pour on it, and reckon it as so much of the water you are to add. The above will make a very rich wine, but half water, with three pounds of sugar to the gallon of liquid will be a very good wine. After dissolving thoroughly the sugar in the liquid, fill the vessel full; set it in a cool place to ferment, and pour off all impurities and keep the vessel full by adding some of the liquid kept in reserve for that purpose, or fill up with water. When the fermentation is nearly or quite done, stop the vessel tight and let it stand, the longer the better; will be good in a few weeks, but much better in a few years.

Blackberry Cordial.

Select the ripest blackberries, mash them well; put them into a jelly bag in small quantities and squeeze out all the juice; for every quart of juice allow one pound white sugar. Put the sugar into a preserving kettle and pour the juice over it. When the sugar is all melted, set it on the fire; add half an ounce cloves, allspice and cinnamon. Boil till well cooked, and when cold, to every quart of syrup add half a pint of French brandy. Stir all well together and bottle the cordial for use. It is best to pound the spices and tie them in a thin piece of muslin, to prevent having to strain again.

Acid Royal.

(MRS. P. B. PRICE.)

Three ounces citric acid dissolved in one quart of water; cover the cherries with it and let it stand six or eight hours; strain off the juice and pour it on another bowl of cherries, and let that remain the same length of time; then strain and add to each pint of juice one pint of white sugar. Boil it in a porcelain kettle; skim, bottle and cork while hot.

Egg Nog--The Best Ever Made.

The yelks of sixteen eggs, twelve tablespoonsful of loaf sugar; beat to the consistency of cream, to this add two-thirds of a nutmeg; beat well together; mix in half pint best brandy, a glassful jamaica rum and two wine glassesful of madeira wine; have the whites beaten to a stiff froth and stir into the above mixture. When done, stir in six pints rich sweet milk.

Cocoanut Candy.

Pare and cut half a pound cocoanut in strips or grate; dissolve half a pound loaf sugar with two tablespoonsful hot water; boil and stir in cocoanut. Flavor with lemon.

Sugar Candy.

(MRS. BUNN.)

One quart white sugar, one pint water, a lump of

butter the size of an egg, one tablespoonful vinegar and the same of vanilla. Pull till white; try in a little water before taking up, if hard and crisp, it is done; put the vanilla in after the candy is taken from the stove before putting the pans to cool.

Butter Scotch.

(MRS. WM. TURNEY.)

One cupful sugar, one cupful molasses, one tablespoonful water, one large tablespoonful butter and a teaspoonful vinegar. Flavor with lemon.

Cream Candy.

(MRS. WM. TURNEY.)

Three pounds loaf sugar and half a pint water. Cook on a slow fire for half an hour; add one teaspoonful dissolved gum arabic and one tablespoonful vinegar. Boil until brittle and pull into long sticks.

Cocoa Candy.

The whites of four eggs, half pound sifted sugar and grated cocoanut. Stir together until stiff; then form into cakes and bake in a moderate oven until brown.

To Keep Silver Always Bright.

Silver, in constant use, should be washed every day in a pan of suds made of good white soap and warm water; drying it with old soft linen cloths. Twice a week (after this washing) give it a thorough brightening with finely powdered whiting, mixed to a thin paste with alcohol, rubbing longer and harder where there are stains. Then wipe this off, and polish with clean soft old linen. Silver is cleaned in this manner at the best hotels.

To Destroy Worms in Garden Walks.

Pour into the worm holes a strong lye made of wood ashes, lime and water; or, if more convenient, use for this purpose strong salt and water.

To Clean Brass.

Rub the tarnished or rusted brass by means of a cloth or sponge, with diluted acid, such as sulphuric, or even with strong vinegar. Afterward wash it with hot water to remove the acid, and finish with dry whiting.

A Strong Paste for Paper.

To two large spoonfuls of fine flour put as much pounded rosin as will lie on a shilling; mix with as much strong beer as will make it of a due consistence, and boil half an hour. Let it be cold before it is used.

Preserving Eggs for Winter.

Pack them in a clean vessel, with the small end down, strewing bran between each layer, then place one or two thicknesses of brown paper over the top, and cover with about an inch or an inch and a half of salt. Cover close and keep in a cool place, and they will be much better than the old method of salting down, which only hardens them.

To Tell Good Eggs.

If you desire to be certain that your eggs are good and fresh, put them in water; if the buts turn up, they are not fresh. This is an infallible rule to distinguish a good egg from a bad one.

Currant Wine.

(MRS. DICK YOUNG.)

One quart currant juice, two quarts water and three pounds good brown sugar. Put into a cask, leave the bung out till fermentation has ceased, then rack off and bottle. Squeeze the juice out of the currants without heating them, and to every quart of the juice use the above proportion.

Blackberry and Currant Wine.

(MRS. ABLE.)

To every gallon of fruit put one quart of water boiling hot; let it stand over night; then extract the juice, and to each gallon add three pounds of sugar. Put it in a keg and let it remain undisturbed for several weeks; then rack off and bottle.

Lemon Sherbet Without Lemons.

(MRS. AGGIE KENNEY, KY.)

Two teaspoonsful of citric acid dissolved in a little water, one teaspoonful and a half essence of lemon, three coffeecupsful white sugar and one gallon water; when this begins to freeze add the whites of two eggs, well-beaten, and then freeze.

Lemon Ice.

(MRS. N. W. EDWARDS.)

To one gallon of water a dozen and a half lemons, squeeze out the juice, and add sugar sufficient to make a pleasantly sweet lemonade. Freeze it, and when nearly frozen, add the beaten whites of six eggs. Stir to mix well, then freeze well.

Gelatine Jelly.

Pour one pint cold water over half a box gelatine; let it stand till soft; add half pint boiling water, one pint madeira wine, three-quarters of a pound white sugar, a quarter of a teaspoonful lemon acid and two drops essence lemon.

Sherbet.

(MRS. BEN. EDWARDS.)

Boil in a quart of rich milk the rind of a lemon with a pound of loaf sugar; when cool, put in the freezer and half freeze. Have ready the juice of five lemons and the whites of three eggs beaten to a stiff froth; add a little sugar to the lemon juice. Add this mixture to the half frozen within the freezer, and let it freeze solid.

Currant Wine.

(MRS. N. W. BROADWELL.)

To each gallon of bruised fruit, add one gallon of water; let it stand twenty-four hours, then strain, and to each quart of the juice add one and a half or two quarts of water and one quart of sugar. Put in jugs and tie a thin cloth over the top for a few days, then put in the cork loosely till fermentation ceases. It can then be poured off and bottled. Cork tightly.

Frozen Custard.

(MRS. PERKINS.)

Two quarts new milk, four tablespoonsful of corn starch and six eggs. Heat the milk to nearly boiling, then add starch, which must be dissolved in a ltttle milk; then add the eggs, well-beaten, with eight tablespoonsful of powdered sugar; let it boil up once or twice. Set the vessel containing this mixture in a vessel with boiling water, and let it boil in that. It will take a little longer, but will not burn if boiled in this way. Let this cool and then freeze.

FISH.

Fish	80
Boiled	80
Boiled Cod	81
Baked	81
Sauce	81
Cod Cakes	82
Spiced	82
Fried	82
Broiled	83
Cat	83

If the Liquor is too Salt	46
Boiled Ham	47
Tongues	47
Mutton Hams, (for Drying)	48
For Corned Beef	48
Sugar Cured Hams	48
Beef and Mutton	49
Ribs of Beef	50
Mutton Chops	50
Leg of Mutton	50
Pork Steaks	51
Spare Ribs	51

Page 9.—**Loal** should be soap.

Page 202—Marble Cake, (Mrs. Ryan's.)—**The white part** should be well-flavored **with** lemon. The **dark part should** have half a tablespoonful, **each, of** spices.

Page 198—Lady Cake.—Should have one cup sweet milk instead of half cup, **and one** teaspoonful soda instead **of** half teacupful.

Page 226—Sponge Cake, (Mrs Ryan.)—Ten ounces flour, instead of sixteen.

Page 239—Imperial Cake, (Mrs. Hodges.)—Should be two **pounds** raisins; one pound **of** them chopped, the other pound **whole.**

Page 67—Mock Venison.—Should be *hind*-quarter.

Page 217—Ginger Cakes.—Teacup, instead of **coffee cup.**

INDEX.

	PAGE.
Advice to Housekeepers	7
To Young Housekeepers	12
House Furnishing	13
Advice to Mothers	14
Modern Cookery and Household Management	16
Four Good Points	19
Four Important Rules	19
Remarks	20
Spoiling	21

SOUPS.

Soups	23
Beef	24
Mutton	24
Portable	24
Mock Turtle	25
Veal	26
Giblet	26
Chicken	26
Gumbo	27
Oyster	28
Winter	29
Noodles for Soup	28
Veal Broth	29

FISH.

Fish	30
Boiled	30
Boiled Cod	31
Baked	31
Sauce	31
Cod Cakes	32
Spiced	32
Fried	32
Broiled	33
Cat	33

	PAGE.
Fish	
Fried Cod	34
Boiled	35
Clam Fritters	37
Potted Shad	37
Stewed Halibut	40
Cod Cakes, (A Yankee Dish)	40
Fried Perch	41
Curry	41
Sauce	42
Fried Oysters	33
Stewed Oysters	34
Scalloped Oysters	34
To Make Stewed Oysters Tender	35
French Stewed Oysters	36
A Codfish Relish	41
Egg Sauce for Salt Fish	41

MARKETING.

Beef Steaks	43
Roasting Pieces	43
Corned Beef Pieces	44
A Stuffed Flank	44
Time for Boiling Meat	45
Fresh Killed Meat	45
Take Care of the Liquor	46
If the Liquor is too Salt	46
Boiled Ham	47
Tongues	47
Mutton Hams, (for Drying)	48
For Corned Beef	48
Sugar Cured Hams	48
Beef and Mutton	49
Ribs of Beef	50
Mutton Chops	50
Leg of Mutton	50
Pork Steaks	51
Spare Ribs	51

	PAGE.
Sausage Meat	51
Tender-Loin	52
Pigs Feet	52
Shoulder and Ham	52
Curing and Smoking Ham	53
Packing Beef	54
To Try Out Lard	54
Mutton	54
Shoulder	55
Leg Boiled	55
Cooking a Loin	56
The Neck and Breast	56
The Haunch	56
Venison Fashion	56
Beef a la Mode	57
Beef Patties	58
To Hash a Calf's Head	58
Spoon Meats	59
Minced Beef	59
Beef and Mashed Potatoes	60
Beef's Heart	60
Beef Collops	61
Beef a la Mode	61
Beefsteak Pie	62
Staffordshire Beefsteak	62
To Mince Beef	63
Potted Beef	63
To Stew a Brisket of Beef	63
Beef Balls	64
Beefsteak with Onions	64
Head Cheese	64
Roast Pig	65
Tripe Stewed	66
Lamb to Fry	66
Calf's Head Pie	66
Mock Venison	67
Mutton Hash	67
Veal	68
Fillet	68
Loin	68
Shoulder	68
Neck	68
Curried	69
Patties	70
Pie	70
Southern Stewed	70
Cutlets, (To Stew)	71
Fricandeau	71
Sweetbread	72
Oyster Pie	72
Loaf	72
Pie	73
Stuffing	73
Minced	73
Patty	74
Breast	74
Dressed with White Sauce	74
Minced	75

	PAGE.
Sandwiches, (Very Fine)	75
Fricasseed Chicken	75
Roast Turkey	75
Goose	76
Ducks	76
Egg Frizzle	77
Sauce for Roast Beef or Mutton	77
Croquettes	77
An Economical Dish	78
French Stew	79
Potatoes Roasted under Meat	79
For a French Pot au Feu	79
Good, Plain Family Irish Stew	80
How to Cut a Chicken to Fry	80
Rabbits Stewed	81
Pot Pie	81
Broiled	82
Potted	83
Broiled Quails	82
Stewed Prairie Chicken	83
Chicken Fried	84
Salad	84
Smothered or Baked	85
Mayonaise	85
To Cook Calf's or Beef's Liver	86

VEGETABLES.

Vegetables	87
To Boil Them	88
Take Care to Wash	88
To Have Clean	88
When They Sink	88
To Preserve Color	89
Potatoes	89
Cakes	89
Boiled	90
Mashed	90
Baked	91
Fried Whole	91
Escolloped	92
Saratoga Fried	92
Fritters	93
Plain Fried	93
Snow	94
Cakes	108
French Batter for Vegetables	93
Tomato Omelet	91
Stew	96
Pudding	98
To Broil	99
To Bake	99
Squash	94
Turnips	94
String Beans	95
Succotash, or Corn and Beans	95
Sweetbreads and Cauliflowers	96
To Stew Red Cabbage	97

INDEX.

	PAGE.
Egg Plant	109
Fried	97
Fricasseed	99
Green Corn Dumplings	97
in Winter	98
Pudding for Meat	109
Beets	99
Young	103
Parsnips	100
Cabbage	100
Asparagus	100
Peas	101
Cold	109
String Beans	101
Mushrooms to Preserve	101
Stewed in Gravy	102
Sweet Potatoes Baked	102
Roasted	102
Boiled	103
Fried	103
Summer Squash	103
Greens and Sprouts	104
Spinage	104
Slaw	105
Hot	105
To Bake Beans	106
Hominy	106
Cucumbers	107
Salsify	107
Corn	106
on the Cob	107
Another Way to Cook	107
Cold	109
Onions to Boil	108
Fried	108

EGGS.

Omelet with Cheese	110
Omelet	110
Eggs Hard Boiled	111
Omelet (Very Fine)	111
Poached	111
Pickled	112
to Keep	112
Plain Boiled	112
a l' Ardennaise	113
sur le Plat	113
Buttered	113
Balls	114

BREADMAKING & YEAST.

Yeast Hop	115
Grated Potato	116
Bottled or Jug	116
Bottled	117
Mashed Potato	117

	PAGE
Yeast, to Make	121
Milk	121
Kentucky for Rolls	139
Kentucky Buttermilk	139
Sally Lunn	118
Snails	119
Biscuit, Soda	119
Souffle	120
Butter	122
Beat	139
Milk	141
Beaten	144
Buns	122
English	129
Spanish	132
Brown Bread	127
French	127
Steamed	127
Boston	128
Boiled	128
Brown Bread	141
Boiled Bread	140
Brown Bread	145
Cracked Wheat for Breakfast	146
Corn Oysters	135
Corn Bread	142
Good	142
Corn Bread	145
Cake, Bread	119
Cream	120
Common Bread	121
Rye Drop	124
Pop Overs	125
Sour Milk Griddle	125
Buckwheat	126
Buckwheat with Sour Milk	126
Corn Meal	126
English Tea	128
Johnny	132
Light	133
Little Milk	134
Rye Drop	137
Flour Griddle	137
Graham Flour	140
Corn Cake	144
Crackers	144
Fritters	135
Spanish	135
Potato	136
Potato	138
"Peculiars," or Graham Puffs	122
Rusk	123
Rusk	131
Rolls, Dutch	128
French	129
Sally Lunn without Yeast	130
Rice Corn Bread	131
Tomato Toast	134

INDEX.

	PAGE.
Muffins	125
Raised	124
Hominy	133
Mush	140
Mush	146
Rice	147
Sally Lunn	146
Waffles	126
German	124
Yankee	136
German	136
Cheap	142
Graham Gems	137
Pancakes, New England	134
Cream	143
Quire of Paper	143

PASTRY.

Very Rich Crust for Tarts	148
Pie Crust	148
Family	148
Pie Crust	152
Puff Paste	149
French Pastry	149
Mince Meat	151
Strawberry Short Cake	158
Mince Meat	158
Peach Cobbler	158
Piecrust Glaze	167
Strawberries Stewed for Tarts	171
Pie Plant Short Cake	172
Pies, Apple	149
Belleflower Apple	150
French Apple	150
Pumpkin	150
Dried Peach	152
Cranberry	152
Pie Plant	152
Cocoanut	153
Soda Cracker	154
Cream	154
Cream	155
Golden	155
Cream	156
Transparent	156
Delicate	156
Cracker	157
Lemon	157
Cracker Mince	158
Gooseberry	159
Lemon	159
Lemon	160
Potato	160
Lemon	160
Mush	161
Silver	161
Lemon	162

	PAGE.
Pies, Mince	162
Cream	162
Golden	163
Cream	163
Egg Mince	163
Molasses	164
Mince	164
Delicate	165
Cream	165
Lemon	166
Corn Starch	166
Transparent	167
Stewart, (Splendid)	167
Summer Mince	168
Mince without Meat	168
Lemon Mince	169
Lemon	169
Lemon	169
Mince	170
Apple Custard	170
Georgetown, Ky	170
Lemon	171
Lemon	171
Cheap Lemon	172
Cream	173

CAKES.

General Directions for Making	175
A Fine Icing for Cake	176
Cold Icing	178
Receipt for Icing	179
Almond Icing for Wedding Cake	198
Almond Icing	220
Sugar Ice	220
Icing for Cake	225
Orange Paste	239
Cakes, Black	176
Currant	177
Custard	177
White	177
Cream	178
Ice Cream	178
Soft Ginger	179
Doughnuts	179
Citron	180
Cottage	180
Delicious	181
Tipsy	181
Silver	182
Ginger Snaps	182
Drop	182
Fruit	183
Spice	183
Ginger Snaps	185
Rolled Jelly	185
Macaroons	185
Tea	185

	PAGE.
Cakes, Black	186
Doughnuts	187
Silver	187
Cream Tea	187
Fruit	188
Cocoanut	188
Coffee	189
Delicate	189
Railroad	189
Sponge	190
Cocoanut Pound	190
Sponge	190
Chocolate Puffs	190
Cocoanut	191
Ginger Snaps	191
Jumbles	191
Fruit	192
White Sponge	192
White	192
White Mountain	192
Pork	193
Fruit	194
Almond Macaroons	194
Feather	195
Cup	195
White Cake	195
Sponge	196
Jumbles	196
Rose	196
Cocoanut Jumbles	197
Mountain	197
Lady	198
Fruit	198
Almond	199
Pound	199
White	199
Cup	200
Sponge	200
Fruit	200
Cream Sponge	201
Union	201
Harrison	201
Delicate	202
Marble	202
Fancy	203
Aunty's	203
Cocoanut	204
Sponge	204
Snow	204
White	205
Ambrosial	205
Sponge	205
Silver	206
Gold	206
Starch	206
Corn Starch, (No. 2)	207
Milwaukee	207
Tipsy, (Sponge)	207

	PAGE.
Cakes, Chocolate Macaroons	208
Chocolate	208
Lemon	209
Filling for	209
Golden	209
Jane's Cream	210
Cocoanut	210
Cookies	211
Cookies	211
Plum	211
Excellent Cookies	212
Jumbles	212
Coffee	212
Sponge	213
Marble	213
Molasses Cup	214
Water Cookies	214
Soft Ginger	215
Soft Ginger	215
Ginger Snaps	216
Ginger	217
Jumbles	217
Raised without Eggs	218
Ginger Snaps	218
Lou's Ginger Snaps	218
Almond	219
Cocoanut Jumbles, No. 1	219
Cocoanut Jumbles, No. 2	220
Tea or Coffee	221
Pork, without Butter, Eggs or Milk	221
Cider	222
Roll Jelly	223
Dried Apple	223
White Fruit	224
Ginger Pound	225
Crullers	225
Cookies	226
Pork	226
Sponge	226
Crullers	227
Doughnuts	227
Snow, (Very Fine)	227
Cream Jelly	228
White Sponge	228
Newport	229
Crullers	229
Ammonia	230
White	230
Ginger	230
Ginger Snaps	231
Snow	231
Cocoanut Macaroons	232
Orange	232
Ice Cream	232
Sponge	233
Sponge	233
Cream	233

	PAGE.
Cakes, Railroad	234
Common Crullers	234
Soft Crullers	234
Rice	236
Corn Starch	236
Tea	236
White	237
Almond Pound	237
Cookies	238
Doughnuts	238
Crullers	238
Citron Marble	239
Imperial	239
Irish	240
Jumbles	240
Doughnuts	241
Splendid Cookies	241
Swiss Cream	237
Cocoanut Jumbles	235
Cocoanut Cookies	229
Cocoanut Jumbles	197
Gingerbread, Sponge	184
Soft	215
Sponge	216
Soft	217
Soft	218
Soft	231

PUDDINGS.

	PAGE.
Directions	243
Sauce, Brandy or Wine	245
Lemon	245
Pudding	246, 247, 265
Cold	246
Boiled Rice	246
Liquid	247
Butter and Sugar	247
Brandy	248
Wine	248
Mrs. R.'s Pudding	248
Sweet	249
Rich Lemon	249
Puddings, Chinese Fun	249
Potato	250, 265, 279, 287
Potato	290
Brown	250
Baked Indian	251
Steam	251, 275, 276
Florentine	252
German	252
Batter	253, 256, 279
Pound, (Steamboat)	253
Tapioca	255, 256
Rice	255, 258
Plum	255, 268
Sago	257, 276
Blanc Mange & Fruit	257
Sponge	257

	PAGE.
Puddings, Snow (Splendid)	258
Lemon	259
Eve's	259
Farina	259
Rice and Apple	260
Cream	260, 282
An Excellent	260
Plain Boiled	261
Orange	261, 283
Bread	262, 269
Apple and Paste	262
Meringue Rice	263
Transparent	266, 290
Apple Roll, or Apple	266
Soda	266
Soufflee	267, 292
Orange Marmalade	267
Nursery	267
Bread and Butter	268
Brown Charlotte	268
Plum, (Plain)	268
Molasses	269
Cracker Fruit	269
Suet	270, 271, 276, 277
Suet	287
Boiled English Plum	271
English Plum	272
The Queen	273
Sallie's Meringue	273
Apple Potato	274
A Welsh	274
Baked Fruit	274
Christmas Plum	275
Jersey	275
Kentucky	278
Nameless	278
Boiled	279
Meringue Rice	279
Pumpkin	280
Fig	280
Jelly	281
Canary	281
Macaroni	281
Corn Meal	282
Cottage	282, 292
Raisin	283
Frozen Almond	284
Almond	284
Citron	285
Poor Man's	287
French	288
Cocoanut	289, 293
Marlborough	289
Boiled Loaf	291
Sutherland	292
Rod Grod	293
To Make Hen's Nest	294
A Trifle	294
Gooseberry Cream	294

	PAGE.
Cheap Dessert	250
German Puffs	251
Lemon Drops	256
Custard	254, 258, 259
Cranberry Roll	262
Cream	262, 263, 264, 265
Charlotte Russe	264, 270
Dumplings, Light Dough	264
Lemon Apple	272
Dried Peach	286
Dried Apple	286
Green Apple	286
Tapioca for Puddings	291
Roly Poly	270

PICKLES.

	PAGE.
General Directions	297
Pickles, Cauliflower	298
Martinoes	298
Cabbage	298, 302, 318
Grape	299
Peach Mangoes	299
Peaches	299, 300, 308, 311
Nasturtiums	300
Sweet Cherry	300
Watermelon Rind	301
Tomato	301, 305, 306
Sweet Tomato	314
Chopped Mixed	301
Cucumber	302, 317, 320
Oysters	302
Butternuts	302
Mangoes	303
Chow-Chow	304, 312, 320
Onions	304, 308, 316
Plums	304, 313
Cucumbers and Onions	305
Eggs	305
East India	306
Buck and Breck	307
Chopped	308
Sweet	309
Gherkins	309
Mushrooms	309
Yellow	312
Virginia Damson	318
Damson Sweet	319
Melon Sweet	319
Yellow Cabbage	320
Cabbage Salad	316
Peach Pickles	317
Pepper Mangoes	317
Catsup, Tomato	310, 311, 314, 316
Pepper	310
Chopped	311
Walnut	313
Plum	318
Universal Sauce	314

PRESERVES.

	PAGE.
General Directions	321
Canning Fruits	323, 324
Corn	338
Preserves, Plums	334
Plums without Skins	325
Pears	326, 334
Cantelope Rind	335
Strawberries	327
Quinces Whole	332
Citron	336
Cherry	337
Tomato	327
Pears for the Table	327, 334
Currants for Tarts	326
Jelly, Apple or Quince	327
Cranberry	328
Currant	329, 330, 335
Apple	329
Crab Apple	331
Quince	332
Raspberry	335
Damson Sauce	338
Jam, Currant	329
Marmalade, Crabb Apple	330
Apple	330, 331
Quince	332
Tomato	337

MISCELLANEOUS.

	PAGE.
Strawberry Ice Cream	339
Italian Snow	339
Itallienne Ice	340
Strawberry Water Ice	340
Lemon Ice	340
Pineapples	341
Peaches	341
Ice Cream	341
Lemon Syrup, (To Save Lemon)	341
Cream Soda, (This is Splendid.)	342
Cheap Ice Cream	342
Wine Jelly	343
Splendid Ginger Pop	343
Elderberry Wine	343
Blackberry Cordial	344
Acid Royal	345
Egg Nog, the Best Ever Made	345
Cocoanut Candy	345
Sugar Candy	345
Butter Scotch	346
Cream Candy	345
Cocoa Candy	346
To Keep Silver Always Bright	346
To Destroy Worms in Garden Walks	347
To Clean Brass	347
A Strong Paste for Paper	347
Preserving Eggs for Winter	347

INDEX.

	PAGE.
To Tell Good Eggs	348
Currant Wine	348
Blackberry and Currant Wine	348
Lemon Sherbet without Lemons	349
Lemon Ice	349
Sherbet	349
Currant Wine	350
Frozen Custard	350

D. WICKERSHAM,

DEALER IN

PROVISIONS!

Staple and Fancy Groceries,

MONROE STREET,

Opp. the Postoffice, SPRINGFIELD, ILL.

A. S. EDWARDS.   J. P. BAKER.   CHAS. EDWARDS.

EDWARDS, BAKER & CO.,

GROCERS,

WINES, LIQORS & CIGARS,

Monroe St., bet. 5th and 6th Sts.,

Branch Store West Side of 5th, third door South of Jefferson Street,

SPRINGFIELD, ILLINOIS.

JOHN T. STUART, Jr.,

East Side Square, - - SPRINGFIELD.

DRY GOODS,

MILLINERY, SMALL WARES, Etc.

The Cheapest Line of Domestic Goods in the City.

Butterick's Patterns, in Every Size and Style.

AGENTS FOR THE SALE OF THE CELEBRATED

Eug. Montalent Paris Seamless Kid Glove.

Price, $1.50.

W. R. BRASFIELD.   R. C. STEELE.

BRASFIELD & STEELE,

WHOLESALE AND RETAIL DEALERS IN

FAMILY GROCERIES,

Provisions, Salt, Wooden and Willow Ware.

All Kinds of Country Produce Wanted.

Monroe House, cor. Monroe and Fifth Sts.,

Springfield, Ill.

OWEN'S
COMPOUND CONCENTRATED FLUID EXTRACT OF
Sarsaparilla
— AND —
Stillingia, with Iodide of Potash.

For Purifying the Blood and Renovating the System.

Performing a radical cure of the following diseases, all of which arise from a foul condition of the blood:

King's Evil or Scrofula, Glandular Swellings, Ulcers of Every Kind, Old Sores, All Skin Diseases, Such as Tetter, Ringworm, Pimples, Eruptions, Boils, Scaldhead, Fever Sores, Weeping Sore Leg; Every Variety Venereal or Syphilitic Diseases, Neuralgia, Mercurial Rheumatism, White Swelling, Hip Joint Diseases, Chronic Erysipelas, etc., etc., etc.

COMPOSED OF VEGETABLE PRODUCTS ONLY!!

It is harmless as well as effectual. Most alteratives now in market contain mercury or arsenic. We will give any chemist in America $1,000 who will detect one grain of metalic medicine in our preparation of Sarsaparilla and Stillingia. OWEN'S SARSAPARILLA has been made and sold in Springfield for 25 years, and we have yet to hear of the first case where it has failed to perform all we claim for it. Although our preparation is put up in smaller bottles than some other similar preparations in market, it is cheapest—being highly concentrated and the dose smaller in proportion

Prepared Only by T. J. V. OWEN, Pharmacist.

Owen Buchu Manufacturing Co., Sole Prop's,

SPRINGFIELD, ILL.

SOLD BY ALL DRUGGISTS.

Our Sarsaparilla and Potash is concentrated so as to be four times the strength of all other one dollar Sarsaparillas.

OWEN'S
Compound Fluid
EXTRCT OF BUCHU,

Is a Reliable Preparation for the Permanent Cure of

KIDNEY DISEASES,

And those Rheumatic and Dropsical Difficulties so often arising from disturbances of the functions of the Kidneys. Thousands suffer from Rheumatism, who direct their attention to that disease only, when the Kidneys are really the seat of the disorder and a
FEW BOTTLES OF

Owen's Extract Of Buchu

Would remove the trouble and effect a permanent Cure. The same is true of

Gravel,	Irritation of the Bladder
Brick Dust Deposits,	Milky Discharges,
Early Indiscretion,	Loss of Power,
Loss of Memory,	Weak Nerves.
Trembling,	Dimness of Vision,
Wakefulness,	Hot Hands,
Dryness of the Skin,	Pain in the Back,
Eruptions on the Face,	Horrors,
Confused Mind,	Private Diseases, &c., &c

OWEN'S EXTRACT OF BUCHU,

Has proved itself to be the most reliable and efficient remedy, for Female Weakness, Debility, Flour Albus or Whites, etc.
IT IS THE BEST SPECIFIC KNOWN.

For Sale by All Druggists.

Prepared by T. J. V. OWEN, Pharmacist,
OWEN BUCHU MANUFACTURING CO., Proprietors,
SPRINGFIELD, ILL.

JOHN H. JOHNSON,
BOOKSELLER and STATIONER,
BOOKBINDER,
BOOK & JOB PRINTER,
— AND —
BLANK BOOK MANUFACTURER,
West Side Square,
SPRINGFIELD, ILLINOIS.

Has always on hand a fine assortment of
SCHOOL BOOKS AND SCHOOL APPARATUS, SLATES, INSTANDS, Etc.,
Gold Pens, Penholders, Pencils and Pencilcases,
Law, Medical and Micellaneous Books, Letter and Note Paper and Envelopes of every description, Visting Cards, Pocket Books, Portfolios, Drawing Materials, Stereoscopes and Views, Writing Desks, Ladies' Work Boxes, Pocket Knives,
And every article pertaining to a First Class BOOK AND STATIONERY ESTABLISHMENT.

PRINTING AND BOOKBINDING
Of every kind done on the shortest notice, and in the very best style, AT REASONABLE RATES.

OLD BOOKS REBOUND.

www.ingramcontent.com/pod-product-compliance
Lightning Source LLC
Chambersburg PA
CBHW020317240426
43673CB00039B/831